The colonial origins of Korean enterprise, 1910–1945

The colonial origins of Korean enterprise, 1910–1945

DENNIS L. McNAMARA

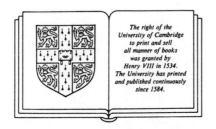

The right of the
University of Cambridge
to print and sell
all manner of books
was granted by
Henry VIII in 1534.
The University has printed
and published continuously
since 1584.

CAMBRIDGE UNIVERSITY PRESS

Cambridge

New York   Port Chester   Melbourne   Sydney

Published by the Press Syndicate of the University of Cambridge
The Pitt Building, Trumpington Street, Cambridge CB2 1RP
40 West 20th Street, New York, NY 10011, USA
10 Stamford Road, Oakleigh, Melbourne 3166, Australia

First published 1990

Printed in the United States of America

British Library Cataloguing in Publication Data
McNamara, Dennis L.
  The colonial origins of Korean enterprise, 1910–1945
  1. Korea. Economic conditions, history
  I. Title
  330.9519

  ISBN 0-521-38565-2 hard covers

IN MEMORY OF MY PARENTS,

LOUIS VINCENT AND LUCILLE O'CONNELL McNAMARA

Contents

Preface

Strong economic growth in the Republic of Korea has gained the attention of scholars, policymakers, and businessmen. Effective state strategies and concentration in private enterprise have enkindled keen interest in the role of the state and the large business combines or *chaebŏl*. The entrepreneurs and firms, planning and accomplishments of the past two decades have drawn most of the attention thus far. We find much less concern for the origins of Korea's development model in the First Republic (1948–60) under Syngman Rhee, or her earlier experience under Japanese colonial rule (1910–45). I began this study of business–state relations in colonial society with the aim of better understanding earlier patterns of capitalism on the peninsula. The relevance of the initial patterns for both the state and large-scale enterprise in postcolonial South Korea quickly became apparent.

The study of business–state relations falls well within the sociological tradition of C. Wright Mills and his emphasis on both "history" and "biography," and the institutions where they meet and define what we know as society. My interest in colonial society has been influenced by the work of French scholars such as Maunier and Balandier and their attention to the interactions between colonizers and the colonized in the "colonial situation," rather than to wider issues of competition among imperial powers or contrasting styles of colonial rule. Within the colonial situation on the Korean peninsula, I look particularly to the experience of capitalism during the years of Japan's colonial rule, how a Korean business elite emerged, adjusted, and created their own forms of enterprise. The ideas and institutions of an indigenous Korean capitalism serve as the subject of the analysis. Thus the domestic debate in the early 1920s over indigenous survival and development draws my attention, as does the business ideology and organization of people like Min Tae-sik, Pak Hŭng-sik, and Kim Yŏn-su. Japanese *zaibatsu* involved on the peninsula such as Mitsui, Mitsubishi, and the companies of Noguchi Jun deserve attention here as well, providing a context and patterns for enterprise in the colony. Continuities between colonial and postcolonial Korean capitalism gradually become apparent as the story of the colonial experience unfolds.

The record of local enterprise in the colonial period reveals familiar patterns of Korean political economy such as the family-controlled *chaebŏl* and an Asian state deeply involved in financing and directing public and private enterprise. The subsequent competition between a capitalist state to the south and a socialist state to the north on the same narrow peninsula has forced Koreans to define their respective political economies in starker terms than in many other decolonized states. Division from the north in 1945, the destruction of war from 1950, the difficulties of reconstruction, and fear of further hostilities have severely constrained discussion and reform of an authoritarian capitalism in the south, lending added weight to persisting earlier patterns. If *capitalism* refers to property rights, *democracy* to political rights, then this study is concerned more with capitalism, though business–state relations in the colony had clear political implications particularly evident in ideologies of private enterprise.

I look here to the colonial origins of large-scale private enterprise and the early shape of a modern Korean capitalism. A discussion of continuities in postcolonial Korea brings out the implications of the colonial experience for subsequent development processes on the peninsula. Review of the institutions, policies, and personalities of the colonial state, and of major Japanese firms and executives on the peninsula through 1945, offers further insight regarding Japanese colonialism and the interplay between state and Japanese private enterprise. And finally, the study looks to theoretical issues of enterprise, state, and class in Korea's modern history, clarifying the content and usefulness of such concepts in an Asian context.

I have brought together three sources of data to draw the picture of local colonial enterprise. A history of the Choheung Bank and its predecessors, and archival materials on Tongil bank loan transactions provided background for understanding the role of Min Tae-sik and Min Kyu-sik at the Hanil/ Tongil Bank. Min Tae-sik's oldest son, Min Pyŏng-do, helped with personal recollections of his days at the Tongil. I complemented company histories of the Hwasin and autobiography of the founder, Pak Hŭng-sik, with interviews of Pak himself and his son, Pak Byung-chul. Here I learned something of frustrations and hopes: the human side of portfolios and corporations, the lived patterns of opportunities and constraints in the colony. Company histories of Kyŏngsŏng Spinning and the Samyang, together with various biographies and autobiographies opened up the world of large-scale industry and commerce in local enterprise. Interviews with Kim Yŏn-su's son,

Kim Sang-hong, and other colleagues at Samyang filled out the picture of colonial enterprise at the family's Honam *chaebŏl*.

A review of Japanese statistical annuals such as the *Chōsen Ginkō kaisha kumiai yōroku* and the *Teikoku ginkō kaisha yōroku* across the period permitted a more objective view of growth and diversification among the Korean firms, and evidence of the strength of Japanese capital investment on the peninsula. The Research Bureau of the Chōsen Industrial Bank collated data and published analyses of capital investment in their monthly research bulletins. I drew biographical material on Korean and Japanese business leaders from directories such as Yamakawa Chikashi's *Jigyō to jinbutsu* and Abe Kaoru's *Chōsen kōrōsha meikan*.

Recently declassified materials from the National Archives of the U.S. Government complemented the Japanese materials. Intelligence reports of the period regarding capital investment in the colony helped complete the picture of enterprise suggested by the Korean-language and Japanese-language materials, and postwar investigations of Japanese *zaibatsu* investments abroad presented a more detailed picture of Japanese private enterprise on the Korean peninsula through 1945. The latter report, titled *Japanese External Assets as of August 1945*, provided information on total assets of Japanese corporations in Korea, Manchuria, and China, as opposed to simply data on capital investment. This resource permitted a much more substantive understanding of the direction and extent of Japanese investment in Korea than was previously possible. Among other materials, I found a useful overview of the economy and polity of Korea through 1945 among the Joint Army–Navy Intelligence Studies (JANIS), titled *JANIS Korea, including Tsushima and Quelpart*. Intelligence officers also published a report titled *Japanese Economic Penetration into Korea as of 1940*, a statistical review of Korean and Japanese corporate investment on the peninsula.

The various sources present the colonial experience in all its complexity. My aim is an intensive, richly textured picture of local enterprise, rather than an extensive summary of local finance, commerce, and industry. A theoretical frame of dependent rather than comprador capitalism gives perspective and analytical depth to the variety of firms and people presented. I argue that the enterprise of the Mins, Pak, and Kim represented dependent rather than comprador capitalism, and in conclusion show how this experience affected patterns of organization and state relations in large-scale enterprise in South Korea's First Republic. I provide two appendices to help the reader with the welter of detail and variety of personalities. The multiple investments of the Mins, Pak, and Kim are presented schematically in separate tables describing their respective portfolios. And if the scheme of the portfolios belies the logic of multiple investments, an appendix of brief biographies introduces the major figures in the study, both Korean and Japanese. A third appendix includes a glossary of the Chinese characters (*hanmun*; *kanji*) used in the spelling of names and terms in the text.

This study has been made possible through the support of a number of mentors and colleagues. I began the project as a postdoctoral fellow in the Center for Korean Studies at the University of California, Berkeley, in 1983. Summer research and travel grants from Georgetown University in 1985 and 1986 permitted further gathering of materials and consultation with scholars in Japan and Korea. Appointment as a Fulbright research scholar at Sogang University in Seoul from the fall of 1987 permitted the time and environment needed for the final writing and preparation of the manuscript. This support represents the confidence and encouragement of mentors and colleagues for which I am grateful. I alone am responsible for the conclusions and only hope the work contributes to a better understanding of a very difficult period in Korea's modern histroy.

Abbreviations

CGKKY
Tōa Keizai Shinpōnsha. *Chōsen ginkō kaisha kumiai yōroku* (A list of banks, firms, and partnerships in Korea), edited by Nakamura Sukeryō. Keijō: Tōa Keizai Shinpōsha, annual. (Cited as CGKKY.)

Chronology
Chōsen Sōtokufu. *Shisei sanjūnen shi* (A thirty-year history of administration). Appendix: "Nempyō" (chronology). Keijō: Chōsen Insatsu Kabushiki Kaisha, 1940. (Cited as Chronology.)

CKN
Zenkoku Keizai Chōsa Kikan Rengōkai, Chōsen Shibu. *Chōsen keizai nempō 1941–1942* (Annual of the Korean economy, 1941–1942). Tokyo: Kaizōsha, 1943. (Cited as CKN.)

DINY
Pak Kwŏn-sang, ed. *Donga Ilbo nonsŏl yuksimnyŏn* (Sixty years of editorials in the *Donga Ilbo*). Seoul: Donga Ilbosa, 1980. (Cited as DINY.)

DISN
Donga Ilbo Sasŏl P'yŏnch'an Wiwŏnhoe, ed. *Donga Ilbo sasŏl nonjip 1 (1920–1940)* (Collection of editorials from the *Donga Ilbo*). Seoul: Donga Ilbosa, 1977. (Cited as DISN.)

DKB
Tōyō Keizai Shinpōsha. *Dairiku kaisha benran* (Handbook of companies on the continent), edited by Akihishi Sawano. Tokyo: Tōyō Keizai Shinpōsa, 1942. (Cited as DKB.)

JEA

Civil Property Custodian, External Assets Division, General Headquarters, Supreme Commander of Allied Forces in the Pacific. *Japanese External Assets as of August 1945*. September 30, 1948, vol. 1, "Korea," and vol. 2, "Manchuria." RG 59. National Archives, 1948. (Cited as JEA.)

ODC

Oriental Development Company (Tōyō Takushoku Kabushiki Kaisha). Cited as ODC.

RG

Research Group. Sorting term at the National Archives, Washington DC.

TGKY

Teikoku Kōshinjo. *Teikoku ginkō kaisha yōroku* (A list of banks and corporations in the empire). Tokyo: Teikoku Kōshinjo, annual. (Cited as TGKY.)

WWJ

Kamesaka Tsunesaburo, ed. *Who's Who in Japan with Manchoukuo and China, 1939–1940*. Also 1943–1944 vol. Tokyo: Who's Who in Japan Publishing Office, 1939. (Cited as WWJ.)

1

Origins

The record of development in South Korea over the past three decades has drawn the praise of businessmen, the envy of Third World leaders, and the belated scrutiny of Western scholars. The story has given hope to many working to alleviate poverty and spur national development in less developed areas. Is there a model of Korean development with lessons pertinent to other areas of the world? Curiosity soon leads us from admiration to analysis, from consequence to cause, from present to past. As yet, however, few studies of the origins of private enterprise or government economic policy in South Korea are available. The commercial and industrial growth of Japan's leading prewar colonies of Korea and Taiwan lead some to suggest the colonial experience contributed greatly to subsequent economic growth, while others find little more than economic exploitation in the years of Japan's rule. Such polemics offer little insight into the beginnings of modern capitalism on the peninsula. If the Korean road to economic prosperity is to influence development strategies elsewhere, we can ill afford to overlook origins in the rush to analyze recent success.[1]

Dramatic changes in the way Koreans lived and worked marked three and a half decades of colonial rule under Japan. A prominent Korean scholar[2] offered the following evaluation:

During the thirty-six year annexation period, Koreans were never allowed to participate in any political activities in a modern sense. However, in the fields of thought, literature and religion, they had access to the trends of the times to some extent; in the economic aspect, although they lived under a capitalistic economic system, the Japanese had complete control over the Korean economy. And in the social aspect, Korean society, whether compulsorily or spontaneously, was gradually growing into a modern society.

Urban residents grew from 3 percent to 7 percent of the total population between 1910 and 1935, and 13 percent by 1944.[3] The Chosŏn Dynasty capital of Seoul and later, headquarters for the Japanese colonial administration, prospered as a major industrial and commercial center with a population of nearly one million. Other cities such as Pusan to the south or P'yŏngyang[4] to the north developed as regional centers of commerce and industry. Urban centers flourished with increased currency circulation, commercial banking, and growth in trading, manufacturing, and regional markets for commercial agriculture. The value of agricultural production nearly doubled through 1940, and the value of mining and manufacturing increased some 1,500 percent from 1910. The total value of agricultural production grew from 550 million yen in 1910 to 900 million yen in 1940, and the value of production in mining and manufacturing jumped from 29 million yen to 498 million yen in 1940.[5] Such data would support the more positive evaluation of the colonial contribution to economic growth.

A closer look at the Korean economy of the time reveals sharp differences between Korean and Japanese capital investment. For instance, firms based in Japan held a large share of the investment on the peninsula, with 76 percent of the total paid-in capital[6] in finance, 73 percent in commerce, and 56 percent in manufacturing. But *zaibatsu* investment on the peninsula was channeled through both Japan-based and peninsula-based subsidiaries. Overall the share of capital on the peninsula controlled by the leading Japanese combines[7] alone by 1940 has been estimated as high as 74 percent of the total capital investment in Korea. Even among only those firms with headquarters on the peninsula,[8] Korean-owned companies represented only 11 percent of the total capital in finance on the peninsula, 26 percent in commerce, and 12 percent in industry. Investment by local entrepreneurs appeared indeed meager in contrast to the capital poured into the colony by the major financial combines and other Japanese investors. One can hardly ignore growth in the scale of Korean capital investments outside of agriculture[9] from 1910, when the capital of the twenty-nine registered Korean firms amounted to a mere eleven million yen. Yet the overwhelming role of Japanese investment on the peninsula in Japanese firms provides plenty of evidence for the exploitation argument.

How deeply did changes in the colonial period affect postcolonial capitalism in South Korea? Certainly some features of a capitalist economy can be traced back to the late nineteenth century. The growth of domestic markets, beginnings of commercial agriculture, and the rapidly expanding scale of foreign trade were evident in the three decades following the opening of Korea to foreign ties in 1876. But the rivalry of foreign powers on the peninsula and domestic unrest, the lack of a reliable currency and of adequate native financial institutions, and the absence of diverse investment opportunities outside of agriculture frustrated wider development of an indigenous Korean capitalism through the turn of the century. Capital investment was limited almost entirely to agriculture with profits accruing through tenant rents.

Although Japanese state and private, corporate and individual interests dominated the economy from 1910, the changes set in place in the next thirty-five years would affect the society and economy of South Korea well after liberation in 1945. Distinctive patterns of business–state relations took shape with the development of finance, the extension of transportation and markets, and expanding opportunities for industrial investment. In this changing environment local precedents in agricultural enterprise such as the prominent role of the Korean family and concentration of ownership and management helped give form to the experience of indigenous enterprise. At the same time institutional methods of state direction and support defined the context in which early entrepreneurs competed to maintain indigenous ownership and control of large-scale enterprises. One can also observe emerging dynamics of class formation among the local business elite evident in networks of managers, friendly local investors, and in ties with Japanese individual and corporate investors. Patterns of corporate organization, state economic policy, and ties among the local business elite, together with ideologies of nationalist enterprise gave shape and substance to the experience of major Korean business leaders through 1945.

Ideologies played a prominent role in the development of large-scale indigenous capitalist enterprise. The term *ideology* here refers to shared understandings of a group, or ideas considered in the context of group action, rather than to ideologies as false or misleading ideas.[10] Clifford Geertz[11] writes more generally of *ideologies* as "symbol systems" or "cultural patterns" that provide "maps for problematic social reality." Such systems include "authoritative concepts" and "suasive images" linking actions with belief and value. Earlier idealistic images of self-strengthening and political autonomy from the late nineteenth century faded with the imposition of colonial control in 1910. Survival of the Korean race and local economic development now surfaced as central issues in efforts to define a modern Korea. The late nineteenth-century dilemma of foreign economic ties coupled with foreign intervention could no longer be resolved simply with total rejection of the Japanese on behalf of national integrity.[12] The poverty of the rural population and growing foreign ownership and control of Korean land and natural resources belied the fallacy of ethnic or national survival in an insulated, self-sufficient economy without careful attention to local development and ties with stronger capitalist allies.

Moderate and radical political activists joined in a strident debate over strategies for growth in the second decade of colonial rule. Local economic development within the colonial situation, or radical change of economic relations in Korean society despite subordination to capitalism and colonial rule, such were the alternatives promoted by Korean nationalist leaders through 1925. Moderates linked equality with wider concerns for survival and development. Leftists looked toward more radical structural changes to insure equality. Whereas differences between the two groups would emerge more starkly by the end of the decade, they had broached basic issues about the shape of Korean capitalist development under Japanese colonial rule. One initial result of the debate was a bipartisan campaign to promote domestically produced goods, giving a boost to the market share of local firms and, more importantly, a legitimation for Korean enterprise under alien rule. Korean business leaders embraced the ideology in a desperate effort to avoid the impression of collaboration despite business ties with the alien administration and Japanese suppliers. Similar to colonial populations in Vietnam, India, and Egypt, the nation as a whole confronted the most difficult issue for a colonized people: Korean economic development under alien rule. Economic leaders in commerce and industry confronted the daunting task of being both Korean and successful within the colonial capitalist economy. The record of their triumphs and failures conveys a great deal about the origins of enterprise in Korea.

The colonial patterns of local enterprise faded for a time in the turbulence of liberation in 1945 and the founding of the First Republic to the south in 1948. Business leaders scrambled to catch up with local rule and newfound opportunities for political voice in a fledgling democracy. All at once they faced a new business partner – a powerful Western capitalist state such as the United States – while facing domestic pressure to curtail ties with Japan. But it was not long before a Korean style of major enterprise again came to the fore, a style quite different from the large enterprises of the West and even from the *zaibatsu* of Japan. Adjustments within an unstable context of new ideologies and institutions certainly forced some change from earlier patterns of business–state relations. But I find a remarkable persistence of earlier patterns such as concentration in family-controlled business groups, the *chaebŏl*, and adaptability to state direction and support.

The structures and ideas of modern Korean enterprise have roots in the political economy of the Chosŏn Dynasty (1392–1910), the colonial experience, and in the immediate postcolonial years of division, war, and reconstruction. I examine the colonial origins of features such as concentration, adjustment to a strong colonial state, and interdependence among an inner group of the native business elite characterizing indigenous large-scale enterprises through 1945. My thesis is that the enterprise of major colonial entrepreneurs such as Min Tae-sik, Pak Hŭng-sik, and Kim Yŏn-su represented dependent rather than comprador capitalism. In conclusion I suggest how the experience of a colonial Korean business elite helped shape subsequent patterns of private enterprise and business–state ties in the First Republic (1948–60).

Enterprise, state, and class

The historical record of colonial enterprise in Korea reveals much about enterprise, state relations, and class ties within a dependent colonial situation. The term *economic dependence* refers to reliance in a colony or peripheral economy on factors of supply and demand in the metropole or core economy. The peripheral economy becomes overspecialized, serving the specific needs of the core rather than diversifying for balanced growth in the domestic economy. An exchange of primary for secondary products develops, typically of agricultural products and minerals for manufactured goods. Dos Santos has described this comprehensive penetration of a stronger capitalist state on colonies of Latin America as "financial–industrial" dependence.[13] I must emphasize at the outset two significant differences in the Korean experience of colonial dependence. First, the proximity of Japan and cultural similarities made possible a more comprehensive penetration than was common in colonies under Western domination. The Japanese controlled public administration, finance, and transport with an extensive infrastructure of Japanese personnel. Japanese private firms came to the peninsula with their own executives, managers, and technicians. There was less opportunity for comprador positions among the colonized population than was common in exotic colonies with climates and cultures alien to the Western rulers and traders. Second, the authorities in alliance with major *zaibatsu* developed Korea as a base for further expansion on the continent in the later years of Japan's rule, and as a chemical and munitions base for the Pacific War. This modified the traditional pattern of primary goods exports and manufactured imports, and encouraged heavy industry and, in particular, development of hydroelectric power on the peninsula. Although the major projects were Japanese-owned and -managed, a few Korean entrepreneurs carved out niches in the economy with their own smaller firms.

Cardoso and Falletto originally suggested the notion of "associated-dependent development' to explain Brazil's postcolonial economic growth despite continued reliance on foreign investment and foreign markets for its agricultural products. Peter Evans[14] extended the argument with the role of the local state as broker and even gatekeeper in ties between local capital and multinational investment. While recognizing the importance of any local accumulation of capital, Evans also underlined differences between locals competing with foreign investors, and locals collaborating with foreign investors in enterprise within Brazil. Although neither Cardoso and Falletto nor Evans focus on issues of local capital in periods of classic dependency, their scholarship has alerted us to the nature and extent of dependence and to the implications of dependent situations for subsequent processes of development or stagnation. Since close ties with the metropole define the very context of large-scale enterprise in colonial commerce and industry, I find Evan's distinction competitors/collaborators for postcolonial Brazil less relevant than that between dependent capitalists and compradors in a period of classic dependence. Nonetheless, I also emphasize issues of competition, of local capital accumulation, and of local experience of large-scale organization, business–state ties, and market development among the native business elite in colonial Korea. The colonial experience of what is termed here "dependent" versus "comprador" capitalism will shed light on postcolonial patterns of development in the Republic of Korea.

Theories of enterprise, state, and class give direction and depth to an analysis of Korean business in the colony, and analysis in turn reveals the distinctiveness of the Korean experience. A close examination of the colonial origins of Korean enterprise helps refine those same analytic frameworks and broaden our understanding of Asian society. Studies of both entrepreneurship and industrial organization, especially of the development of Japanese combines or *zaibatsu*[15] provide a framework for examining early Korean enterprises. Schumpeter[16] emphasized innovation in his definition of the entrepreneurial function as "carrying out new combinations" of the means of production. The place of family, a kinshiplike network of close associates, and a group of interdependent investors in innovation and risk taking is evident in the profiles of major colonial Korean entrepreneurs, as is the cooperation that Hirschman has observed among aspiring business leaders in the economies of developing nations.[17] He emphasized

the ability – so important in underdeveloped countries today – to enlist cooperation of official agencies in such matters as customs duties, permits, exchange control regulations, etc.; the ability to bring and hold together an able staff, to delegate authority, to inspire loyalty, to handle successfully relations with labor and the public, and a host of other managerial talents.

Entrepreneurs such as Min Tae-sik and his brother, Min Kyu-sik in finance, Pak Hŭng-sik in commerce, and Kim Yŏn-su in industry developed closely held and tightly managed enterprises.

I am especially interested in the scale, structure, and control of local large-scale enterprise. No one would suggest colonial Korean firms competed with the likes of Mitsui or Japan Nitrogenous Fertilizers, the leading zaibatsu on the peninsula. Yet size was important. Larger Korean firms did challenge less extensive Japanese firms, a considerable accomplishment in itself, and far outpaced most of their smaller local competitors. I use financial statistics to gauge the scale of corporations: authorized capital, paid-in capital, and estimated total assets. Authorized capital represents the ceiling on capital investment, an indication of the class of firm and its competitors, and paid-in capital represents the actual capital invested by stockholders.[18] Then, I look to corporate structure and especially management personnel with an eye to issues of both nationality and tenure. A dual focus on intracorporate and intercorporate dynamics permits a more comprehensive view of local enterprise. Finally, whereas ownership can be determined by stockholdings, and management by personnel data, control of indigenous enterprise in a dependent situation demands closer scrutiny. Zeitlin offers a useful definition of *control*: "When the concrete structure of ownership and of intercorporate relationships makes it probable that an identifiable group of proprietary interests will be able to realize their corporate objectives over time, despite resistance, then we may say that they have 'control' of the corporation."[19] I would add scrutiny of both intracorporate and intercorporate relationships as well as analysis of ownership itself to specify strategies for control among local capitalists in colonial Korea. Such dynamics were significant, for one can discern the initial shape of Korean large combines or chaebŏl in such features as concentration of capital, ownership, and management control.

Research on the ideas and efforts of Japanese entrepreneurs from the Meiji period (1868–1912) through World War II, particularly their relations with the state, also shed light on the format of business–state relations in the colony of Korea.[20] I find studies of prewar business policy organizations especially pertinent. Takeshi Ishida has coined the term "governmentalization" to describe the pervasive power of government direction in such groups originally organized to represent the interests of private enterprise.[21] Studies of prewar business law in Japan have also been helpful in view of the similarities between legislation in the home islands fostering the growth of large-scale joint-stock firms, and colonial legislation promoting and controlling the development of joint-stock enterprises on the peninsula.[22]

Regarding the economic role of the state, scholars have drawn attention recently to the state as an autonomous actor in processes of development[23] rather than simply an arena for class struggle, or a more neutral representative of a variety of major interest groups. Alexander Gerschenkron initially alerted us to the prominent role of the state in late-developing capitalist societies, and Rosovsky brought attention to the role of the Japanese state. Chalmers Johnson and others have examined the prominent role of the "developmental state" in East Asian societies more generally.[24] The foil for such interventionist, aggressive economic direction by the state remains the weak or "soft" state. Gunnar Myrdal examined the ineffectiveness of "soft states" in the economic development processes of recently decolonized societies of Southeast Asia, where "policies decided on are often not enforced, if they are enacted at all, and in that authorities, even when framing policies, are reluctant to place obligations on people."[25] The latter issue of social compulsion arose in the context of nominally democratic and sovereign societies, as did most of the recent studies of state intervention on behalf of economic growth. One might question the pertinence of such concepts for a colonial situation of total control by an alien state.

Japanese colonialism has been distinguished with its emphasis on state-directed development processes along the model of Meiji Japan.[26] Although the colonial state was unaffected by local demands for political participation and vigorously pursued various authoritarian methods of social compulsion, the government-general (*sōtokufu*) aggressively pursued development of economic infrastructures and promotion of investment on behalf of wider strategic priorities. Given the prominence of economic priorities and of state-directed strategies for growth, I apply the concept of a "strong state" to the Japanese colonial administration and probe methods of economic direction on the peninsula through 1945. Evans and Rueschemeyer have examined the efficacy of state economic intervention by looking to both the relative autonomy of state leaders from the leading economic elite, and to the corporate cohesiveness of the state in implementing its economic plans, that is, autonomy versus capacity.[27] The government-general enjoyed absolute autonomy from most sectors on the peninsula, despite occasional reliance on local Japanese and Korean business leaders for policy adjustment and implementation. The military rulers at the helm in Korea remained remarkably independent within the wider Japanese Empire, formally accountable to neither the Japanese Diet nor the prime minister until 1942.[28] Of greater interest here, however, was their means of maintaining such autonomy and particularly their capacities for economic direction within the colony. The colonial state enforced compliance with its economic direction through legislation, direct and indirect investment, and control of business policy associations on the peninsula. I give careful scrutiny to the role of the colonial state on the peninsula, its relations with the major Japanese zaibatsu, and its distinctive methods of direction and control over local business leaders.

The colonial state in Korea – the government-general and affiliated institutions – played a major role in private enterprise. Adaptability to state economic priorities was a prerequisite for successful large-scale enterprise. Certainly adaptability is demanded of native entrepreneurs in any colonial situation in which an alien state and alien enterprises hold the upper hand. Colonial state supervision accompanies offers of state support, leaving local business in a dilemma between growth and alien control. Hirschman's cooperative entrepreneurship became a trademark of successful large-scale local enterprise outside of agriculture in colonial Korea. Yet one cannot help but be impressed with the persistence of native ownership and management in a few major firms despite close relations with the state and large Japanese firms. Dependent on the colonial state for credit financing and even subsidies for high-risk ventures, a few entrepreneurs found ways to adjust to administration priorities without losing ownership and internal direction of their large-scale investments. Practices common among Korean large landowners, such as concentration of capital and adaptation to a centralized state, were already apparent in the political economy of the late nineteenth century and earlier. With the transportation and financial networks developed during the colonial years, and the competition on the peninsula with Korean and especially Japanese private enterprise, distinctive features of concentration in enterprise, state relations, and class ties came to the fore in the few large-scale indigenous firms that survived and prospered through 1945.

Class dynamics among major Korean business leaders also helped to distinguish business–state relations in the colony. Balandier wrote of cultural continuity yet change apparent in ties among local elites in a colonial situation: "Certain ways of forming links, certain social ties persist, even when the structures within which they operate are radically altered or destroyed, while at the same time new ties appear as a result of the colonial situation and the social conjunctures it creates."[29] The term *class* here refers to the small group of local capitalists in colonial Korea.[30] I am especially interested in continuity and change among a small segment of that class, an indigenous group of primary owners and top managers of major business enterprises whom I refer to also as the "business elite." Zeitlin, Useem,[31] and others have highlighted their distinctive interests:

The inner group, in short, may constitute a special segment of the capitalist class, if a *class segment* can be defined as a subset of class members sharing a social location with partially distinct interests. Though the common concern with capital accumulation unites the inner group with the remainder of the capitalist class, at the same time, the inner group's greater stake in class-wide interests sets it apart.

An interdependent network of native entrepreneurs distinguished by corporate ownership, salience in business-policy associations, and close ties with colonial state officials came to play a major role in local enterprises in the last decade of colonial rule. The network assured contacts with leading Korean business figures in finance, commerce, and industry, and opportunities for mutual investment in projects with strong growth potential. Issues of interdependence and cooperation among a select elite examined in the literature on "interlooking directorates" and an "inner circle" of primary owners,[32] merit careful examination.

Useem observed an inner group or circle of senior corporate officers with positions on boards of other leading firms and leadership roles in major business policy associations. He offered the metaphor of an "inner group," suggesting an axis of inner group "centrality" ranging from "those connected with a single major firm to those with two connections, three connections and at the far end of the axis, many connections."[33] Useem later argued that this "politicized leading edge of the leadership of major corporations has come to play a major role in defining and promoting the shared ideals of large corporations in the industrial economies of the United States and Great Britain."[34] Although the Korean capitalist class was very small, particularly the industrial and commercial elite as opposed to the agrarian elite, and the inner circle suggested here was only a segment of the Korean capitalists, still the Kims, Pak, and the Mins represented a very significant politicized leading edge of the local elite. Their ideologies, investment activities, and joint efforts with leading Japanese businessmen on the peninsula strongly influenced patterns of business–state ties in the origins of Korean large-scale enterprise.

Useem traced a three-stage progression from "family capitalism" to "managerial capitalism," and finally to "institutional capitalism," with the inner group playing a salient role in the latter transition. However I look to a group of Korean entrepreneurs with little direct political power in the colonial state, and in a political economy best described as "family capitalism" with large indigenous enterprise under family ownership and management. The composition and role of a politicized leading edge of the leadership of major native Korean firms will be examined, particularly their efforts to adapt to state direction and support. I cite ample evidence of multiple corporate connections, of "institutional governance" positions in business associations and educational foundations, and of consultative posts with the government-general. But I will also underline two major differences from the inner circles in modern capitalist states of the West: the combination of management and ownership in the Korean elite, and the absence of substantive political voice in policy-making within the colonial state. The similarities and differences force us to recognize the contextual character of Korean colonial dependence and the distinctive dynamics of local dependent enterprise.

How does a local business elite survive, much less prosper, in the shadow of a well-financed colonial state with absolute authority? I devote careful attention to distinctive modes of adaptation evident in the ideologies, state relations, and investment portfolios of the Korean inner circle. I find Korean colonial business ties with the Japanese less amenable to the heuristic distinction between collaboration and patriotism applied to local political activists. Businessmen must carry on their business. Big businessmen with large-scale investments had to deal with the colonial administration and thus were obviously more vulnerable to collaboration, but also more important in the development of native enterprise. If close ties with the administration define collaboration, then the Korean businessmen in this study must be judged collaborators. This relationship tells us much about the comprehensive economic control of the state but little about dynamics in the origins of Korean capitalism. A more useful analytic dichotomy would contrast the "comprador"[35] role prominent at the time in neighboring China, with the "dependent capitalist." Compradors work mainly within foreign enterprises, investing their talents and capital for the most part in an alien firm in their own land. Dependent capitalists, by contrast, invest often in their own local enterprise, though nonetheless under the wider control of an alien administration and markets controlled by foreign investors. Kang Tong-jin termed the leading Korean entrepreneurs as "compradors," citing Han Sang-yong as evidence of a successful government policy to encourage "comprador capitalism."[36] I find his argument more cogent in the case of Han Sang-yong, but less convincing in the case of the three major entrepreneurs examined here. Kajimura Hideki[37] offers a more useful distinction between indigenous capital developed in a dependent economy, and Korean capital developed with Japanese participation, or "comprador capital" (*maep'an chabon*). I cite efforts to maintain Korean ownership and management as evidence to distinguish "compradors" from "dependent capitalists" (*yesok chabonga*).

Relations with Japanese business leaders helped define the dependence of Korean business leaders. The inner group of Korean business leaders could at least keep abreast of policy changes through association with Japanese business leaders on the peninsula. The latter ties became more salient with the industrialization projects of the late colonial period. On the one hand, we find one or two familiar Japanese managers active in indigenous firms, such as Kawaguchi Makoto at the Tongil or Chogō Eiji at Hwasin, or Nakatomi Keita as auditor of Kyŏngsŏng Spinning. On the other hand, we find Korean corporate owners investing in major Japanese enterprises, developing ties with such eminent business figures on the peninsula as Sakoma Fusatarō, Akita Hideo, Ōhashi Shintarō, Ariga Mitsutoyo, and Hashimoto Keizaburō. A part in major Japanese ventures on the peninsula afforded contact also with zaibatsu interests such as Mitsubishi, Mitsui, and Japan Nitrogenous Fertilizers (Nippon Chisso Hiryō).

Theories of enterprise, state, and class provide direction but not the content of an historical study. The business record of three prominent colonial Korean families serves as the centerpiece of this study, representing major native enterprises in finance, commerce, and industry. The term *indigenous* denotes native ownership and management, the criteria of dependent versus comprador capitalists. Even though there were very few large-scale indigenous firms in a colonial economy dominated by state corporations and branches or affiliates of Japanese zaibatsu, I argue that the initial experience of extensive corporate funding, direction, and organization, as well as state and class relations in these few enterprises, affected indigenous capitalist enterprise well after liberation. Apart from the more narrowly defined issue of dependent capital, Korean scholars[38] have debated the thesis of "national enterprise" (*minjok kiŏp*) or "national capital" (*minjok chabon*) linking colonial enterprise with subsequent political and economic development processes. Kang Man-gil added considerable light to a highly charged emotional debate with distinction among three connotations of the term "national capital:" (1) capital owned by a Korean, (2) that part of Korean-owned capital used for the benefit of Koreans, and (3) that part of Korean-owned capital invested directly in the nationalist movement. I have seen no documentary evidence of investments in the nationalist movement by the Mins, Kim Yŏn-su, or Pak Hŭng-sik. My term "indigenous capital" (*t'och'ak chabon*) coincides with the first and possibly the second of Kang's connotations. Certainly the local entrepreneurs themselves boast of native ownership and benign use of native capital for the wider benefit of the Korean populace throughout this study. I present their story and look directly to the degree and nature of their dependence, and in the process hope to shed light on the more complex question of national capital in a colonial situation.

Indigenous enterprise

Han Sang-yong, Kim Sa-yŏn, the Min bothers and Kim brothers, Pak Hŭng-sik, Hyŏn Chun-ho, Ch'oe Ch'ang-hak, and others faced a dilemma in colonial Korea. The classic dependency of Korea's colonial situation left local entrepreneurs with two alternatives: more independent, local enterprise, usually of a small scale due to limited capital resources, or a career in foreign enterprises on Korean soil. I would not deny the significance of Korean experience in foreign business organizations[39] on the peninsula, in state institutions such as the Bank of Chōsen or Industrial Bank,[40] or in the colonial government itself. Their accumulated expertise through 1945 played a role in subsequent institutional developments. But with neither the direct responsibility of working within a native enterprise that would continue after liberation, nor the wider symbolic significance of a competitive Korean investment in an economy dominated by foreigners, work in alien ventures was quite different from participation in local firms, particularly in major Korean enterprises.

A small number of independent local businessmen combined local resources with state support to develop a third alternative: locally owned and managed large-scale enterprise. I look to these local banks, commercial firms, and industries and to their owners and executives, the dependent capitalists. Unlike the legacy of the compradors, one finds continuity here of capital, organizational structure, and management personnel between colonial and postcolonial Korea. The colonial experience of dependent capitalism reveals much of chaebŏl origins, and more generally of enterprise, class, and business–state relations. With criteria of indigenous ownership and management, and prominence in major areas of the colonial economy, I have selected Min Tae-sik and his brother Kyu-sik of the Hanil/Tongil Bank, Pak Hŭng-sik of Hwasin, and Kim Yŏn-su of Kyŏngsŏng Spinning as the central figures in this study. My task will be to show that indeed these select entrepreneurs were dependent rather than comprador capitalists, to explain their methods of maintaining indigenous enterprise, and to probe the implications of such experience for organization and state relations in large-scale private enterprise in postcolonial South Korea.

The Min brothers grew up in a family of prominent aristocrats and government officials in the last years of the Chosŏn Dynasty. The father's experience and investments in the Hansŏng Bank and later the Hanil Bank paved the way for the careers in finance of his sons, Min Tae-sik and Kyu-sik. Born the eldest son of Min Yŏng-hwi, Min Tae-sik[41] (1882–1951) was a high-ranking military officer in the administration of Emperor Kojong at the end of the Chosŏn Dynasty, and a government advisor in 1904 just prior to annexation. After travel to the United States, he returned to manage a family mining venture. Together with Han Sang-yong of Hansŏng and Pak Yŏng-ch'ŏl of the Chōsen Commercial Bank, Min Tae-sik stood among the leading local banking figures in the colonial period. He organized his agricultural and real estate holdings under the family-owned Kyesŏng Company in 1935, a holding company also for investments in other enterprises. He served as president of the Hanil Bank from 1920 through its reorganization as the Tongil in 1931, until financial problems at the bank and pressure from the government-general for new management forced his resignation in 1936.

Born in 1888, the younger brother Kyu-sik attended the family's Hwimun School and studied privately before going on for a college degree at Cambridge University. Returning to Seoul in the spring of 1920, he immediately assumed the post of managing director of the Hanil Bank and three years later, president of the family's industrial venture, the Chosŏn Silk Weaving Company. Astute in both agricultural and commercial investments, he organized the Yŏngbo agricultural and real estate firm as a holding company for his landholdings, buildings, and investments in other commercial and industrial ventures.[42] Min Kyu-sik served as president of the Tongil Bank and then the Choheung Bank until 1945, and thereafter as a director. He remained a prominent figure in finance in the First Republic as president of a finance company and later the Korea Commerce and Industry Bank.[43]

Unlike the aristocratic financiers of the Min family, Pak Hŭng-sik gave the impression of an ambitious and aggressive merchant from northern Korea. Pak was born in South P'yŏngan Province near Chinnamp'o in northwestern Korea in 1903. After the deaths of his older brother in 1910 and his father in 1916, the young Pak supported his mother with some landholdings he later parlayed into local printing and cotton investments. He moved to Seoul in 1926 and quickly established Sŏnil Paper Goods with capital accrued from the earlier ventures and bank loans. The company's success led to a further investment in his famous and widely successful Hwasin Department Store on Chongno Avenue in Seoul. Pak was counted among the leading entrepreneurs of the day with domestic investments in wholesaling and retailing, trading ventures in China and Southeast Asia, and minority shares in other joint-stock firms. He led the Hwasin chaebŏl through the liberation and the First Republic in the south under Syngman Rhee, specializing in trade and textile production.[44]

Perhaps the most famous and successful of the colonial Korean entrepreneurs, Kim Yŏn-su was the younger brother of the eminent educator and politician, Kim Sŏng-su (pen name Inch'on, 1891–1955).[45] The adopted son of Wŏnp'a Kim Ki-jung, Sŏng-su graduated from Waseda University in 1912 and returned home as a teacher and administrator at Posŏng Middle School. He was appointed president of Kyŏngsŏng Weaving Company (Kyŏngsŏng Chigyu) in 1917, and founded the famous Kyŏngsŏng Spinning and Weaving Company, or more simply, Kyŏngsŏng Spinning, together with Pak Yŏng-hyo two years later. He remained at the firm as a director through 1927, and later as an advisor, while maintaining a large block of shares in the company. Sŏng-su founded the prominent vernacular *Donga Ilbo* newspaper in April of 1920, serving as president intermittently though 1927, and thereafter as a director. In line with his early interest in Korean education, he also later helped found Posŏng College, the present-day Korea University. Sŏng-su emerged as a leader of the opposition party after 1945, and served briefly as vice-president of the Republic in May of 1951.

But it was his less prominent younger brother who directed the family's investments. The son of a prosperous landowner, Kim Yŏn-su (1896–1979) was a native of the Koch'ang area in North Chŏlla Province. He attended middle school in Tokyo and later graduated from the Economics Department of Kyoto Imperial University. Upon his return he took charge of the family's agricultural properties, expanding the family-owned Samyang Company with agricultural estates in Korea and Manchuria, plus holdings in other commercial and industrial ventures. He left his mark on Kyŏngsŏng Spinning as executive director from 1922 to 1927, and president from 1935 to 1945. In addition to the direction of major agricultural and industrial ventures, Yŏn-su was active in finance as executive and representative director of the Haedong Bank. He resigned his post at Kyŏngsŏng Spinning in 1945, but retained a large block of shares in the company until 1958. His efforts in the First Republic were directed toward development of the Samyang Company in trade and sugar production.[46]

To fill out the picture of how one did business in the colony, I follow the careers of selected individuals with prominent roles in Korean enterprises or associated firms. The Min brothers, Pak Hŭng-sik, and Kim Yŏn-su stand out as key figures, but other prominent colonial Korean business leaders such as Han Sang-yong of the Hansŏng Bank, Hyŏn Chun-ho of the Honam Bank, Ch'oe Ch'ang-hak of Samsŏng Mining, Ha Chun-sŏk, and Kim Sa-yŏn deserve attention as well. Contrasts and comparisons within this circle of investors provide a more substantive picture of the main actors themselves. Nor are Japanese associates and fellow investors ignored. The story of state and enterprise is a story of both organizations and people. The human networks of fellow "friendly" Korean investors, of Japanese associates and fellow investors set the stage for the enterprise of the Mins, Pak, and Kim.

Apart from entrepreneurs I also look to enterprises. I give close scrutiny to the major joint-stock ventures of each of the families: the Hanil/Tongil Bank, the Hwasin Department Store, and Kyŏngsŏng Spinning. To convey some sense of context, I contrast the history of each of these enterprises with Japanese firms on the peninsula of similar scale, and with comparable Korean firms that did not survive as indigenous enterprises. Where did the Mins, Pak, and Kim put their money and direct their entrepreneurial and administrative energies? A distinctive pattern of investment portfolios and election to corporation boards was apparent by the last decade of the colonial period. The pattern included four concentric levels of business activity. First of all, there was an inner core of family-owned companies, usually in agriculture and real estate. The Kyesŏng or Yŏngbo Companies of the Min family were typical, as was Kim Yŏn-su's Samyang Company. Wholly owned family companies with a large paid-in capital, the firms served as holding companies for other commercial and industrial investments, while providing consistent, extensive profits for investment elsewhere. Pak Hŭng-sik was the exception here because his family lacked extensive agricultural holdings. Instead, he developed the Hwasin Department Store and Hwasin Chain Stores along this pattern of nearly wholly owned and closely managed family enterprises. The other three levels of investment among these entrepreneurs were more conventional joint enterprises, but the family-owned enterprise remained the center of their investment portfolios.

The second level of investments included major investments with administrative responsibility in complex joint-stock enterprises, such as the Hanil/Tongil Bank of the Min family, Kyŏngsŏng Spinning under president Kim Yŏn-su, and Hwasin Trade under president Pak Hŭng-sik. In each of these ventures, the most prominent native enterprises of the period, one major entrepreneur made a large commitment of capital, developed a tight, kinshiplike management group, and elicited the smaller capital contributions of friendly investors. To date, this second level has received most of the scholarly attention,[47] with some reference to the inner core of wholly owned family enterprises. I have found strong interrelationships between the two circles for each entrepreneur, however, particularly in capital investment and executive recruitment.

The third and fourth levels of business activity by these entrepreneurs have been largely ignored by scholars thus far, since case studies of particular entrepreneurs and their major enterprises have absorbed most of the attention. A focus on business–state relations rather than enterprise itself demands attention to common patterns of investment and networks of mutual support. Here one begins to see the need for diversified investment portfolios in the colonial era, investments not unrelated to the family-owned agricultural companies or their major joint enterprises. A third level included smaller investments by Kim or Pak or the Mins in medium-sized joint ventures, without major administrative responsibilities. What distinguishes this group of ventures is a team of major Korean entrepreneurs and a few former Japanese government officials. The Korean business elite here put together capital in ventures often parallel to their own agricultural or commercial companies. For example, Min Kyu-sik, Kim Yŏn-su, and Pak invested heavily in the Chosŏn Engineering Company for mining and military equipment. Kim and Pak put up the funds for Shibuya Reiji's Daikō Trade based in Mongolia, and Min Kyu-sik served as a director for the Chōsen Trade Promotion Company. Kim Yŏn-su was the minor partner in the Okkye Gold Mine Company with Japan Gold Promotion Company. Pak and other Korean entrepreneurs appeared as major investors in the Japanese-managed Keijin Enterprises.

A fourth level of activity in major Japanese ventures on the peninsula differed only in scale and major ownership from the third level. Whereas Koreans were among major investors in the joint enterprises of the third level, the scale of investment on the fourth level excluded all but the minor participation of Korean capital. For instance, Min Kyu-sik's older brother, Min Tae-sik, served many years on the boards of Ōhashi Shintarō's Keijō Electric and Chōsen Beer companies. Pak Hŭng-sik was on the board of the North Korea Paper and Chemical Manufacturing Company, and served with Kim Yŏn-su on the board of Chōsen Petroleum, one of the ten largest Japanese investments on the peninsula. If class ties with other Koreans and Japanese investors were reinforced through investments in the third circle of firms, Min, Pak, and Kim were in contact with executives of Mitsui, Mitsubishi, and Noguchi Jun's Japan Nitrogenous Fertilizer companies in this fourth circle.

The multilevel portfolios provide a more comprehensive perspective on this dynamic of adaptation of dependent capitalists in colonial Korea, especially when set in the context of Korean ideologies for colonial enterprise. A review of colonial state economic policy and the role of Japanese investment on the peninsula suggests the conditions under which the local businessmen learned to adapt. I begin the story of local enterprise and the colonial state with the domestic debate over a benign capitalism in the exciting second decade of colonial rule. The story continues with the economic policies and modes of intervention of the colonial strong state. A further chapter on investments in Korea by major Japanese private firms in harness with the state fills out the picture of the state's direct and indirect economic role and introduces the basic pattern of business–state relations in the colony. Within this context of Korean ideologies, state economic policy, and the place of Japanese private investment, I look carefully at the enterprise of three local business leaders in finance, commerce, and industry. Here I hope to convey something of the fabric and feeling of local large-scale enterprise in the colony. Early forms of corporate organization, dynamics affecting formation of a business class, and relations with the state draw careful scrutiny. A review of major private enterprise in postcolonial South Korea opens a concluding chapter evaluating the legacies of the colonial experience and the origins of Korean enterprise.

2

Benign capitalism

Pak Hŭng-sik pleaded ignorance when accused of cooperation with the Japanese colonial rulers: "I was a businessman unversed in politics."[1] Unversed perhaps in nationalist politics, Pak was certainly adept in persuading the government of his credibility and hardly shy about his contribution to the growth of commerce on the peninsula. The Min brothers, Kim Yŏn-su, and Pak proved themselves masters at the practical business ideology necessary to gain government support and a share in the domestic marketplace. They faced a challenge in the colony not only of nationalist identity under alien rule, but also of capitalist enterprise in a feudal society. Byron Marshall wrote of "business ideologies" as "ideas expressed by or on behalf of the business class with the manifest intent of creating attitudes favorable to private capitalism."[2] Cogent ideologies are necessary to support large-scale ventures, particularly in the early stages of capitalist development. Local capitalists could find no moral justification for the pursuit of private profit in their own Korean Confucian tradition. The absence of earlier ideologies complicated immediate tasks such as persuading landowners of transfer capital from agriculture to commercial and industrial investments. Add to this the fact that ideologies carried the further burden of somehow legitimating indigenous enterprise under the political rule and economic domination of Japan, and you can sense the complexity of their task.

If the challenge itself to create attitudes favorable to capitalism within an agrarian colony appeared daunting, the nationalist fervor of the 1920s proved oddly conducive to a unique brand of economic nationalism supportive of even dependent, indigenous enterprise. Pak and his colleagues in colonial enterprise formulated business ideologies in the shadow of a broader debate over the shape of a modern Korean economy. Even though few would describe the second decade of colonial rule under Governor-Generals Saitō Minoru and Yamanashi Hanzō as "lenient," Koreans in these years enjoyed freedoms of expression and association unknown prior to 1919 and outlawed during the military mobilization of the 1930s.[3] The March First Demonstrations for independence in 1919 enkindled a wide-ranging debate over the shape of an indigenous economy.

A Korean "Declaration of Independence," signed by thirty-three intellectuals and religious leaders was read publicly at a restaurant in Pagoda Park in Seoul on the first of March in 1919, accompanied by shouts of *tongnip manse* ("long live independence") in local demonstrations throughout the peninsula. The government-general estimated about one million Koreans participated, while Korean sources claimed double that number[4] or about 12 percent of the population. The ambitious organizers defied[5] the colonial authorities with a public declaration of a Korean cultural and racial identity. Imperial subjugation had deprived Koreans of their separate existence as a nation, their right to spiritual growth, and their distinctive contribution to a world culture. More to the point, the patriots complained their ancestral lands amounted now to little more than a "colony," and their race little more than "savages."[6]

The demonstrations for independence gave vent to widespread anger with the repressive methods of the colonial administration, but also gave voice to nationalist aspirations. The content of a Korean racial identity would be hotly contested in the ensuing years, due in part to wider freedom of expression and association following the demonstrations. Newspapers such as the *Donga Ilbo* (*East Asia Daily*) and the *Chosŏn Ilbo* (*Korea Daily*), and the *Kaebyŏk* (*Creation*) journal were established in 1920. The local press provided open fora for discussions of a modern Korean identity, particularly in the initial years prior to tighter administration control of publications from 1926.[7] Labor, farm, and youth groups burst on the scene among moderates and especially leftists.[8] Students, young intellectuals, laborers, and farmers would support the founding of the Korean Communist Party in 1925 through such groups as the Tuesday Society (*Hwayohoe*), the North Wind Society (*Pukp'unghoe*), and the Seoul Youth Association of the Korean Youth League Federation (*Chosŏn Ch'ŏngnyŏn Yŏnhaphoe*).[9]

Basic themes in what would later emerge as two radically different models of a modern Korea now took center stage. A more moderate nationalism was apparent in the "Products Promotion Campaign (*Chosŏn mulsan changnyo undong*),"[10] with leaders advocating the use of native products, industry, and commerce as a path to economic self-sufficiency. Even limited economic autonomy was recognized as a basis for national survival and ultimately for national autonomy. Turn-of-the-century themes of reform or self-strengthening now included "modern" or "scientific" attitudes, structural development in the economy, and more equitable distribution. Progressive or "leftist" intellectuals were critical of inequalities and particularly of the advantages of major capitalists. Leftists promoted "class consciousness" and even class revolution,[11] while moderates emphasized cultural changes such as "greater freedom, equality, justice and humanistic concerns."

Arguments over the shape of an indigenous economy focused on issues of class division but not class composition, of private property but not private enterprise, and only by intimation on the issue of a Korean nation, but certainly not on a Korean state. Meanwhile the entrepreneurs themselves were learning to succeed through concentration in private enterprise, finding a place in the development priorities of the colonial administration, and forging class ties in a polity and economy radically different from that of their fathers and grandfathers. Their professed ideal was a benign if unequal capitalism, both locally owned and ultimately beneficial for the nation. They spoke of Korean financial, commercial, and industrial development, fully aware of the vulnerability of their enterprises in a dependent economy closely managed by the colonial administration and heavily influenced by strategies and business interests in the home islands of Japan. They promoted "Korean finance," "our Kyŏngbang" or "commercial Korea," while relying on loans and even subsidies from state-affiliated banks and cultivating ties with high-ranking bureaucrats and major Japanese business leaders on the peninsula. Such was the ambiguity of large-scale indigenous enterprise in the colony, the dilemma of local development in a dependent economy.

Entrepreneurs and political activists alike took part in discussions on the shape of an indigenous economy. An older brother of Kim Yŏn-su, Kim Sŏng-su had helped organize both Kyŏngsŏng Spinning and the *Donga Ilbo* newspaper in 1919, and continued as a major stockholder and advisor at the spinning company throughout the colonial period. Kim Yŏn-su himself returned from studies in Kyoto in the midst of the debate in 1921 and quickly became involved as a major business figure with the Samsu (i.e., predecessor of the Samyang agricultural firm), the Kyŏngsŏng, and the Haedong Bank. Min Kyu-sik's brother, Min Tae-sik, had succeeded his father as president of the leading indigenous bank,[12] the Hanil, in 1920, and Kyu-sik himself took over as managing director at the same time after his recent return with a Cambridge University degree. Pak Hŭng-sik, however, was busy with a printing venture and cotton brokerage firm in a far northern province before moving to Seoul finally in 1926. He would gain prominence as the leading advocate of Korean commerce only in the next decade.[13]

The initial fervor of the debate had crested by 1925 with some resurgence surrounding the founding of the short-lived unified front, the Sin'ganhoe, two years later. The practical rhetoric of the entrepreneurs muted the exciting clash between moderates and progressives. Still the broader debate provided the intellectual context for the prosaic business ideology of solidarity on behalf of a benign but doggedly competitive capitalism. The Native Products Campaign provided the ideas and opportunity for a local business ideology, but it was the entrepreneurs themselves who put ideas together with products and organizations. A review of their ideology of a benign capitalism offers insight into the formative ideas of Korea's early capitalist development, particularly the transition from agrarian to industrial and commercial capital.

Native products campaign

The Korean Products Promotion Society (*Chosŏn Mulsan Changnyohoe*) led the effort to promote indigenous products as a way of self-strengthening. Cho Man-sik, a Presbyterian Elder and General Secretary of the P'yŏngyang YMCA,[14] had established the organization in P'yŏngyang in July of 1922. The Society was already in Seoul by January of the next year with branches in various rural areas by the fall of 1923, but enjoyed only brief success.[15] One scholar traced the society's decline to the extremism of the youth groups, failures of organization, and pressure from the government-general. Cho Ki-jun concluded that the movement failed to gain support among either the land-based Korean elite, or among the wider Korean population too poor to live solely with Korean products.[16] The impact of the self-strengthening movement was felt far beyond the society and its branches, however, spurring an intense discussion on the shape and substance of a modern Korea. The debate in the *Donga Ilbo*[17] and *Kaebyŏk* through 1925 provides a chronicle of their aims, their perception of Korea's most pressing problems, and their strategies for change characteristic of the moderate nationalists. Statements from the moderates in turn provided targets for leftist criticsm.

A series of editorials[18] in the *Donga Ilbo* in the spring of 1921 raised the initial theme of the debate: industrialization for the survival of the Korean race. The world was now divided into strong nations with vigorous industry and developed commerce such as Britain, Japan, and the United States, and the weak nations such as India, China, and Korea. "Those who immerse themselves in this (commercial and industrial) culture will survive, those unable will perish."[19] A similar theme was apparent a year later, emphasizing a national identity reflected in Korean lands and cities, opposition to foreign ownership, and a call to "choose life, not the death of our people, prosperity not poverty."[20] Articles in *Kaebyŏk* highlighted the desperate economic plight of the nation.[21] One author lamented not only a lack of capital and technology, but also Korea's inferior position in foreign markets and the consequent need for maritime and continental transportation links. But the central focus through 1925 in this journal was on agriculture and the plight of the peasants rather than industrial problems. The editors made repeated calls for reform of the colony's agricultural policy.[22]

The writers took aim at both colonial dependence and obsolete economic attitudes among the wider populace. Economic dependence on Japan was widely recognized as a structural constraint on the emergence of an economically autonomous Korea, rather than as a path toward independence. An early newspaper editorial described Koreans as "economic slaves," pressing the government-general to insure at least an equal competition with Japanese companies in development of Korea's resources.[23] Nationalist demands included specific programs to dilute Japan's tight control of capital in the domestic economy through their Bank of Chōsen (Chōsen Ginkō) and the Chōsen Industrial Bank (Chōsen Shokusan Ginkō).[24] Despite their tone, the nationalists here were realistic enough to promote reform within the colonial framework, somehow resigned to alien rule but unwilling to surrender hopes for ultimate autonomy.

The critics looked within as well, focusing on native attitudes and structures pertinent to development. A series of editorials[25] in May of 1921 decried the traditional emphasis on agriculture persisting in the 1920s and reluctance to invest in industry or commerce. The editorials called for a change in Korean attitudes and structures parallel to the Industrial Revolution in the West, arguing that an agricultural nation could not survive among the industrial nations. Koreans must develop scientific methods and applications such as chemical industries to compete among the strong nations; they must come to respect and revere industry, as agriculture had been respected in the past; they must redirect capital investment away from agriculture toward urban industries and export markets. Beyond simple promotion of industrial strategies, other editorialists[26] argued that economic development was the very key to national survival and chided their readers that this was merely common sense in any "modern nation (*kŭndae kukka*)."[27]

If there were problems of both Japanese economic control and obsolete Korean attitudes and structures, the proposed solutions involved both the Japanese and Koreans. The writers demanded administration policies promoting indigenous industries: profits to Koreans, opportunities for Koreans to compete with Japanese industries, and policies supporting indigenous development.[28] In line with the thrust of the Products Promotion Society, they advocated self-development strategies such as purchase of native products,[29] and establishment of native economic organizations including banks[30] and large enterprises. Yi Kwang-su in particular emphasized the need for well-funded Korean corporations to compete with Japanese firms,[31] coupled with the need for educational organizations to change attitudes regarding industrialization. The plea for education coincided with repeated calls for the application of scientific methods, especially for research and planning regarding native industries and products.[32] Among areas for study, one writer began with innocuous topics such as a national inventory of Korean products, and a survey of what production facilities were necessary or desired. He concluded more forcefully, calling for a study of how the Japanese were taking money away from Koreans and, finally, a study of strategies to educate Koreans about the very need for a native products campaign.[33] The latter plea indicates the continuing difficulty of changing attitudes and economic practices in this agrarian society.

In contrast, leftists took issue with the basic structure of Korea's economy: The problem was not simply poverty or the Japanese, but class divisions and unequal access to resources. Yi Sŏng-t'ae attacked the middle-class interests of the Products Promotion Campaign – the capitalists would benefit from stronger local markets but not the workers.[34] He railed against capitalists manipulating the patriotism of the wider population for their own class interests, that is, "economic domination (*kyŏngjejŏk chŏngbok kwangye*)." The theme of exploitation by greedy capitalists continued in Ok Ch'on-suk's *Kaebyŏk* articles, as he explained the theory of surplus profit and the social consequences of private property.[35] Ok trained a harsh light on Robert Owen's transition from kindly paternalism in factory management to a socialist commitment. He argued that it was ultimately the greed of British capitalists fostering poverty, unemployment, and exploitation of the workers that spurred Owen's commitment to a socialist ideal. Such criticism proved divisive within the Korean nationalist movement, supported and often led by educated and often wealthy members of the middle class such as Kim Sŏng-su.[36] The seamy side of benign capitalism had been exposed.

Others wrote in a similar vein but with closer attention to the structural defects of the capitalist model: The problem was not capitalists, but capitalism. A perceptive set of articles in the *Donga Ilbo*[37] pointed to the growth of capitalism among advanced nations as a threat to the very existence of the dominated races in colonies like India and Korea that lacked the bases of capitalism – freedom, communications, and an adequate base of investment capital. Here the author contrasted capitalists with labor, linking aspirations for national survival and autonomy with equality between the two groups. He scored capitalism for class differences and persistence of inequality despite the ideal of political freedom, debunking the notion of freedom without equality.

The slogans[38] of the Korean Communist Party would later make the division clear between moderates and leftists, denouncing the moderates (*minjok kaeryang chuŭija*) as well as Koreans working within the bureaucracy of the Japanese administration as opportunists. But the leftist arguments in the *Donga Ilbo* and *Kaebyŏk* through 1925 reflected for the most part only idealism and hope for greater justice in the economic and social order, rather than a commitment to socialism as such. More progressive themes were not yet linked with strategies for change apart from the ideology and platform of the Korean Communist Party itself. Yet the progressives did agree on the central role of equal and free individuals, an issue not as salient among the moderate nationalists, and shared an uneasiness with the role of Korean capital in an inequitable economy.

Articles by leftist writers reflected deep-seated anger with capitalist excesses and strong sympathy for those left behind in the process of capitalist development. Such feelings would lead to calls for radical structural change. The leftists would criticize the moderates for class interest in promoting a Korean capitalism, and denounce the industrialized capitalist nations for inequality, prosperity of the few, and economic growth without true freedom. Yet within the colonial situation the leftists could find comparatively little support through 1925, despite a formidable ideological and organizational base. Harassment and repression by the colonial administration frustrated growth of a leftist movement in the colony, preventing formulation of a concrete, realistic program for a more equitable society. Realism or survival would bring the moderates into cooperation with the alien colonial rulers; under the careful surveillance of the colonial rulers, the ideal of indigenous unity never proved cohesive enough to join moderates with the leftists. The alternative of radical change would find little support among the broader Korean populace, leaving withdrawal or adaptation as the only viable responses.

Yi Kwang-su[39] perhaps best represented the theme of benign capitalism (i.e., unequal but for the benefit of all) aligned with this native products campaign. Born in 1892, Yi graduated from the Meiji Academy (Meiji Gakuin) and later studied philosophy at Waseda University. He published his first novel in 1917, became active in the Korean student movement in Tokyo opposing colonial rule, and later returned to the peninsula. He won initial acclaim with a major article in *Kaebyŏk* in 1922 and joined the editorial staff of the *Donga Ilbo* the following year. His vernacular novels over the next two decades gained a wide following. After investigation and brief internment in 1937 for nationalist activities, Yi became associated with pro-Japanese groups. In 1949 he was brought to trial for antinationalist activities and later disappeared during the occupation of Seoul by North Korean forces in 1950.

In a series of editorials in the *Donga Ilbo*[40] in January of 1924, Yi argued for a competitive local economy to insure at least economic survival despite Japanese domination. The problems were both external and internal, but the solution was not the fundamental structural change advanced through socialist revolution. He opted rather for local political and especially economic organizations within the colonial situation to give shape and substance to the idea of a Korean people. Limited autonomous economic development was linked with national integrity in the shape of a benign capitalism.[41] Yi rallied for changes in economic attitudes as a means toward autonomous economic development and national survival. Both structural reform and education were the keys to a modern Korean identity. Despite Yi's resolution, the problem of national integrity under Japanese rule would hound the moderates throughout the colonial period. How can a people develop an economy and culture while subordinate to a foreign nation? The leftists would eventually reject the gradualist approach as collaboration, demanding radical structural change away from a Japan-aligned capitalist model.

Native enterprise

The ideology of an unequal but widely beneficial Korean capitalism with at best limited autonomy, helped sustain the efforts of large-scale Korean enterprise in the colony. The Tongil and Haedong Banks, Kyŏngsŏng Spinning and Hwasin enterprises were known as Korean firms, indigenously owned and managed. Min Tae-sik and Kim Sŏng-su, and later Min Kyu-sik, Kim Yŏu-su, and Pak Hŭng-sik built native enterprises with Korean managers and Korean investment capital, serving Korean markets. One obvious continuity among the three was their promotion of solidarity among Korean producers, investors, and consumers in the development of indigenous enterprise. Less directly stated but nonetheless clear was their sense of competition and commitment to survival. Local ownership and direction here would coincide with the initial sense of "native" capital, but the ideology of the "native products" campaign would further suggest benefit for the wider population. Korean business leaders paraded the fact of indigenous ownership and advertised the wider benefits of their enterprise in an effort to gain agrarian capital for investment and bolster their nationalist credentials.

Credible financial institutions were critical in the transition from agrarian capital to the more fluid capital demands of industry and commerce. Min

Tae-sik of the Hanil Bank argued for solidarity between producers and consumers as a basis for trust, and also for the institutional credibility of the banks themselves. He had joined the chorus of national solidarity on behalf of native enterprises already in 1923. Addressing a meeting of the Products Promotion Society, Min insisted "producers and consumers must cooperate, face difficulties together, if this campaign is to last."[42] Cooperation was linked on the one side with stronger enterprises, and on the other with strengthened consumer confidence. A year earlier he had promised to correct banking abuses of the past to restore confidence in banking functions, and called for encouragement of a savings mentality among the populace.[43] Reflecting on the economy in 1926, Min wrote of the strength of financial structures and called for greater consumer confidence and investment.[44] He was less optimistic about finance structures in the early years of the next decade, yet still emphasized cooperation and hopes for greater capital availability.[45]

As director of the Haedong Bank, Kim Yŏn-su in 1933 echoed Min's call for consumer confidence, praising the inflation control policies of the Japanese cabinet and its effect on business in Korea.[46] Kim had been involved earlier in well-publicized efforts to establish a spirit of cooperation between Korean producers and consumers at Kyŏngsŏng Spinning. The company highlighted its national roots with traditional terms used for brand names such as "T'aeguksŏng," and English labels with "Made in Korea" prominently displayed.[47] Sales to Korean consumers were critical in the company's early survival against Japanese competition. Cooperation among Korean investors in capital formation was also necessary to maintain growth in a capital-intensive large-scale industrial venture, as highlighted in reports of the company's need for increased funding.[48] The ideal of a Korean company owned by a large number of smaller Korean investors seemed implicit in the company's founding ideology. Yet by March of 1925, the number of investors decreased from 194 to 89, while capital investment by the remaining stockholders increased. Here difficulties in gaining the support of the agrarian elite might explain the growing concentration.

Kim Yŏn-su campaigned also for basic attitudinal and behavioral changes in support of a more rationally organized and efficient society. In a "New Year's Message on Family Life," he cautioned the populace regarding mistreatment of illegitimate children and the practice of concubinage, scapegoating, and a lack of accountability among his countrymen.[49] Rationality was also emphasized in recruitment policies at the Samyang Company. The firm employed at least six hundred families in Chŏlla Province by 1931, and one thousand by 1940, with a similar number in Manchuria.[50] Here Kim discouraged smoking, gambling, and the custom of early marriage, while promoting productive use of leisure time such as the weaving of straw rice bags. The more positive theme of solidarity among workers and managers stood out as the main emphasis among these admonitions. Kim set a high priority on a spirit of teamwork with other tenants on the agricultural estate in an effort to root out divisiveness that impeded production.[51] Efforts toward greater rationality in production among employees, joint investment efforts among investors, and the interplay between Korean producers and consumers were all part of the wider solidarity necessary for successful large-scale native enterprise.

Pak Hŭng-sik made a public commitment to product reliability and mutual trust with consumers in a New Year's pledge of 1933.[52] He outlined a future of rayon textile production and other improvements in consumer products, and challenged his audience to an "unprecedented public spirit" of solidarity. He envisioned domestic industrial development, technical education, and especially a strong sense of self-reliance among Koreans. Pak later developed an ambitious system of Hwasin chain stores across the peninsula, a project demanding extensive organization and cooperation with merchants in rural dry goods stores. In a recruitment ad run in vernacular newspapers,[53] he explained cooperation with local merchants in terms of wider national development and service to consumers:

Korean commerce is not yet developed. The system of distribution is obsolete, barely surviving with primitive methods. Business has declined and the consumers are greatly inconvenienced.... The chain stores will serve as a major economic unit of Korea and as a means of achieving domestic development and as a means of training merchants. They will play an important role in developing the Korean economy.

Here was benign capitalism at its best: improved distribution to better serve the customer, train merchants, and spur domestic development.

The entrepreneurs highlighted solidarity in hopes of promoting their enterprises and securing a place in an indigenous capitalist economy on the peninsula. However, the solidarity did not prevent intense competition with their fellow capitalists, Korean or Japanese. If the wider benefits of capitalism were somehow benign, competition among fellow nationals was not. Patterns of investment in their own ventures, in joint investments with other Korean and Japanese investors, and in major Japanese projects on the peninsula belied a priority of growth and profit characteristic of capitalism elsewhere. Such a priority led to vigorous rivalries with other Korean competitors and at times with Japanese business interests.

For instance, Min Tae-sik struggled to maintain the market share of the Seoul-based Hanil Bank in the face of increasing competition from the Japanese-owned Chōsen Commercial and Hansŏng banks. A scramble to expand through takeovers of major Korean regional banks was his only hope. He concluded a merger with the Hosŏ Bank of South Ch'ungch'ŏng Province in 1931 to form the Tongil, only to agonize through internal financial difficulties and strains in the wider economy through the early years of the merger. The bank's first president, Cho Pyŏng-t'aek, was quick to point out that whereas Japanese banks on the peninsula had received subsidies, the Hanil/ Tongil had to survive without such support.[54] The most pressing problem was capital availability in a tight economy. Min continued his aggressive pursuit of regional banks to assure a domestic capital supply but met stiff opposition among regionally based capitalists. The intervention of a local shareholder, Chŏng Chae-hak,[55] foiled Min's bid to take over the Kyŏngsang Haptong Bank in Taegu in 1932. Mergers and the subsequent financial costs and organizational difficulties caused problems for consumers and bank investors alike, but Min and the Hanil survived.

Land was precious in the agrarian society of colonial Korea, particularly in the fertile plains of the Chŏlla provinces. Massive Japanese investment in land and later in land reclamation intensified competition in agriculture, yet Kim Yŏn-su both integrated and expanded the landholdings of his father into the extensive agricultural estates of his Samyang Company between 1924 and 1940. The company reinvested tenant farm profits into purchase of neighboring plots, often from owners in debt.[56] Competition for land with fellow Korean agricultural investors faded in the later colonial years as the company turned its energies to lucrative land reclamation projects, trying to gain the support of the government-general for such capital and labor-intensive projects in competition with Japanese investors. The Samyang was busy in Manchuria relocating Korean farmers, organizing and managing agricultural estates toward the end of the colonial period, again in competition with Japanese firms. Kim Yŏn-su was among the very few Korean industrialists able to compete with larger Japanese firms. The remarkable accomplishments of both his agricultural and industrial firms gave greater credibility to his practical ideology of wider benefits through competition.

Pak Hŭng-sik wrote of fierce competition with Ch'oe Nam's Donga Department Store across from Hwasin property in the Chongno district.[57] In a published announcement of Pak's takeover of his rival, however, the competitive aspect was deemphasized in favor of the contribution of Hwasin customers to the company's success and the consequent wider benefits for the consumer of improved service.[58]

This is to announce that we have taken over 'Donga Department Store' in its entirety.... We realize that we have achieved such development and expansion thanks to your continued patronage. In order to fulfill our mission as proprietors of a department store suitable to the new age, we effected renovations in every aspect of management, and we framed our policy for offering good-quality merchandise at cheaper prices, feeling high responsibility for our society.

On the other hand, Pak boasted of Hwasin's uniqueness as a Korean department store challenging Japanese competitors of the more prestigious Chungmu district of Seoul, such as Mitsukoshi, Chōjiya, Minakai, and Hirata. Pak found a niche in the dry goods department and chain store business on a level above the larger Chongno district Korean merchants, and below the elaborate Japanese department stores in Chungmu. His ambition and competitive spirit were evident throughout the later colonial years, whether in paper with Sŏnil Paper, in domestic commerce with Hwasin Department Store and Hwasin Chain Stores, or in foreign trade with Hwasin Trade.

If the capitalism of Min, Kim, and Pak was benign in promoting solidarity for mutual though unequal growth and prosperity and solidarity for economic survival and possibly eventual Korean autonomy, it was likewise competitive, with strong priorities of growth and profit. Competition was evident even in educational foundations aimed at enhancing their nationalist credibility. The father of Min Tae-sik and Kyu-sik, Min Yŏng-hwi, had founded the Hwimum School,[59] later supported with a major block of shares in the Tongil Bank. Kim Yŏn-su donated the Myŏnggo Agricultural Estate (184 acres) to the Chungang Middle School in 1929, the Sint'aein Estate (612 acres) to Posŏng School in 1932, and established the Yangyŏnghoe Educational Foundation by 1942 with a capital of one million yen.[60] A latecomer to the educational efforts, Pak Hŭng-sik[61] built a new Seoul campus for the Kwansin Commercial School, formerly Hyŏpsŏng, and established the Kwansin Educational Foundation in 1940. If the educational contributions of the Mins in Hwimun, of Kim in Posŏng College and the Yangyŏnghoe, and of Pak later in the Kwansin Academy promoted enlightenment and industrial training, the schools also made the enterprises more competitive with a stream of promising young technicians and even managers.

If their enterprises were advertised as native firms with Korean management, ownership, and capital, close ties with government offices and Japanese business leaders would eventually erode their claim to national capital for the wider benefit of the nation. Progressive critics had earlier sounded the alarm about capitalist exploitation and raised hopes for a more egalitarian economy on the peninsula. But their fears and hopes were lost in the more pressing problems of Japanese dominance from without, or long-standing, obvious abuses of tenant farmers within. The vernacular print media gave little attention through 1940 to larger issues of a benign capitalism, egalitarian ideals, or possible exploitation in indigenous finance, industry, or commerce, and then ceased publication during the war. The years of the Pacific War brought new pressures on the local entrepreneurs now closely linked with the state, and further eroded their claim to private enterprise for the wider benefit of the populace.

Min Kyu-sik, Kim Yŏn-su, and Pak Hŭng-sik, figured prominently in the Wartime National Service Council. Each contributed two hundred thousand yen for the Japanese war effort in September of 1941, signing a resolution in support of the organization. Pak spoke grandly at the time of patriotic fervor for the war, of a "national project," and of the contribution of "our peninsula people"[62] to the war effort. But the most blatant example of Pak's service for the colonial state was his role in the Korean Aircraft Manufacturing Company (Chōsen Hikoki Kōgyō),[63] established in October of 1944 with an authorized capital of fifty million yen. The firm built a plant at Anyang and assembled a workforce of twenty-eight hundred employees to produce aircraft away from Japanese islands vulnerable to attack. Pak was appointed president. Representatives from the government-general, the Japanese Air Force, the Chōsen Industrial Bank, and the Oriental Development Company served on the board. Pang Ŭi-sŏk and Kim Yŏn-su served as directors, as did Yi Ki-yŏn of Sŏnil, and Min Kyu-sik was an auditor.

Kim and Pak were finally brought to trial for colonial antinationalist activities only after liberation from colonial rule. Although both were acquitted of all charges and continued their enterprise in the First Republic under President Syngman Rhee, their credibility as nationalist business leaders was tarnished in the last years of colonial rule. Yet local consumer confidence and investment had sustained the few fledgling Korean enterprises in the face of strong Japanese competition. Solidarity with consumers helped open a niche in Korean markets to be retained and expanded against both Korean and Japanese competitors. The growth of their enterprises in local markets through 1945 indicates some success in legitimating pragmatic goals of survival, profit, and growth with the moderate nationalist approach of native enterprise for limited economic autonomy in a colonial, capitalist economy. Their ideology of benign capitalism may not have captured the minds and hearts of the population through 1945, but it did provide some legitimation for local large-scale enterprise in finance, commerce, and industry.

Conclusion

The debate in the early colonial years over the design of the economy, and the subsequent business ideology and enterprise of local entrepreneurs raised three critical questions for the development of capitalism on the peninsula. In the first place, would self-development on a large scale, at least of major native enterprises with limited autonomy, even be possible, much less feasible, within the tightly controlled colonial economy? The very small number of major indigenous enterprises through 1945, and the difficulty of maintaining Korean ownership and direction even within these firms in the late years of colonial rule indicate the difficulty of organizing and sustaining such investments. The remarkable record of survival and growth of these few firms deserves further scrutiny, given their symbolic significance in efforts for autonomous development, and their contribution to the early shape of Korean business ideology and organization.

Two further questions apparent already in the second decade of colonial rule concerned the shape of a Korean capitalism. How could a more advanced industrial and commercial capitalism develop in an agrarian Korean economy? The strong emphasis of the colonial administration on agrarian development reinforced earlier patterns of real estate speculation, of profit taking with high tenant rents and usurious loans, and of commerce limited to grain trading and associated consumer items. Lack of access to investment capital plagued the efforts of major Korean entrepreneurs throughout the colonial years. Investors were reluctant to turn from the high returns on agrarian investments to the long-term commitment of funds necessary in industrial ventures, and they had doubts about the prospects of local enterprise. Again, the record of a relatively small share of indigenous investment in financial, commercial, and industrial ventures on the peninsula reflects the difficulty of the transition from an agrarian economy to the complex set of social and economic relationships necessary in an industrializing society. The rise of agrarian elites such as the Min and Kim families to financial and industrial leadership gives some sense of the dynamics of this transition.

A further issue of national capital became apparent toward the end of the colonial years with the shape of large-scale Korean industrial and commercial organization established in a few prominent enterprises. If Korean industrialization, finance, and trade were necessary for the survival of the Korean race, would the ideology and enterprise of a few business leaders like Min, Kim, and Pak suffice? Moreover, what would define wider benefit in a benign local capitalism under colonial rule, apart from the financial success of the individual local capitalists? At what point would intimate ties with the state and alien capitalists render the very ideal of national capital meaningless? And looking to the future, what would be the economic and social legacy of national capital (i.e., locally owned and of some wider benefit) surviving the alien government controls and intense competition with larger and better-funded Japanese firms through 1945?

Both the Japanese colonial state and Japanese private investment strongly affected efforts toward a benign capitalism on the peninsula. I examine state controls and alien investment, together with Korean enterprises such as the Tongil Bank, Hwasin Department Store, and Kyŏngsŏng Spinning in subsequent chapters. Our story comes to a close with the economic legacy of the colonial years in the First Republic under President Syngman Rhee. The analysis does not provide definitive answers to questions of an egalitarian capitalism in a society of long aristocratic traditions, to contradictions of inequality and divisive competition within a benign capitalism, or to the ambiguities of survival versus development of national capital. The study does tell a great deal about the degree and nature of colonial dependence, the early shape of major local enterprise, and the legacy of colonial concentration and business–state relations.

3

Colonial state

Japanese authorities gave wide publicity to the economic and social benefits of colonial rule in their *Annual Report on Reforms and Progress in Chōsen*. They too promoted an image of benign capitalism, but without nationalist concerns for indigenous ownership or an autonomous national economy. Yet even the Korean businessmen who might profit from such growth found themselves scrambling to survive and succeed in a closely supervised environment dominated by Japanese investment. The prominence of military leaders selected to direct the colony and the stringency of their control were evidence of the strategic importance of the Korean peninsula: a buffer against continental aggression and a base for expansion into Manchuria and China.[1] The state never wavered in its commitment to security and control, to economic development of the peninsula as a self-sufficient colony within the empire, and later to establish Korea as a forward base for expansion into the Japanese-controlled territory of Manchukuo. The government-general kept a tight rein on an often hostile Korean populace fiercely proud of their own cultural traditions and long accustomed to domestic self-rule as an independent nation within the Chinese orbit. They denied Koreans political participation while encouraging a closely supervised role in the economy.

The colonial state has been aptly characterized as growth-oriented and interventionist in economic affairs, promoting the peninsula as a base for mineral, agricultural, and eventually manufactured exports. The March First Demonstrations rudely awakened the authorities to a more cohesive and formidable civil society than had been recognized in the first decade of colonial rule. Nonetheless the "structuring" role of the colonial state far exceeded what Alfred Stepan[2] has observed more generally: "The administrative, legal, bureaucratic and coercive systems of the state attempt not only to structure relations between civil society and public authority in a polity, but also to structure many crucial relations within civil society as well." The economy of the peninsula represented one area of crucial rela-

34

tions for the colonial state. The very opposite of Myrdal's soft or weak state constrained by anxieties over domestic political consensus, the Japanese administration on the peninsula proved itself a strong state primarily concerned with military security and economic productivity. Yet the Korean inner circle gained some limited voice in economic matters. Oddly enough, it was to the state's benefit to permit at least a small, successful Korean elite to showcase local development, and provide evidence of a benign capitalism to counter leftist criticism.

The state offered direct and indirect support for a small network of local entrepreneurs representing an indigenous business elite. Overt support included the granting of peerage with annual stipends in 1911 to seventy-five eminent aristocrats and government officials from the late Chosŏn Dynasty, and subsequent appointments to the prestigious Central Advisory Council. One finds a less direct role in formation of a business elite in state supervision of business policy associations. Common interests and mutual support between a local elite and the state distinguish the "relative autonomy" of the strong state in contemporary developing economies, making possible effective policy direction and implementation.[3] Some understanding by the state of the opinions and investment interests of Japanese and a small group of Korean investors was necessary for effective policy formation and implementation even in colonial Korea. Only in large-scale private enterprise can we find exception to the absolute autonomy of the colonial state, and even here the state retained the upper hand.

Stephen Krasner[4] has distinguished three levels of state power vis-à-vis domestic society: (1) power to resist private pressure, (2) power to change private behavior, and (3) power to change social structure. Few could challenge the administration's power to resist pressure, though the business elite could at least represent its distinctive interests. The issue of private behavior was more complex. Imotani Zenichi[5] has argued that the colonial administration promoted change away from an aristocratic society toward a class-based society along economic criteria, a behavioral change paralleling the structural transition from agrarian to commercial and industrial capital. Although he agrees with the conclusion of structural reform, Norman Jacobs[6] has recently concluded that despite the changes, the Japanese did not disturb underlying cultural continuities. Jacobs referred specifically to cultural trends in Korea characteristic of Max Weber's model of a "patrimonial society." For instance, he described law in Korea as "the didactic expression of ethical rulership" whose purpose was "to preserve the moral character of authority rather than protect private interest." Reviewing the Japanese colonial legacy, Jacobs argued the authorities modernized patrimonial goals and procedures in Korea, such as more efficient patrimonial administrative control, without promoting deeper cultural changes.

Whatever their cultural efforts, the Japanese colonial authorities showed remarkable determination in reshaping business on the peninsula, particularly the structure of corporate organization and methods of state economic direction. Shikata Hiroshi[7] cited three changes in the early years of colonial rule: reorganizing the financial system, modernizing institutions for the circulation of money, and clarifying landownership. He concluded with the most salient characteristic of Korean capitalism at the time: the initiative and leadership of foreign capital. The Mins, Kim, and Pak represented only a segment of a small capitalist class in Korea scrambling to find a place in a Japanese-dominated colonial economy. If "effective" economic planning and implementation characterizes the strong state, whether in colony or sovereign nation, both the aims and beneficiaries of growth are quite different. Agriculture and later extractive and production industries in the colony were developed in line with the interests, capital resources, and markets of the main islands. If Koreans found benefit in the growth of transport and finance networks, they also found themselves working in Japanese-owned and -managed firms where profits reverted to the main islands. The Korean enterprises examined in this study were exceptions to the general rule of alien ownership and direction characteristic of major investments in a dependent colonial economy.

Three phases of administration policy marked the years of colonial rule.[8] The initial nine years under Generals Terauchi and Hasegawa have been characterized as "military rule" (*budan seiji*), highlighted by the extension of Japanese military and police controls into all areas of civilian life on the peninsula. Authorities developed the peninsula primarily as a source of grains with the rapid expansion of rice and soybean exports to Osaka, Yokohama, and Nagasaki, and as a market for light manufactures of textiles and cooking utensils from Japan. The rallies for independence on the peninsula in the spring of 1919, together with the ascendancy of liberal forces in Japanese politics, spurred policy adjustments in the next decade under Admiral Saitō Minoru, characterized as the years of "cultural rule" (*bunka seiji*). The salient Japanese military and police presence on the peninsula faded a bit, and controls eased on assembly and public expression among the local population. The demand for grains to feed the fast-growing urban population in the home islands dictated colonial economic policy, resulting in strong promotion of rice production for export on the peninsula through the second decade of colonial rule. The bureaucracies of the government-general mobilized resources for irrigation and reclamation projects to increase acreage under cultivation, improve seeds, and expand the supply of fertilizers.

Events in Manchuria and elsewhere on the Chinese mainland, and later the Pacific War led to a new phase of policy in the final fourteen years of colonial rule. Efforts toward a limited "assimilation" (*Naisen ittai*)[9] replaced the more relaxed cultural policy, with the colony and its population forced to play a more prominent role in the hard-pressed Japanese Empire. The Japanese scholar Yanihara Tadao[10] questioned the logic of assimilation among a colonial population deprived of even basic political rights: "It would appear, therefore, that the assimilation policy expressed in the form of paternalistic protection in the economic and social spheres of life can be carried out only under the guardianship of an oppressive bureaucracy in control of political and military affairs." The authorities never resolved the tensions between paternalism and bureaucratic oppression on the peninsula. However, Generals Ugaki and Minami did encourage and support Japanese and a few Korean firms with large investments on the peninsula to invest in similar projects in Manchukuo. State-subsidized development of Korean hydroelectric power and mineral resources to the north encouraged Japanese investment in large-scale chemical and heavy industrial plants supporting the war effort.

If autonomy and capacity represent measures of state strength, I am particularly interested in capacity or "infrastructural power"[11] to penetrate civil society in the colonial situation. The Japanese colonial state on the peninsula through 1945 attempted to structure economic relations in civil society mainly through legislation, and development and control of critical transport and finance infrastructures. One feature of colonialism in Korea was the meticulous process of pursuing state-mandated change through legal reforms announced and implemented with the full authority of the government-general. The administration legislated reforms in finance and agriculture, promotion of mining and energy development, and finally mobilization of corporate interests on the peninsula for the Pacific War effort. The government-general and its associated institutions designed and built transport and finance systems on the peninsula for both strategic purposes and the growth of commerce and industry. A railroad system crisscrossing the peninsula in an X pattern had been completed first from Sinŭiju in the northwest to the port city of Pusan at the southeast tip of the peninsula, and later from Chŏngjin in the northeast to Mokp'o in the southwest corner. In 1910 the rails carried 2 million passengers on 700 miles of rail, and in 1920 carried 16 million passengers, a number equal to the entire population, on 1,400 miles of rail. Close to 900 thousand tons of freight was carried in 1910 and 3.5 million tons in 1920.[12] The railroads carried 126 million passengers on 4,213 miles of track in 1941, and 24 million tons of freight.[13] Besides transportation infrastructures, the development of large-scale commerce and industry also required reliable and widespread currency circulation, and the functions of sound central and development banks. The Bank of Chōsen and the Chōsen Industrial Bank provided a firm basis in finance and credit for private investors in projects on the peninsula, and always under state supervision.

I find the colonial government was largely successful in establishing a capitalist framework on the peninsula along the lines of Japan's late Meiji period experience of state and economy,[14] though with more direct government control. Continuities in the East Asian cultures and societies of Japan and Korea supported the administration's efforts. Cultural and historical precedents from the late Chosŏn Dynasty in patterns of agrarian capital concentration, in the role of centralized state control in the economy, and even in class ties based on landholdings and education were not inconsistent with changes in colonial business–state relations. The Min brothers, Pak Hŭng-sik, and Kim Yŏn-su developed large-scale enterprises in an economic environment strongly affected by the direction of the colonial state. Laws, access to credit, and, at times, official positions both in and outside of government corporations helped to define their experience of business–state relations and, more broadly, their experience of capitalism in the colonial years. I am interested in how local entrepreneurs aligned their enterprise to the strong state economic policies and controls of an alien administration.

Economic direction

Authorities vigorously set about structuring capitalism on the peninsula through economic legislation, direct and indirect state investment in private enterprise, and ties with business leaders through business policy associations. The administration emphasized protection of private rights in efforts to revise civil law,[15] although rights of private property and economic organization were subject to the scrutiny and control of the state. The Japanese residency-general on the peninsula prior to annexation faulted Korean law as an inadequate basis for private rights.[16]

The Koreans had little or no conception of private rights as these were understood elsewhere in the Orient. Thus such maladministration existed for a long time that public officials were accustomed to pay only scant respect to the private rights of the people, and the latter on their side, did not complain against official extortion. In short, civil law guaranteeing private rights had practically no existence. This was undoubtedly one of the main causes of the people's impoverishment. Changes were needed in the Korean law so that it should become competent to protect life and property.

The colonial legal framework established a new pattern of relations between major business leaders and the state. Legislation developed within the administration and promulgated by decree gave authority, content, and practical direction to state economic policy, assuring compliance through incentives and constraints. Banking laws, the Corporation Law, and the clarification of property ownership through the Cadastral Survey established a basic format for economic activity already in the early years of colonial rule. Amendments to the banking laws and repeal of the Corporation Law spawned further adjustments in business in the second decade of colonial rule. Although various ordinances for strategic industries and economic control in the last few years of Japanese rule reoriented the economy toward war supplies,[17] the more fundamental reforms of the first two decades merit closer scrutiny. The reforms provide a legal outline of a colonial model of capitalism, though only the actual record of indigenous enterprise under alien rule can tell us of the mix of ideology, law, and entrepreneurship distinguishing the Korean colonial experience.

A Banking Law (*ginkōrei*) of 1906 solely for Korean banks gave notice of a prominent state role in finance: "The Minister of Finance will supervise all banking activities, and establish laws to insure bank stability and security for commercial finance." The law clarified procedures for obtaining government approval, organizational requirements as joint-stock companies,[18] and the functions of managers and the board of directors.[19] The authorities kept pace with the growing complexity of peninsular banking activities with revisions of 1912, finally ordering uniform regulations for Japanese- and Korean-owned banks alike. The reform further clarified requirements for establishing branches, for accountability of management to stockholders and for contents and publication of semiannual reports.[20] Expanding financial markets and fears of instability had spurred tighter banking regulations in the home islands of Japan by 1927.[21] Growth in finance on the peninsula likewise led to further revisions in 1928, including capital requirements and required deposits with the Central Bank.[22]

The authorities also established a legal basis for commercial and industrial investment. The Corporation Law (*kaisharei*) of 1910 required a license from the government-general prior to establishment of a business firm or foreign subsidiary in Korea. Whereas the formal intent of the Korean legislation was control of speculation,[23] the laws also set precedents regarding company organization and periodic reports that continued after repeal of the regulations[24] in 1920. The legislation effectively discouraged the founding of registered joint-stock firms, but a number of joint-stock firms did receive authorization under the law, including Korean firms such as the Chosŏn Mining Company of Min Tae-sik and Kim Sŏng-su's Kyŏngsŏng Spinning.[25] A revision of the Commercial Law and Corporation Law[26] in Japan in 1911 specifying legal responsibilities of founders and management was applied to Korea by 1922, further structuring intracorporate relations and business–state ties for the early Korean firms. But the most dramatic state effort to structure private enterprise was yet to come. The Critical Industries Ordinance (Jūyō Sangyō Tōseiho) of March 2, 1937, encouraged and provided support for industrial investment in Manchuria, and on the other hand restricted support for plant development on the peninsula. Various control ordinances would further constrain local enterprise and promote consolidation through the Pacific War years.[27]

At the same time legal structures were being formulated for business and finance on the peninsula, the authorities also set about clarification of land ownership, ostensibly to encourage capital circulation in the agrarian economy. They announced a Land Survey Law five months prior to formal annexation in August of 1910, mandating the temporary Land Survey Bureau to conduct a cadastral survey.[28] The Bureau assumed the monumental task of sorting out lands of the crown from private property, and distinguishing between cultivators and owners with the stated objective of clarification of property rights for tax purposes and property transfers.[29]

A complete land survey of the Peninsula is of great importance in order to readjust the land system which, till recently, was in an almost chaotic state. Its chief objective is to secure justice and equity in the levying of the land tax, and to determine accurately the cadastre of each region as well as to protect the rights of ownership, thereby facilitating transactions in sale, purchase and other transfers.[30]

Upon completion eight years later, the study had established a clearer legal framework for taxation and the transfer of property, of benefit to larger landowners especially, but not to the tenants. The survey hastened extension of landholdings by public and private Japanese firms such as the Oriental Development Company and Fumi Industrial, and also the expansion efforts of the family of Kim Yŏn-su and others among the local business elite.[31] The survey also clarified the capital assets of large Korean landowners, encouraging the transfer of capital between agricultural and commercial or industrial projects evident in the Min family's Kyesŏng and Yŏngbo companies.

Other laws established requirements for investment and constraints on irresponsible management. But the state also wielded considerable positive incentives for business on the peninsula through the credit and subsidies of state banks. The state played a key role in the colonial economy through changes in civil law relating to finance, with legislation affecting the mobilization of capital and credit resources, but also with its own massive resources for investment. The government-general and associated agencies held 19 percent of total Japanese assets on the peninsula by 1945, amounting to 14.9 billion yen out of a total of 88.6 billion yen of real estate and plant investments.[32] Agencies of the state with major investments included banks and the Oriental Development Company.

The Oriental Development Company (ODC, Tōyō Takushoku) was established in 1908 for agricultural migration to Korea, and later expanded into a development company with extensive landholdings and finance capital for agricultural and industrial projects.[33] The firm operated branches in China and Manchuria as well as Korea by 1942, with an authorized capital[34] of 100 million yen and 62.5 million yen paid-in, and an annual budget of 512.5 million yen. The belated appointment of Pak Hŭng-sik to the board of directors at the ODC in 1942 was the sole exception to a roster of Japanese nationals. Among the largest shareholders, the Finance Ministry in Japan held 3 percent of the shares,[35] and the Secretary of the Imperial Household 2.5 percent. The ODC owned and managed large tracts of land on the peninsula and invested heavily in major utilities and resource development projects.[36] The firm held large blocks of shares in leading utilities such as the Chōsen Railway Company, Chōsen Electric, Nansen Hydroelectric, Chōsen Electric Transmission, and the Chōsen Yalu River Hydroelectric Generation Company. Mining investments included equity in Chōsen Petroleum, Chōsen Anthracite Coal, Chōsen Magnesite Development, and its own Tōtaku Mining.

Resources for investment capital and credit at the Bank of Chōsen and the Chōsen Industrial Bank assured the state a major role in capital formation on the peninsula, whether in support of other banks, or providing credit and subsidies for large-scale projects in agriculture, business, and industry. The Bank of Chōsen functioned as a government-supported central bank on the peninsula, and later as the main financial institution for Japanese expansion into Manchuria. Within the peninsula the bank was responsible for currency circulation and foreign exchange, treasury operations for the government-general, and for the wider credibility of banks on the peninsula, at times providing commercial banks with funds for loan operations or even reorganization.[37] The government-general was the leading stockholder in the bank with about 4 percent of the shares.[38]

The Chōsen Industrial Bank specialized in medium- and long-term financing for agriculture and industry on the peninsula, based on a system of regional development banks established under the Korean Bank Law of 1906. The colonial authorities reorganized the regional system into the Chōsen Industrial Bank in June of 1918 with a substantial increase in capital and debt ceiling, and a network of forty-seven branches across the peninsula. The bank operated seventy-four branches two decades later, the most extensive banking operation on the peninsula,[39] secured with a paid-in capital of 15 million yen in 1927, raised to 37.5 million yen by 1941.[40] The Japanese Imperial Household and the government-general were among the major stockholders in the joint-stock corporation, although the Chōsen Savings Bank and the Hansŏng Bank held even larger blocks of shares by the third decade of colonial rule.[41]

The Industrial Bank supported enterprise on the peninsula through indirect financial support such as credits or subsidies, and also through direct investment in projects of high priority to the government-general. The bank invested directly in infrastructure development on the peninsula, especially in transporation, and in various projects coinciding with the wider economic plans of the state. Such projects were usually undertaken in co-operation with other state-supported institutions such as the Bank of Chōsen, the ODC, the Chōsen Savings Bank, and Chōsen Trust,[42] and also the Seigyōsha.[43] Financial help for agricultural development, particularly for irrigation and land reclamation projects, represented a major area of Industrial Bank activity. Subsidies and low-interest loans for extensive land reclamation projects proved lucrative for larger firms with sufficient capital and technology to undertake the risky projects, but few Korean firms participated until the third decade of colonial rule when the Samyang Company added considerable acreage through projects supported by the bank subsidies.[44] Annual subsidies from the bank helped Kyŏngsŏng Spinning weather the first decade and a half of slow growth, and a timely bank loan equal to the Kim's equity investment in South Manchurian Spinning and Weaving Company, or simply South Manchurian Spinning, supported the latter venture.[45] The bank also provided extensive medium-term loans in support of Pak Hŭng-sik's Hwasin Chain Stores project, making possible a four-month grace period between local merchants' receipt of goods and their reimbursement to Hwasin headquarters.[46]

Personalities prominent in transactions between the colonial state and indigenous enterprise tell a more human side of colonial enterprise. Activities of current and former colonial officials merit special attention. I find the career of Ariga Mutsutoyo, president of the Industrial Bank, of special interest given his ties with major Korean investors such as Kim Yŏn-su and Pak Hŭng-sik. Ariga intervened to arrange Industrial Bank loans for the Hwasin Chain Stores project, earning high praise from Pak Hŭng-sik:[47]

Ariga was known as a pro-Korean banker and formed warm friendships with Kim Sŏng-su and Song Chin-u, prominent national leaders. Although most Japanese enterprises treated Korean employees with discrimination, Ariga prohibited the practice in his bank. Ariga was a man of good reputation.

Pak was not the only beneficiary of close ties with the bank. The record of support from the Industrial Bank for the growth and expansion of Kim Yŏn-su's textile firms was remarkable. Here ties between Ariga and Pak Yŏng-ho made a difference. The sole Korean representative under Ariga, Viscount Pak[48] served as a director of the Industrial Bank from its founding until 1930, when he was offered the more prestigious post of advisor. The tenure of Viscount Pak Yŏng-ho as president of Kyŏngsŏng Spinning for sixteen years coincided with the years of Ariga's leadership at the bank.

During his years (1919–37) as president of the bank, Ariga Mitsutoyo played a major role in funding both Japanese and Korean enterprise in agriculture, commerce, and industry on the peninsula. His career pattern of experience in the bureaucracy prior to investment and leadership in private enterprise was not uncommon among Japanese active in major Korean and Japanese firms. Ariga had passed the civil service examination and joined the Tax Bureau in Japan after graduation from Tokyo Law Academy in 1898. He soon came to Korea as an official in the finance section of the residency-general and the government-general, before appointment as a director and then president of the Industrial Bank at age forty-seven in 1919. Successful direction of the bank led to his appointment to the Japanese House of Peers in September of 1934. Stepping down as president of the bank in 1937 at age sixty-one, he turned his energies to private enterprise on the peninsula closely tied to government support. In the last decade of colonial rule, Ariga held the post of president at such prominent Japanese firms as Chōsen Refining, the Japan High Frequency Heavy Industry Company, and Kankō Hydroelectric.[49] One can hardly overestimate Ariga's role in colonial business history, prominent in both the state–zaibatsu alliance and among an inner circle of leading Korean businessmen.

One finds a surprising number of larger Japanese ventures on the peninsula with strong Industrial Bank participation in which one or another Korean entrepreneur took part. The bank and the Oriental Development Company held 20 percent of the equity in the Chōsen Land Improvement Company where Min Tae-sik and Pak Yŏng-hyo served on the board, and the bank owned 16 percent of the shares of Kankō Hydroelectric where Kim Yŏn-su was among the board members. The Industrial Bank and Chōsen Trust together owned one-third of the total shares in the Keishun Railway Company, and with Chōsen Savings they owned 8 percent of the stock of the West Chōsen Central Railway Company. Kim Yŏn-su was active in both railway companies, as well as in Chōsen Refining. The Industrial Bank alone held one-fourth of the shares available in the latter company, which in turn invested in other mining and manufacturing ventures. Pak Hŭng-sik was on the board of North Korea Paper and Chemical Manufacture in which Chōsen Trust, the Industrial Bank, the Bank of Chōsen, and the ODC held 7 percent of the shares. Frequent dealings with the Industrial Bank through native-owned enterprises led to prominence in peninsular business circles, and in turn to contacts with major Japanese business leaders interested in Korea.

Apart from these large-scale Japanese ventures supported by direct Industrial Bank investment, there was one rather unique investment with Korean businessmen. Daikō Trade was a joint venture among Pak Hŭng-sik's Hwasin Trade (18 percent of the shares), Kim Yŏn-su's Kyŏngsŏng Spinning (10 percent), and the Industrial Bank, the Bank of Chōsen, and the Japanese Imperial Household (18 percent). Founded only in 1939, the company specialized in trade with Mongolia with a paid-in capital of five hundred thousand yen.[50] Such direct investment by state-supported firms in Korean investments was the exception in colonial Korea. On the one hand, few Korean firms were large enough to undertake the large-scale infrastructure or industrial projects of interest to the state until the waning years of colonial rule. On the other hand, wary of government interference, Korean investors with strong native-owned enterprises did not welcome direct state investment, but also did not spurn credit and subsidies. Indirect rather than direct state investment proved to be the key to survival and prosperity in large-scale local enterprise.

Both the content and implementation of laws and the activities of these state firms profoundly affected the design of business–state relations through 1945. One can hardly overemphasize the state role in the colonial economy, whether through economic legislation or the massive presence of state-directed and supported joint-stock companies such as the Industrial Bank and the ODC. But there was more. A third area of state efforts to structure the economy was evident in strategies to control organizations of business leaders. Appointment to peerage was explained as recognition of past contributions to the Korean state, an effort by the administration immediately after annexation to gain the support of native aristocrats and political leaders.

The Korean Aristocracy Law was promulgated on August 29, 1910, the day of annexation.[51] An official explanation for the law can be found in the *Annual Report*, preceding the announcement of the number of surviving peers each year.

In August of 1910, regulation concerning the peerage of Chōsen and matters relative to it were promulgated by Imperial Ordinance, and on the 7th of July, by virtue of them, the blood relatives of Prince Yi, other than those accorded the status of princes of the Blood, men of high birth, and those who had rendered great services to the state, to the number of 76 in all, were created peers, ...among whom were 6 Marquises, 3 Counts, 22 Viscounts and 45 Barons.[52]

Sixty-one of the peers survived through 1929, with each receiving both title and an annual stipend.[53] The status and stipend accorded aristocrats facilitated their emergence as leading business figures in the early colonial years, such as Marquis Pak Yŏng-hyo of Kyŏngsŏng Spinning and Viscount Min Yŏng-hwi of the Hanil Bank.

If peerage was recognition for the past, appointment to the Central Advisory Council was recognition for political support and/or economic cooperation from the second decade of colonial rule.[54] The council was consulted on rare occasion by the governor-general on economic topics such as inheritance laws (1921), industrial development (1929), and tenancy regulations (1931). As members of the civil service, council members received a salary from the government-general. Among the entrepreneurs of interest here, Kim Yŏn-su and Pak Hŭng-sik protested after 1945 that they never accepted their appointments to the council, although Min Kyu-sik did. Other leading business figures among this elite group of Korean investors did serve on the council, even if Kim and Pak were prominent enough to decline the offer and still maintain relations with the administration. Recognizing earlier prominent officials with peerage, and later business figures with appointment to this advisory body, the administration reinforced the prestige of these leaders at least among the Japanese business elite and no doubt among some of the Korean business elite. More to the point, appointment strengthened the credibility of indigenous business leaders in the eyes of the administration and their affiliated joint-stock corporations.

The state also played a part in major business policy associations on the peninsula, an effort to generate new patterns of business–state relations. The Keijō Chamber of Commerce and Industry[55] was established in 1916, followed by chambers in other major cities the next year. Fourteen cities across the peninsula could boast of chambers by 1935, and an umbrella group, the Chōsen Chamber of Commerce and Industry, appeared in

1932.[56] The associations gathered and published information on business trends, monitored the enterprises of association members, responded to government inquiries, and consulted on economic policy, all under the banner of promoting trade and industry.[57] The state regulated the chambers with detailed bylaws published as government ordinances, and by mandating membership for all large-scale and medium-sized business. Election of officers, annual budgets, and changes in operating procedure were all subject to government approval. Regulations[58] enforced from 1915 suppressed separate Korean and Japanese chambers of commerce, leading to Korean participation in the Keijō Chamber of Commerce and Industry and other branches, though hardly on an equal footing.

The venerable Keijō (Seoul) chamber[59] had originally been organized as a Japanese businessmen's group in 1888. The designation of a second vice-presidency for a Korean national provided an important opportunity for institutional governance among the Korean inner circle. Whereas Koreans soon represented at least half the membership, only three to five appeared annually among the fifteen or so directors, with Han Sang-yong of the Han-sŏng Bank, Kim Han-gyu, Pak Yŏng-gŭn, and later Kim Sa-yŏn quite prominent. Min Tae-sik, president of the Hanil Bank and later the Tongil Bank, served one term (1929–32) as vice-president of the chamber. Kim Yŏn-su served later as a board member and Pak Hŭng-sik as a special member.[60]

Former bureaucrats with extensive business experience in Korea headed the organization, such as Watanabe Sadaichirō (1924–32)[61] and his successor, Kada Naoji (1932–9). Watanabe originally worked for the partnership of Okura Kihachirō before coming to Korea in 1905. An engineer, he was active in the Seoul–Ŭiju railroad construction, and later as a supervisor of irrigation construction for the administration. He rose to the presidencies of the Kōkai Company and of Chūyō Trade by 1935, and served as a director of the Chōsen Engineering and Architecture Association. Kada Naoji[62] was employed as a civil engineer in the colony of Taiwan before coming to Korea in 1917 to pursue business interests, originally in lumber. He later served as president of Chōsen Leather (Chōsen Hikaku) with a paid-up capital of 1.5 million yen by 1942, and also of Chōsen Agriculture Promotion (Chōsen Kanno). The chamber leaders here represented important links between the colonial state and local enterprise.

Besides chambers of commerce and industry in major cities on the peninsula, there were also more specialized associations[63] where the inner group of the Korean business elite held positions of institutional governance. For instance, Kim Yŏn-su served as vice president of the Chōsen Industrial Association (Chōsen Kōgyō Kyōkai) with Shibuya Reiji of the

Bank of Chōsen and, later, Daikō Trade as managing director.[64] The eminent Katō Keizaburō,[65] former governor of the Bank of Chōsen, was president of the association. Born in 1874, Katō graduated in law from Nippon University in 1898. After some years of government service, he won appointment as president of the Hokkaido Industrial Bank in 1924. He assumed the presidency of the Bank of Chōsen three years later. The Industrial Association was particularly active in making recommendations (*kengi*) on administration industrial policy.[66] While helping to design government-directed industrial development, the association also gave high priority to collegiality among its members and the sharing of expertise. Termed "associations under state guidance" (*yūkei kikan*),[67] the activities and organization of the chambers and of the industrial association were subject to the supervision and regulations of the colonial administration.

Why did the Korean inner circle take part in such organizations? Useem[68] offered three reasons for similar activities among an inner group of the U.S. business elite:

(1) The multiple corporate connections of inner group members tend to foster the formation of informal transcorporate networks; (2) inner group members are expected to be especially prominent in institutional governance because of the integrative position the inner group holds within the capitalist class; (3) by virtue of their stronger connection with the primary holders of corporate ownership, inner group members are also more likely to be promoted for governance positions.

Despite unequal participation, the business groups served as a source of contacts for Korean business leaders with one another and with Japanese investors and administration officials. Business association activities reinforced the multiple intercorporate connections of the Korean inner circle, while prominence as local corporate leaders led to governance positions.

The colonial authorities represented the interests of the empire on the peninsula. The administration took the role of a strong state in the economy, pushing their development plans forward with legislation and state-backed and -directed financial institutions. If their economic policy was growth-oriented and interventionist, it was also distinctively capitalist, promoting the rights of private property and the growth of private enterprise in line with the state's wider strategic aims. A format for business–state relations emerged in which the state played a more prominent role in the economy than was typical even in Meiji Japan. The pattern of business–state relations was obviously more complex than this brief review would suggest, and even the three areas of intervention depicted here were not necessarily internally consistent. The abstract rule of law, for instance, contrasted sharply with the skeins of personal relationships that gave dynamism and direction to the associations of business leaders. Informal controls such as personal ties supported formal controls. Legislation and bureaucratic procedures can provide direction but not the day-to-day content of business–state relations.

If the strong state was one partner in the business–state relationship, what can be said of the other partner, the business people who survived and prospered? I examine the role of Japanese private investment on the peninsula, and then look closely at the investments of major Korean business leaders in subsequent chapters. But the profile of the colonial state outlined here already says much about how one did business on the peninsula. Adaptation to government economic direction, credibility with the administration, and close contacts with present and former government officials were prerequisites for successful large-scale enterprise in the colony, for Japanese and Koreans alike. Lacking large-scale capital resources of their own or political leverage in the tightly controlled colony, native business leaders had few channels for influencing the directions of government economic policy.

Overriding concerns of security and later military and economic expansion into Manchuria reflected the interests of the home islands and absorbed the attention and resources of the colonial administration on the peninsula. But military security and expansion beyond Korea were not inconsistent with development of transport and finance infrastructures. The railroads were a case in point, constructed at considerable cost, though in time returning extensive annual revenues for the administration.[69] The state estimated public expenditure in railroad construction at about 384 million yen by 1930, 504 million yen by 1935, 600 million yen by 1937, and 900 million yen in 1940. The state soon began to see returns. The publicly owned railroads cleared 10 million yen in 1930, 24 million yen in 1935, and 32 million yen in 1937. In 1937 alone, revenues from the railways, telecommunications, and monopolies on ginseng and other precious commodities represented 41 percent of the total revenue in the budget of the colonial government. Security priorities led to railroad development, and in turn to economic development. Given such clear priorities, even with some stronger voice in policy formation I doubt Koreans could have altered the state's single-minded commitment to regional military security, agricultural and later industrial complementarity with the main islands, and finally the colony's economic self-sufficiency within the empire.

Conclusion

The picture of a growth-oriented and interventionist, albeit alien, colonial state provides a context for understanding concentration, state relations, and class ties among major Korean business leaders through 1945. The absence of restraints on state intervention coupled with the state's pervasive influence in the economy and careful direction, constrained but did not inhibit the pursuit of private profit. One could argue that the very constraints imposed and anxieties over further state intervention encouraged concentration in private enterprise to sustain local direction and ownership. Korean entrepreneurs faced difficulties in gaining the credibility of the state for native enterprises. The few who did gain credibility, however, were then able to gain extensive support for various enterprises, again contributing to concentration of capital among a few established local entrepreneurs. Effective management demanded formal education in Japanese law, business practices, or technology, long experience of dealing with the state, and a network of personal contacts with pertinent officials. There were not many Korean or Japanese managers with such experience who could gain the confidence of major Korean investors without long service in the organization. The extensive role of the strong colonial state in the economy thus encouraged concentration in management as well.

The thirty-five years of colonial business–state relations provided an experience of economic growth for major native business leaders in line with the priorities of an alien state. Alignment with the priorities and projects of the colonial state led to the growth of a few native enterprises, to the accumulation of indigenously owned capital, and to the emergence of a few extensive, locally managed investments in major areas of the economy. At the same time colonial authorities advertised the economic benefits of state-directed and state-supported growth, local entrepreneurs spoke of a benign capitalism taking shape in their locally owned and managed enterprise. The more immediate question here is not the profile of the strong state or even its infrastructural power, but the actual dynamics of enterprise among a small native business elite. It is clear they had to carefully align their investments to find a niche in the development plans of the colonial administration. We will examine how they adjusted yet maintained indigenous ownership and direction in later chapters.

The role of the colonial state in class formation among Korean business leaders deserves more attention. The state's direct role in peerage selection and appointment to the Central Advisory Council, and indirect role in the supervision of business policy associations has been noted. I will examine interactions among a few major Japanese business leaders on the peninsula and a small coterie of Korean businessmen. A review of indigenous enterprise in the colony will shed light on processes of class formation among leaders like the Mins, Pak, and Kim Yŏn-su, and their interactions with officials such as Ariga Mitsutoyo, Katō Keizaburō, and Shibuya Reiji. The prominence of former administration officials in private enterprise added a further dimension of state direction to emerging class ties, and permitted the Korean business elite access to information and certainly contact with central figures in policy formation processes. The leadership of Min Tae-sik, Pak Hŭng-sik, and Kim Yŏn-su in various associations of leading native and foreign business figures provided entree to discussions of industrial and commercial policy. Such organizational activity, and more importantly, joint investment with prominent Japanese business leaders on the peninsula, moderated the autonomy of the colonial state vis-à-vis local business leaders.

The profile of the colonial state suggests a curious model of Japanese capitalism in its leading colony of Korea. The principle of private property and limited economic rights were protected by law, but the state exercised close controls on private enterprise and supported massive investment from the home islands, precluding all but a few Koreans from competitive major enterprise. If private rights distinguish a modern capitalist society, there was little place for the Korean individual in colonial capitalism. Cumings has pointed to the "overdevelopment" of finance and transport infrastructures and the underdevelopment of human resources. In the same vein, Kublin had earlier concluded: "Japanese policy was above all devoted to uplifting Korea but unfortunately not its people."[70] There were other anomalies. The state invested in finance and transport structures and provided support for private enterprise in strategic areas of agriculture and later industry, but only in line with wider concerns of military security and a firm base of industrial and military expansion in Manchuria and China. The model of Japanese capitalism evident in the Korean experience of colonial rule was an odd blend of military priorities, authoritarian rule, and the remarkable mobilization of Korean labor and Japanese capital for the construction of economic infrastructures, Japanese mining, and heavy industrial plants.

4

Japanese investment

If the colonial state helped structure the economy on the peninsula, so also did the massive business combines[1] from the home islands. Japanese corporate investors left behind estimated assets of 3.5 billion dollars in 1945, representing 67 percent of total Japanese assets in Korea. Leading zaibatsu such as Mitsubishi, Mitsui, and Noguchi Jun's Nichitsu[2] dominated the corporate share. Contrasting cultural with economic assimilation, the colonial scholar Yanihara Tadao concluded: "the invasion of the peninsula by Japanese capital is tantamount to an assimilation of Korea by the capitalistic structure of Japan."[3] Whatever the Japanese achieved culturally on the peninsula, they certainly succeeded in transferring the model of close relations between state and major private enterprise. The small number of Korean entrepreneurs can hardly be termed a third party in business on the peninsula. They rather went about their farming, commerce, and food processing in the shadow of a formidable alliance between colonial state and major zaibatsu.

The design of colonial state relations with the home island corporate giants permeated the colony's business climate in the formative years of large-scale local enterprise. There were parallels in the concentration of capital and ownership between the large Japanese firms and the native enterprises of the Mins, Pak and Kim. The pattern of close business–state relations evident among the Korean economic elite also coincided with well-established patterns among their prominent counterparts directing Japanese corporate investment on the peninsula. Prewar Japanese business organization and business–state ties provided a format for capitalism on the peninsula.

Centralization of ownership and capital distinguished the Japanese zaibatsu through 1945. Concentration in ownership and sometimes management permitted close control by a family or kinship group such as the Iwasakis of Mitsubishi. We can further characterize the early Japanese combines with concentration of capital in a group of companies in diverse fields of

investment, often with a monopoly position. The zaibatsu gained prominence in the prewar economy through control of extensive capital assets with
affiliated firms of the ten largest combines holding 35 percent of the total
paid-up capital in Japan in 1945.[4] Both intercorporate competition and an
interventionist state encouraged the transition from family companies to
joint-stock industrial and commercial combines. Ironically the late Meiji
state had to prod reluctant, private family firms toward reincorporation as
public joint-stock companies with enforcement of the Commercial Law of
1893 and Civil Law of 1898 guaranteeing the rights of private property. But
limited and unlimited partnerships remained attractive since neither were
required to disclose their assets or financial condition.[5]

Efforts continued in the Taishō era with tax reforms of 1913 legislating
progressive taxation[6] for all but joint-stock companies. At the same time,
demand for industrial capital and diversification in the more competitive
postwar economy of the 1920s contributed to reorganization as joint-stock
companies among the zaibatsu. Owners developed strategies to preserve
core ownership despite expansion. Flagship companies owned by the
families reorganized as partnerships or limited partnerships with closed
holdings; the flagship companies in turn held large blocks of shares in their
affiliates. Sale of stocks to friendly associates among the affiliates, particularly those with personal connections to the firms,[7] supplies capital for
expansion without diluting family control. Parallels were evident in the
family enterprise of the Kyesŏng and Yŏngbo companies of the Min families
and the Samyang of Kim Yŏn-su, though their reliance on agricultural rather
than commercial or light industrial capital reflected the agrarian character
of the local economy.

Apart from similarities in organization and the role of personal networks,
there were also obvious differences in state ties for the local elite. If business –state relations were important for both the prewar Japanese zaibatsu
and the early Korean chaebŏl, there was little similarity in the content of
these relations between the two types of combines. Tracing the place of
business leaders in Japanese political development through the turn of the
century, Scalapino found evidence of growing political influence. They
played a unifying role in party and bureaucratic alliances with the advent of
constitutional government in Japan at the end of the nineteenth century.
They enjoyed growing political leverage with industrialization at the beginning of the twentieth century, and soon a business elite emerged with better
education, more capital for political party support, and more self-confidence
as leaders in Japanese society. Industrial and commercial interests occupied
important positions in the major parties and in the bureaucracy by the

1920s.[8] The business elite consolidated its position in state affairs through the influence of businessmen's associations on the formation of economic policy.[9] But still the strength of the Japanese state could not be ignored even among such powerful local elites. Ishida Takeshi[10] wrote of a "governmentalization" of interest groups in prewar Japan where "the specific purposes of interest groups become fused with government purposes." And if Japanese business was the weaker partner in business–state ties in the home islands, even more so was the local business elite in colonial Korea. Despite Korean participation in local business policy organizations, the legacy of economic power without experience of substantive political voice would haunt businessmen and politicians alike in the First Republic.

Dramatic corporate growth in private enterprise marked the years of colonial rule in Korea. Statistics alone suggest a remarkable increase in the number and size of registered firms, mostly joint-stock companies. One hundred and fifty-two companies were listed with a total paid-in capital of 15.9 million yen in 1911, and 5,413 companies were registered in 1938 with a paid-in capital of 1.08 billion yen.[11] Firms with Korean presidents and capital were generally smaller ventures in commerce and agriculture such as rice mills and breweries, whereas Japanese investment was common in both smaller and especially larger enterprises. Japanese capital on the peninsula was divided equally between firms registered in Japan and affiliates registered in Korea. The aggregate paid-in capital of Korean branches with headquarters in Japan amounted to some 1.1 billion yen in 1940, while Japanese holdings in Korean-registered companies amounted to 1.02 billion yen. One hundred thirty-two companies registered in Japan were listed with production establishments in Korea in 1940, spread evenly among mining and manufacturing, with a few also in agriculture and lumber.[12]

A review of only the larger Korean and Japanese firms registered in Korea in 1940 gives some idea of ownership, areas of investment, and productive facilities. Of some two thousand firms, 68 percent were owned by Japanese nationals, 5 percent by Korean nationals, and 27 percent were joint investments including both Japanese and Koreans among major shareholders. The Japanese and the joint investments were led by Japanese nationals, with Korean presidents appearing only in the companies owned by Koreans. The joint investments point up the importance of the distinction in colonial Korea between ownership and administrative control. The Japanese in private enterprise commanded not only far more extensive capital resources, but also exercised leadership in the economy through administrative control of 95 percent of the capital of larger firms.

Apart from commerce and services, differences in production facilities alone indicate major differences between Japanese and native-controlled firms. Manufacturing firms represented 62 percent of the Japanese firms, with mining (15 percent) and agricultural (12 percent) firms less common. Manufacturing firms represented 69 percent of the locally owned firms, with agricultural firms (14 percent) a distant second. What I find noteworthy is not the preeminence of manufacturing among local production units, but the disparities evident in strong alien and weak local investment in mining, and the relatively small share of agricultural investment among local large-scale firms. Clearly, local investment in natural resource extraction and development of land-based capital into publicly registered agricultural firms was slow to develop on the peninsula, further evidence of the deliberate pace in the transition from agricultural to commercial and industrial capital. A final comparison of the largest of the Japanese versus locally controlled firms gives some sense of the competitive environment in which local entrepreneurs pursued their business activities. Among the Korean-controlled firms in 1940, only 16 were registered with a paid-in capital of one million yen or more, including the enterprises of the Mins, Pak, and Kim, compared with 238 Japanese-controlled firms of that scale on the peninsula.

The scale and direction of Japanese private investment in the colony of Korea, in tandem with the direct and indirect investment of the state and its associated agencies, established patterns for large-scale enterprise on the peninsula through 1945. Competition and at times cooperation with Japanese investors were part and parcel of large-scale enterprise for the native economic elite. Patterns of corporate organization and government relations characterizing the pre-World II Japanese zaibatsu strongly affected concentration of capital, ownership, and control in the initial years of large-scale native enterprise in Korea. I look first to the character and direction of three of the largest Japanese corporate investments in the colony, their alliance with the state through such key organizations as the Industrial Bank, and then to the leading Japanese firms in areas where the Mins, Pak Hŭng-sik, and Kim Yŏn-su tried to compete. I am interested in the adaptations of Japanese private enterprise to the policies of the colonial state.

Investors and the state

Two sources of zaibatsu power caught the attention of American government investigators in Tokyo in 1946: their monopoly position and close relations with the Japanese state. The Americans appeared surprised with the monopoly position of prewar zaibatsu and quickly faulted the Japanese government for the absence of antitrust legislation. Their criticism in retrospect appears simplistic, but their interviews with executives at the time regarding the monopoly position quite insightful. The executives cited four reasons for the reluctance of smaller Japanese concerns to compete with the zaibatsu: (1) the financial strength of the combines due to control of their own banks and influence in other financial institutions; (2) the comprehensive scope of zaibatsu interests, including control of critical supplies and raw materials; (3) dependence of smaller firms on the cooperation of zaibatsu trading agencies to gain access to markets beyond local traders; and (4) the potential of zaibatsu concerns to hire away the best talent from smaller firms. The local firms of the Mins, Pak, and Kim could not compete directly with the Japan-based large-scale firms of the leading zaibatsu, but the scale and direction of zaibatsu investment in Korea strongly affected the economic priorities of the colonial government, access to Japanese and other markets beyond the peninsula, and other facets of local enterprise such as the availability of skilled labor, the supply and availability of credit, and so on.

Early Korean chaebŏl cherished dreams of advantages similar to the zaibatsu. The Mins, Pak, and Kim all endeavored to gain control of financial institutions for support of their capital-intensive investments but none succeeded, leaving them much more reliant on government-controlled finance institutions than the zaibatsu. The local elite also displayed great imagination and entrepreneurial energy. The inner circle of Korean entre-preneurs nurtured business groups, accumulating extensive capital within a few closely controlled companies, and later branching out with interests in agriculture, finance, commerce, and industry. Whereas none of the chaebŏl compared in scale with the zaibatsu, the Korean combines with their diverse interests stood in sharp contrast to the more conventional native investments simply in agriculture or simply in commerce. Also, Pak Hŭng-sik and Kim Yŏn-su vigorously promoted and invested in trading agencies, the former with wider commercial aims, the latter with both commercial aims and practical concerns of marketing his textile products.

Turning from monopoly to state relations, the report concluded: "one of the strongholds of zaibatsu power has been their ability to strongly influence and frequently control governmental actions affecting their common interests."[13] The report cited examples of prominent figures with strong business and government connections, including Hideo Kodama, second-in-command in Korea under Governor-General Saitō from 1929 to 1931, and Seihin Ikeda of Mitsui.[14]

Hideo Kodama (Nissan, Hitachi, and Manchurian Investment) has been Civil Admin-istrator of Korea, Minister of the Interior, State Minister without Portfolio, and Min-ister of Education. Some of his relations by marriage are connected with Sumitomo, and his sister is the wife of Shigeto Hozumi, who is directly interested in Shibusawa and also Grand Chamberlain to Crown Prince Akihito. Seihin Ikeda (Mitsui) has served as Governor of the Bank of Japan, advisor to the Ministry of Finance, Counsellor to the Home ministry, Member of the Cabinet Advisory Council, Minister of Finance, and Minister of Commerce and Industry. His daughter is the wife of Takaya Iwasaki, who also has political connections through the marriage of the eldest daughter of Hisaya Iwasaki to Renzo Sawada, who had a long career in the foreign office and diplomatic corps. In addition, the present Finance Minister, Meizo Shibusawa, and the present Premier, Kijuro Shidehara, are related by marriage to the Iwasaki family, as are a number of other individuals who hold or have held important government posts.

Close business–state relations evolved through a variety of ties including family relationships and friendships, and appointment of people with strong business interests to government posts. The investigators overestimated the power of zaibatsu to affect government policy, particularly from the late 1930s, but observations about intimate business–government ties were quite perceptive and relevant to patterns of business–state relations in Korea as well.

A closer look at zaibatsu activity in colonial Korea reveals how the big players did business on the peninsula. Among the largest of the Japanese zaibatsu active in the colony of Korea, Mitsui was active in trade and later industrial ventures, while Mitsubishi was distinguished by heavy industrial investments, and Nichitsu by hydroelectric and chemical projects. The Mitsui Honsha listed a paid-in capital of 400 million yen in 1946, with affiliates such as Mitsui Bussan (paid-in capital, 100 million yen), the Teikoku Bank (148 million yen), Mitsui Mining (300 million yen), Mitsui Chemical Industry (101 million yen), and Mitsui Steamship (70 million yen).[15] Mitsui showed early interest in commerce on the peninsula, later turned to light industrial investments, and ultimately to heavy industrial projects at the end of the colonial period. Mitsui Bussan (Mitsui Trade) established a branch in Seoul in 1909 and later in Pusan, with stations in seven other major port cities across the peninsula by 1941. The firm prospered with exclusive rights for the export of Korean red ginseng, a popular medicinal herb. Mitsui Trade commanded estimated assets in Korea in 1945 of 125.5 million yen.[16]

Ginseng had long been a government monopoly in Korea and a highly prized export item in relations with China. Together with the railroads and tobacco monopoly, the ginseng monopoly organized by the government-general served as an important source of state revenues. The state granted Mitsui the trade rights in the original ginseng ordinance of 1908, reaffirmed in the Red Ginseng Monopoly Law of 1920.[17] U.S. investigators provided a rare glimpse into foreign enterprise, national strategy, and Korean labor in a study of Mitsui's red ginseng monopoly.

After the Japanese annexation, Mitsui Bussan Company was given the exclusive license to export red ginseng. Extract and a powder substance of red ginseng was distributed by the Ginseng Wholesale Ltd. Co., directly to pharmacies and stores in Korea and Japan. Mitsui loaned money to the ginseng cultivators at Kaesŏng each year to assist the farmer to pay cultivation expenses. Repayment of these funds to Mitsui was a charge against the Monopoly Bureau for the purchasing price of the red ginseng. Mitsui paid an additional amount to the Government General Account, very small compared to the selling value of the manufactured red ginseng in China. In addition to making a huge profit on selling ginseng, the company utilized red ginseng to purchase scarce articles for Japan's economy. During the war, materials necessary for war were exchanged for red ginseng and the Japanese Army used red ginseng to bribe Chinese spies. Also in 1944, Mitsui monopolized the export of white ginseng and bartered over ten million yen for materials of war. To the cultivators, they distributed 600,000 yen as a subsidy in lieu of payment.[18]

The alliance between colonial state and a leading zaibatsu here raised the traditional production and trade of ginseng into a fabulously profitable agricultural industry with strategic benefits. The monopoly added nearly two million yen annually to government revenues between 1918 and 1935.[19] Production and sales continued to grow in the next ten years. Pak Hŭng-sik boasted of finally gaining about one-half of the annual sales rights of red ginseng from Mitsui in 1944 to help defray the 600 million yen necessary for purchase of aircraft manufacturing equipment.[20]

Mitsui did not confine itself to trade. Among smaller ventures in light industry, the Mitsui Bussan owned the Tōyō Silk Manufacture Company in Seoul, founded in 1929, and an affiliate, Tōyō Cotton Trade of Osaka, owned Nanboku Cotton Manufacture,[21] founded in 1919. Mitsui Mining purchased Sansei Mining from the Korean "Gold King," Ch'oe Ch'ang-hak in 1929,[22] and a Mitsui affiliate, Nippon Flour Milling, operated mills on the peninsula.[23] Mitsui played a role in heavy industrial investment in 1940 on the peninsula mainly through minority holdings in other Japanese firms such as Ōji Paper and Ōji Securities, the Kanegafuchi firms, and Tokyo Shibaura Electrical Equipment.

With a paid-in capital of 240 million yen in 1945, the Mitsubishi Honsha of the Iwasaki family held large blocks of shares in Japanese affiliates such as Mitsubishi Heavy Industries (one billion yen), Mitsubishi Mining (407 million yen), Mitsubishi Chemical Industries (110 million yen), and in the Mitsubishi Bank (135 million yen).[24] The firm entered the business world of the peninsula only in the later decades of colonial rule, with a Japan-registered subsidiary, the Tozan Agricultural Company (Tozan Nōji), operating farms in central and southern Korea, and a refinery operated by Japan Corn Products in P'yŏngyang. The combine also joined with the colonial state in larger ventures on the peninsula. Mitusbishi, the Oriental Development Company, and the Industrial Bank established a joint venture for shipbuilding in Pusan in 1937. They registered Chōsen Heavy Industries (Chōsen Jūkōgyō)[25] with an authorized capital of 7 million yen by 1942, 5 million paid-in, with Mitsubishi and the ODC each holding 37 percent of the shares, and the bank 18 percent. The company's assets in Korea in 1945 were estimated at 65.7 million yen.

Among opportunities for investment, mining attracted the lion's share of Mitsubishi capital in line with strong administration support for development of mineral resources.[26] Mining represents an excellent example of a mutually beneficial alliance between state and zaibatsu based on common interest. The state offered subsidies and loans for gold mining investments, including support for transportation facilities and technologies such as electric-powered extraction equipment. The administration also implemented a five-year Gold Production Plan from 1938 to boost production. Mitsubishi Mining teamed up with the state-supported Japan Iron Manufacture to found a venture[27] in 1939 with operations in the Mozan area of North Hamgyŏng Province and elsewhere on the peninsula. Based in Tokyo with only a branch in Seoul, the Mozan Iron Mining Company (Mozan Tekkō Kaihatsu) listed an authorized and paid-in capital of 50 million yen in 1942, with Mitsubishi Mining holding 49.9 percent of the shares, and Japan Iron Manufacturing 24.9 percent. The assets of the Mozan mining venture alone were estimated at about 400 million yen in 1945.

The mother company and Mitsubishi Mining held 29 percent of the shares in another mining venture, Chōsen Anthracite Coal,[28] and the ODC and its affiliate Tōtaku Mining, retained a further third of the shares. Founded in 1927, the Chōsen Anthracite Coal Company (Chōsen Muentan) listed an authorized capital of 50 million yen in 1942, 40 million yen paid-in, but the firm's mining assets by 1945 were evaluated at 540 million yen. How extensive were Mitsubishi mining interests in the colony of Korea? The estimated assets of just Mozan Iron Mining and Chōsen Anthracite Coal together amounted to close to a billion yen in 1945.[29] The colonial metropole typically extracts raw materials from the colony for industrial purposes at home. One difference late in the Korean colonial experience was the development of refineries, munitions plants, and light manufacturing in textiles in the colony itself, using a portion of the extracted minerals for energy generation. The tremendous capital and technological resources mobilized in the alliance of colonial state and major zaibatsu made such investments at home and abroad possible and profitable.

Unlike the transition of Mitsui interest from trade to a variety of investments on the peninsula, Nichitsu (Japan Nitrogenous Fertilizer) invested mainly in hydroelectric power, chemicals, and refining, and associated ventures in heavy industry. Even the awesome scale of Mitsui and Mitsubishi investments on the peninsula fades in comparison with the incredible enterprise of just one Japanese entrepreneur: Noguchi Jun. Noguchi began with a fertilizer plant and hydroelectric power plants in the late 1920s at Hŭngnam in South Hamgyŏng Province. He diversified into explosives and synthetic oil in the 1930s and later invested in tandem with the state in massive hydroelectric power projects on the Yalu River bordering Korea and Manchukuo. The estimated assets of Nichitsu in Korea in 1945 amounted to an astonishing 4.5 million yen,[30] better than a third of direct Japanese investment in the peninsula.

The colonial administration supported development of hydroelectric power with long-term bonds and commercial loans for Nichitsu power company investments in the 1930s. Nichitsu founded the Chōsen Hydroelectric Power Company in 1933.[31] The affiliate and the Oriental Development Company in turn organized the Chōsen Electricity Transmission Company in 1934.[32] Colonial authorities then entrusted the company with power transmission from dams on the Changjin River in the north to the major population centers of P'yŏngyang and Seoul.[33] More extensive projects would fellow. Government officials from both Manchukuo and the colony of Korea published plans for joint development of hydroelectric power on the Yalu in 1937.[34] Electric companies were established in both jurisdictions, sharing some 700,000 kilowatts of power.

The strategic importance of the Yalu River development caught the attention of U.S. intelligence analysts.[35]

By far the largest (generation facility) is the Sui-hō hydroelectric plant, with a large dam on the Amnok-kang (Yalu River) about 40 miles northwest of Sinŭiju, North P'yŏngan Province. This development, serving both Manchuria and Korea, is believed to have been completed in 1944 with a capacity of 450,000 kilowatts, 180,000 kilowatts of which was probably available for generation of 60-cycle current for use in Korea. Original plans called for a capacity of 630,000 kilowatts.

The researchers estimated 75 percent of Korea's hydroelectric power capacity was controlled by Nichitsu, and went on to describe generation facilities on the peninsula.

There are 3 groups of 4 hydroelectric plants each in the mountains of Northern Korea, and another group in which only 2 plants are believed to have been built, although others have been planned. Within each group the plants are connected by aqueducts in series, a single dam serving each group. Water storage is believed to be adequate to maintain full production capacity during the relatively brief dry season. Capacities of the groups are estimated to be as follows: Changin (Chōshin) River –

347,000 kilowatts, Pujŏn (Fusen) River – 202,000 kilowatts, Hoch'on (Kyosen) River – 355,000 kilowatts, Kanggye (Kōkai) – 189,000 kilowatts.

An affiliate of Nichitsu, Chōsen Electricity Transmission held 10 percent of the shares of the Chōsen Yalu River Hydro-electric Generation Company, the government of Manchukuo held 50%, and the ODC 20 percent. The Yalu River company received 110 million yen worth of loans from the Bank of Chōsen between 1937 and 1943. The total assets of this firm alone in 1945 were estimated at 408 million yen.[36]

Energy is a critical element in the transition from agrarian to industrial capital, though hydroelectric power developed to the north in Korea served mainly Japanese strategic aims rather than consumer industrial purposes within the peninsula – development yes, but colonial development oriented to the interests of the metropole. Chōsen Nitrogenous Fertilizers was founded in 1927 for the purpose of mining and fertilizer production, as Noguchi began transferring his fertilizer production to northern Korea with access to hydroelectric power. Prior to merger with Japan Nitrogenous Fertilizers in 1941, the Korean affiliate listed a paid-in capital of seventy million yen.[37] The affiliate in turn developed subsidiaries such as Chōsen Synthetic Oil for the manufacture of glycerine from sardine oil, utilizing the sardine fishing grounds off Korea's shores.[38] Another affiliate, the Chōsen Nitrogenous Gunpowder Company emerged as one of the most prominent munitions centers in the empire with plants in Hŭngnam and Haeju.[39]

If Mitsui's red ginseng monopoly and Mitsubishi's mining efforts were evidence of a coincidence of interests between the state with strategic concerns and profit-oriented zaibatsu, profitable Nichitsu investments in munitions on the peninsula alarmed Japan's leading foe, the U.S. military. Intelligence analysts[40] warned U.S. leaders of the importance of the Korean chemical industry within the empire.

Korea's proportion of the total capacity available to Japan is greatest in industries closely associated with munitions manufacture – especially nitrogen fixation and glycerol refining, of which Korea has 20% and 25% respectively of the capacity of Japan, Korea, Manchuria and Formosa. The products of these industries are used in whole or in part by munitions plants within Korea. The most important chemical-plant development in Korea and one of the most important in Japan's Inner Zone (i.e., Japan, Korea, Manchuria, North China, and Formosa) is at Hŭngnam and the nearby town of Pon'gung, usually discussed with Hŭngnam.

The report continued with a detailed analysis of production facilities, products, and the connection with Nichitsu hydroelectric power projects.

Aerial photographs show the Pon'gung plant to have been greatly expanded since about 1941. At these locations the Chōsen Chisso Hiryō Kabushiki Kaisha [Chōsen Nitrogenous Fertilizers] has the largest ammonia-synthesis and sulfuric-aid plants in the Japanese Empire, as well as installations for the production of nitric acid, caustic soda, chlorine, calcium carbide, calcium cyanamide, calcium superphosphate, glycerol, hardened oil, and other chemicals. The development includes nonferrous metal smelting, and alumina and aluminum installations. Power is supplied by the Changjin River and Pujon River hydroelectric plants, and the Hŭngnam steam plant, all of which have been developed by and are controlled by the Chōsen Chisso Hiryō K.K.

The alliance of colonial state and this zaibatsu played a prominent part in the wider military strategy of the empire.

Leading Japanese zaibatsu with projects on the peninsula adapted to the strategic interests of the colonial state and thereby gained state support for profitable private investment. The major zaibatsu interests in colonial Korea set a pattern that strongly influenced business–state relations among Korean entrepreneurs. Adjustment to state priorities and access to state subsidies and loans would be important in the enterprises of the Mins, Pak, and Kim as well. Obviously the massive mining, utility, heavy industrial, and commercial ventures of the zaibatsu were beyond the ken of the Koreans with their limited base of agricultural capital. They would compete directly with less extensive Japanese ventures on the peninsula in banking, light industry, and retailing. If relations between zaibatsu and the state set a pattern for business on the peninsula, rivalry with smaller Japanese firms set the tempo for the Korean inner circle in the scramble for government support, market share, and for expansion within and beyond the peninsula.

By 1938, only the Tongil, Honam, and Kyŏngsang Consolidated Banks continued under native management. Their combined paid-in capital of 5.4 million yen paled in comparison to the capital of 66 million yen among the six commercial banks under Japanese leadership.[41] The Tongil of Min Tae-sik and Min Kyu-sik faced stiff competition from the Chōsen Commercial Bank and the Hangsŏng Bank, while also trying to contend with the commercial operations of the Bank of Chōsen and the Chōsen Industrial Bank. How did the Tongil fare in the competition? The Commercial Bank[42] listed a paid-in capital of 4.97 million yen in 1942, the Tongil 2.77 million, and the Hansŏng 1.87 million yen. The Commercial Bank operated thirty-seven branches across the peninsula, the Tongil sixteen, and the Hansŏng eighteen. More significant than the immediate differences in capital base were the varying capabilities of major owners to expand the capital of the respective banks. The state-owned Chōsen Trust Company was the major stockholder with 36 percent of the shares in the Commercial Bank, the Bank of Chōsen the largest shareholder (47 percent) in the Hansŏng, and Min Tae-sik's Kyesŏng Company the leading shareholder (18 percent) in the Tongil. Wartime constraints, government pressure toward consolidation in the banking industry, and the competition would ultimately erode the independence of the Tongil.

If state regulations, state investment, and intense competition pushed locally owned firms out of finance, the larger world of industry appeared more benign. Cotton mills absorbed a great deal of capital, technology, and skilled labor in Korea, and were the third largest sector of industrial investment on the peninsula in 1938. Among firms with headquarters on the peninsula, Japanese textile companies were registered with an aggregate paid-in capital of twenty-five million yen. Korean companies held an aggregate paid-in capital of only six million yen,[43] with Kim Yŏn-su's Kyŏngsŏng Spinning alone registered with nearly half that amount. Kyŏngsŏng Spinning faced formidable competitors from Japan. Major cotton mills were clustered in Yŏngdŭngp'o, an industrial area between Seoul and the port city of Inch'on. Kyŏngsŏng had constructed a plant here in 1923, only to be joined by huge Japanese competitors a decade later. Kanegafuchi Cotton Spinning had opened a plant in Yŏngdŭngp'o with one and one-half times the number of spindles, looms, and workers of Kyŏngsŏng, and a second plant of similar size in Kwangju to the southwest. Tōyō Cotton Spinning in Yŏngdŭngp'o operated nearly twice the number of spindles as their Korean competitor, and another plant of similar scale in Inch'ŏn.[44] Kanegafuchi Spinning of Tokyo and Tōyō Spinning of Osaka registered a paid-in capital in 1941 of 75 and 72 million yen respectively, compared to the 2.8 million yen of Kyŏngsŏng.[45]

The larger Japanese textile ventures on the peninsula in the last decade of colonial rule overshadowed two long-established, smaller cotton spinning operations: Kim's Kyŏngsŏng Spinning and the Japanese-owned Chōsen Spinning of Pusan. Founded already in 1918, majority shares in Chōsen Spinning were purchased by Chūgai Investments of Japan in 1932, with the Commercial Bank and later Mitsubishi Trust as major investors. The company was registered with a paid-in capital of 5 million yen by 1931 and 7.5 million yen by 1942,[46] comparable to the size of Kyŏngsŏng Spinning in the closing years of colonial rule. Kim's venture grew dramatically in the last decade of colonial rule, gaining near parity with Chōsen Spinning, but still far behind the larger Japanese textile investments.

There were a few local success stories in commerce as well, though only in the shadow of Japanese investment. Even excluding the larger Japanese trading firms, Korean-owned companies held only a quarter of the total paid-in capital of commercial ventures with headquarters on the peninsula in 1938.[47] Locals could hardly compete in foreign trade with the likes of Mitsui Trade, or in wholesaling on the peninsula. Most Korean commercial concerns were small-scale local ventures, with a few larger rice dealers or produce wholesalers in the Tongdaemun or Chongno areas of Seoul. One exception was the Hwasin Department Store of Pak Hŭng-sik, and his Hwasin Chain Stores Company with affiliates across the peninsula. The department store competition in Seoul was intense. The renowned Japanese store Mitsukoshi, established only in 1905, had opened a station in Seoul three years later and a branch in 1929. The Chōjiya Store started an affiliate in Seoul in 1921, and the Minakai in 1922. The Japan-based Mitsukoshi stood apart from the rest with a paid-in capital of 20 million yen in 1941.[48] The Minakai was listed with a paid-in capital of 2.8 million yen, the Chōjiya of 2 million, and the Hwasin and Hwasin Chain Stores with 500 thousand yen each.[49] The Hwasin fared remarkably well among the competition through the end of the colonial period.

Local businessmen learned to survive and at times prosper in a context of strong state intervention and direction, of massive zaibatsu investment in heavy industry, trade, and agriculture, and of smaller-scale alien investment competitive with the largest native efforts in banking, light industry, and retailing. The Mins, Pak, and Kim adjusted to state priorities on the peninsula, whether in the more open economy of the 1920s, the Manchurian expansion of the next decade, or the more restrictive economy during the Pacific War. The state and the leading zaibatsu established a format of business–state relations that could not be ignored. Competition for scarce government support kept the local economic elite alert to precedents and necessary adjustments.

Conclusion

Concentration in ownership, access to extensive amounts of capital, and monopoly positions within an industry or market were the hallmarks of the leading prewar Japanese trade and industrial combines. The major Korean combines of the Mins, Pak, and Kim emerged in the shadow of the Japanese zaibatsu. Korean entrepreneurs did well to retain ownership and direction of their enterprises for the most part, avoiding direct investment from the massive Japanese combines. And even though the characteristics of concentration and close state relations could be seen in the early Korean chaebŏl as well, the Korean combines differed from the Japanese combines in three very significant ways.

There were obvious differences in scale and development history, particularly in foreign investment. The small scale of Korean chaebŏl through 1945 precluded investment in heavy industries on the peninsula comparable to the investments of the major Japanese zaibatsu. Certainly the state made extensive investment more attractive and secure for the zaibatsu, but the very scale of investment capital demanded of the companies narrowed the field of eligible investors to a few major combines. Also, the relatively short history of relations with the Japanese state left the Korean chaebŏl at a disadvantage for gaining a share in major state-supported heavy industrial investments. Koreans lacked the contacts and the credibility nurtured by the zaibatsu since the late nineteenth century or earlier. A record of state-supported foreign investment in trade and transport, and later in mineral extraction and industrial development further distinguished the zaibatsu. Korean combines took at least an indirect part in the grain trade with Japan, but never enjoyed the opportunities for foreign trade and investment afforded their Japanese counterparts with secure transportation routes, financial networks, and diplomatic relations or colonial ties supporting penetration of foreign markets. Pak's Hwasin Trade and Kim's South Manchurian Spinning were only belated efforts at the end of the colonial period to establish their enterprises beyond Korean borders.

And finally, the absence of internal financial institutions represented a critical structural dependency distinguishing the early chaebŏl from the zaibatsu. The Teikoku Bank and Mitsui Trust, the Mitsubishi Bank and Mitsubishi Trust, and the Sumitomo Bank and Sumitomo Trust served important roles in capital accumulation and in the investment capabilities of the major Japanese combines.[50] The absence of even a single indigenous bank dedicated to industrial investment seriously impeded the process of Korean capital accumulation through large-scale trade and investment ventures. The Tongil Bank itself became dependent on the central bank, and was eventually merged with what amounted to an affiliate of the Bank of Chōsen by 1943, the Hansŏng Bank. Pak Hŭng-sik invested in two indigenous efforts, the Tongil and Honam banks, only to see both merged with Japanese-controlled banks at the end of the colonial period. Kim Yŏn-su failed in his effort to develop a capital base at the Haedong Bank sufficient for support of major industrial investments.

Besides differences between the Japanese and early Korean combines, the review of Japanese investment in the colony sheds further light on the peculiar model of Korean colonial capitalism. The priority of Japanese state interests in colonial capitalism on the peninsula has been noted. The review here suggests that the orientation of private Japanese business interests toward state strategies reinforced state direction and priorities in the colony. As the state made its presence felt in the economy through legislation and direct and indirect investment, an expanding Japanese corporate presence became part of the fabric of colonial economic life. Japanese businessmen rather than the state provided practical direction through daily economic transactions such as equipment purchases from Japanese suppliers, marine transport about and beyond the peninsula, and leadership of business policy associations. The interpenetration of state and private Japanese capital in the major industrial and commercial ventures on the peninsula proved a formidable combination.

5

The Mins and finance

The Min clan from Yŏhŭg near Yŏju in Kyŏnggi Province gained prominence at the end of the Chosŏn Dynasty with the decline of the Andong Kim clan.[1] Viscount Min Yŏng-hwi (1852–1935; pen name, Hajŏng) and his sons, Tae-sik and Kyu-sik, turned their energies mainly to finance, with interests in agriculture and industry as well. The father had been appointed to the board of the Hanil Bank in August of 1912. Within three years Min Yŏng-hwi won executive control, relinquishing the presidency to his son Tae-sik only in 1920. The family retained executive responsibilities and the major block of shares in the Hanil and its successor from 1931, the Tongil Bank. Aristocratic status[2] and long experience of high political office served the family well in relations with the state and other Korean investors during the colonial years. Education abroad was a further advantage for the younger of the sons, Kyu-sik, a graduate of Cambridge University. Min Tae-sik's son, Pyŏng-do graduated from Keio University before returning to Korea for a career in the Bank of Chōsen and the Tongil.

A study of Min family enterprise opens up the world of banking in the turbulent years of colonial rule. One can feel the competition by looking to Min family efforts to take over the Hanil Bank, then other smaller Korean banks, and finally to sustain ownership if not control of the Hanil's successor, the Tongil Bank. By observing family adjustments to banking ordinances and other government intervention, and their scramble to gain support from the central bank, we learn from the inside of hopes for autonomy and realities of dependence among even major Korean entrepreneurs. More than either industrial or commercial enterprise, banking involved the close supervision and support of the Bank of Chōsen and the government-general. And, finally, Min family enterprise tells us of class formation in the colonial years. As members of a well-known noble family from the late Chosŏn Dynasty, Min Tae-sik and his brother Kyu-sik were among those of the earlier aristocracy achieving the status of major entrepreneurs in the colonial period.

The Mins served as one link with the past among the emerging class of large-scale Korean capitalists.

The colonial authorities played a major role in banking on the peninsula, in line with earlier experience at home. The Meiji government established banks in the home islands in the late nineteenth century to stabilize the economy and spur industrial development. Hugh Patrick explained that the Japanese banks served a "supply-leading" rather than "demand-following" function; their purpose was more to encourage investment in industrial and commercial areas than to earn short-term returns on capital invested.[3] The Bank of Chōsen functioned as a central bank on the peninsula, owned mainly mercial Bank served a similar function in Korea, though often on behalf of Japanese investors better funded and more accustomed to large-scale investment than local businessmen. Japanese banks dominated investment on the peninsula, holding most of the deposits, providing most of the loans. The Bank of Chōsen functioned as a central bank on the peninsula, owed mainly by the Japanese Imperial Household and the government-general, while the Chōsen Industrial Bank provided large-scale loans in agriculture, commerce, and industry.[4] The smaller Chōsen Commercial Bank was likewise mostly owned and operated by the administration and Japanese nationals, and with a paid-in capital of only 4.9 million yen in 1941, it still over-shadowed ordinary Korean banks.

State investment in the Hansŏng Bank from the 1920s left the Tongil and a few other regional banks as the sole Korean-owned banks on the peninsula. Even though the Tongil and the Honam survived the next decade, tight capital and stiff competition with the Industrial and Commercial banks dictated at best a minor role for the smaller banks even in local large-scale industrial and commercial ventures. The Mins, Pak, and Kim recognized finance as a crucial area for the development of an indigenous Korean capitalism, but the record of local bank growth through 1945 suggests a difficult transition from immovable capital typical of an agrarian society to fluid finance capital in the form of currency and shares in joint-stock companies characteristic of a commercial and industrializing society. Investment banking in support of large-scale industrial and commercial development never gained widespread support among Korean landowners accustomed to large, rapid returns on agricultural investments through tenant farming. Korean scholars[5] have identified high tenant rents as the main source of profits for land investors through the turn of the century on the peninsula. The Research Bureau of the Chōsen Industrial Bank[6] wrote similarly of "expectations of high yield investments such as tenant rents, in line with the tradition of a self-subsistent, agricultural economy, rather than more reasonable yields evident in industrialized economies." A subsequent study cited how landowners even used banks more for hoarding and storing capital than for productive investment.[7] Reflecting on his own discouraging experience in finance, Kim Yŏn-su[8] lamented the continuity between the high-interest loan practices and land rents among wealthy landowners of the late Chosŏn Dynasty, and the lack of interest in finance among colonial period landowners. In contrast to such short-term profit motives, he had hoped for long-term industrial financing with his Haedong Bank but gained little outside support from landowners. Chung Young-iob[9] concluded that most local investment even during the colonial period was "for land purchase and usury" rather than more productive investment.

There were exceptions. A number of well-known aristocrats[10] from the late Chosŏn Dynasty invested in finance from the early colonial years. Count Yi Wan-yong and Barons Yi Yun-yong and Pak Pu-yang appeared as major stockholders in the Hansŏng Bank in 1921, and Viscount Min Yŏng-hwi served as an auditor. Marquis Pak Yŏng-hyo, the first president of Kyŏngsŏng Spinning, served as a director of the Chōsen Industrial Bank and Marquis Yun Tŏk-yŏng as an auditor in 1921. But few could match the career in finance of Han Sang-yong.[11] Educated in Japan, he returned to Korea at the turn of the century of a career in the Hansŏng Bank. A relative by marriage of Count Yi Wan-yong, Han was welcomed by the aristocratic owners with promotions to managing director (1910–23), and then to a five-year tenure as president. Han gave new meaning to the term "comprador capitalist" by using his experience and talents in finance on behalf of mainly Japanese-owned firms. Hao[12] defined the comprador as a "Chinese manager of a foreign firm in China, serving as middleman in the company's dealings with the Chinese." Besides ordinary comprador functions, many operated their own businesses as independent merchants. But Han Sang-yong was no merchant, nor simply a bank manager. He had acquired considerable skills in finance that he parlayed into top executive positions at various firms supported by Japanese investment.

The fate of the Hansŏng Bank provides insight into Han's early career in alien-owned enterprises. The Chōsen Commercial Bank, the Bank of Chōsen, and the Mitsui Corporation already held shares in the Hansŏng from 1921, as did Viscount Min Yŏng-hwi, though the Korean royal family held the largest block. Of the expanded lot of 120,000 shares of the Hansŏng Bank in 1927, the Korean royal household and relatives retained their position as the largest stockholders, with Japanese firms and individuals listed with only smaller holdings. The Chōsen Industrial Bank had gained 28,000 shares by 1931 of the bank's consolidated total of 60,000 shares with other

Japanese interests well represented.[13] Remaining active in finance, Han later held posts in Korean firms such as Chosŏn Life Insurance (Chosŏn Saengmyŏng Pohŏm), but mainly in prestigious Japanese investments such as Chōsen Trust (Chōsen Shintaku). He took part as a director and often major investor in a number of other prominent industrial and financial concerns during the colonial years, though never as a major stockholder in larger native enterprises comparable to the Mins, Pak, or Kim. Foreign ownership of the Hansŏng contrasted with local ownership of the Hanil/ Tongil; the comprador capitalism of Han Sang-yong provides a foil for the dependent capitalism of the Min family.

At the same time, other Korean landowners and merchants invested in indigenous banks such as the Hanil and Haedong in Seoul, and regional banks like the Hosŏ and the Honam. But apart from the aristocrats and other Korean investors, I find most significant the banking activities among the three entrepreneurial families of interest here. Kim Yŏn-su had himself taken control of the Haedong Bank from 1927 through 1938. Pak Hŭng-sik held a major interest in the Tongil Bank by 1940, as well as shares in the Honam Bank and other finance companies. Min Yŏng-hwi's descendants and their companies represented the largest shareholders in the Tongil Bank in 1940. Despite their efforts, the small scale of local banks in the colonial period deprived Korean enterprises of native sources of large-scale financing. Limited capacity for loans to large enterprises and competition for deposits with better funded Japanese banks slowed the growth of indigenous financial structures.

Three factors discouraged the emergence of indigenous banks supporting large-scale investment on the peninsula: (1) the reluctance of wealthy landowners to transfer their capital from land capital to finance capital; (2) the overwhelming presence of state-affiliated banks with commercial services on the peninsula, dominating the banking industry; and (3) constraints on indigenous banks from 1937 due to Japan's military involvement in China and then in the Pacific War. Legislation regarding investment and banking activities favored larger, better secured banks. Wider problems of inflation and state funding through its own banks for strategic projects further constrained the activities of indigenous banks.[14] No independent Korean-owned bank survived through 1945 to help bolster indigenous investment in commerce and industry. Yet as one banking official[15] concluded: "Although the Korean financial system served Japanese interests, forty years of Japanese occupation resulted in the evolution of a fairly highly specialized banking system in Korea." The experience of a central bank, a development bank, a savings bank, smaller commercial banks, as well as trust and insurance companies would provide a basis for rebuilding a Korean financial network after liberation. Colonial "overdevelopment" in finance provided structures but neither the experience in credit financing nor the capital for a range of local investment in large-scale projects.

A result of the merger of the Hansŏng and Tongil banks in 1943, only the Choheung remained among the various Korean attempts to develop indigenous banks. Strong Japanese investment in the Hansŏng Bank[16] contrasted with indigenous Korean investment, local ownership, and control of the Tongil Bank by the Min family until the mid-1930s. As one of the leading indigenous banks in the colonial period, the early growth of the Hanil/Tongil, its later consolidation, fading indigenous presence in management, and finally merger with the Hansŏng suggests the fragility of indigenous banks. The record of the Min family in the Hanil and Tongil banks portrays a colonial legacy of experience in financial entrepreneurship without the institutional continuity of indigenously owned and managed banks.

Enterprise

Min Yŏng-hwi's descendants did not devote all their energies to the Tongil. One can observe a clear pattern[17] of Min family business activity by the last decade of the colonial period: (1) an inner core of family-owned companies in agriculture, real estate, and textile production; (2) major investments with executive responsibility in complex joint-stock enterprises, such as Chosŏn Silk Weaving and the Tongil Bank; (3) a further level of smaller investments in medium-sized Korean and Japanese ventures without managerial commitments; and (4) an outer level of participation in major Japanese investments on the peninsula. The family of Min Tae-sik owned the Kyesŏng Company with agricultural holdings in Ch'ungch'ŏng and Kyŏnggi Provinces, while the family of his younger brother Kyu-sik owned the Yŏngbo Company.[18] The two families in turn jointly owned the Yŏnghwa Industrial Company.[19] Among the three firms, the diversity and growth of Min Kyu-sik's Yŏngbo firm deserve special attention. Secured with a paid-up capital in 1940 of 2.5 million yen, the Yŏngbo managed family assets in agricultural and urban real estate, including large buildings in Seoul such as the Yŏngbo (five stories), the Chongno (five stories), and the Yŏngbo Taejŏmp'o (three stories). The firm also functioned as a holding company for investments in other companies such as Yŏnghwa Industrial, Hansŏng Cotton Manufacture, Tōhō Development, and Chosŏn Silk Weaving (Chosŏn Kyŏnjik).

The family founded the latter in February of 1923 with a capital of 175 thousand yen. By 1941 the capital had been increased to 200 thousand yen with Min family members listed as the major shareholders of the total of four thousand shares. Min Kyu-sik had served as president in the early years, and later as a director. He was listed again as representative director in 1943, though then with mainly a Japanese board and a paid-in capital of 500 thousand yen.[20] Although shareholders were not listed, I assume that the addition of seven Japanese nationals to the board of Chosŏn Silk Weaving coincided with their investment in the company. Originally a family-owned company, it became a major joint investment with administrative responsibility for Min Kyu-sik at the end of the colonial period.

Beyond the inner level of major family investments and a second level of investments with family administrative responsibility such as the Tongil Bank and Chosŏn Silk, Min Kyu-sik participated in other Korean ventures without management responsibilities. The third level included firms in finance, commerce, and industries such as textiles and breweries. For instance, Korean businessmen interested in diversifying or expanding organized Chōsen Life Insurance,[21] Chosŏn Engineering, and Chosŏn Industry and Management[22] with a paid-in capital of less than a million yen each. Min Kyu-sik joined other prominent local investors in these smaller joint enterprises, and took part as well in the leading native enterprises of the day, appearing on the board of Pak Hŭng-sik's Hwasin, and of Kim Yŏn-su's Kyŏngsŏng, South Manchurian, and Tonggwang textile ventures.

The younger of the Min brothers also invested in two companies under Japanese management. Interests in agricultural development and trade in Manchuria led to participation in the Tōhō Development Company[23] of Hirayama Masao. Founded in June of 1935, the company specialized in agricultural administration, grain sales, and land development in Korea and Manchuria with an authorized capital of 500 thousand yen. Min contributed 46% of equity, Hirayama 47%, and the company set about purchasing land with the aim of aiding "Japanese and Manchurian farmers with cultivation, for the harmony of the common farming population."[24] The company had amassed holdings of some 14,700 acres of land in the Jientao Province of northern Manchuria by 1941. Hirayama oversaw the venture from headquarters on Chongno Avenue in Seoul in a building shared with the Yŏngbo Company and other Min investments. Min also served on the board of Yokose Umatake's Chōsen Trade Promotion Company[25] together with Nakatomi Keita, auditor of Kyŏngsŏng Spinning. But these companies were at best medium-sized ventures in comparison with Min family activities in larger Japanese investments in the colony.

The older of the two brothers, Min Tae-sik gained notoriety in a fourth level of major Japanese investments prominent in the daily lives of most of the population. His position as chief executive officer of the Tongil Bank, which held large blocks of shares in the state-owned Bank of Chōsen and the Chōsen Savings Bank, assured his place in financial levels as evident in his appointment to the board of the Chōsen Trust Company,[26] a leading state-funded credit institution. I find his prominence especially significant in early Japanese colonial ventures such as Chōsen Land Improvement and Keijō Electric under Ōhashi Shintarō.[27] Min appeared on the board of the Chōsen Land Improvement Company (Chōsen Tōchi Kairyō)[28] with Marquis Pak Yŏng-hyo, president of Kyŏngsŏng Spinning. The company constructed and managed irrigation systems and provided administrative assistance for irrigation associations. Founded in 1926 with the backing of the Industrial Bank and the Oriental Development Company, the firm listed an authorized capital of five million yen in 1931 and a quarter of that amount paid-in, with the bank and the ODC each holding 10 percent of the shares.

If the land company had earlier been active in irrigation associations in rural Korean life, Keijō Electric prospered with urban growth in the colonial center of Seoul. Major late Meiji Japanese entrepreneurs such as Shibusawa Eiichi helped organize Keijō Electric (Keijō Denki) in Tokyo in 1908.[29] When the company finally moved its headquarters to the Namdaemun Section in Seoul twenty-five years later, president Ōhashi Shintarō was working with an authorized capital of 15 million yen and 12.6 million paid-in. Born in 1863 in Niigata-ken, Ōhashi rose to the presidencies of Chōsen Smokeless Coal, Taiwan Electrification, Nippon Glass, and Oyodogawa Hydroelectric Power. He was elected chair of the board of Chōsen Beer, Dai Nippon Brewery, and Electric Chemical Industrial. He served as a director of such leading firms as Daiichi Life Insurance, Tokyo Electric Light, Hokkai Hydro-electric Power, Nippon Yūsen, and the Ōji Paper Manufacturing companies, among others.[30]

Keijō Electric[31] registered an authorized capital of 23 million yen in 1942 with 19.8 million yen paid-in, and estimated assets three years later of nearly 500 million yen.[32] Major shareholders included Daiichi Life Insurance, Ōhashi Honten, Chōsen Trust, and the Chōsen Commercial Bank. The venture originally provided electricity for lighting and streetcars in the city of Seoul, and diversified by the mid-1930s into import of railway cars, buses, and automobiles, and operation of the Seoul-Inch'ŏn bus line. Annual profits averaged between 8 and 12 percent annually from 1927 to 1931, and jumped to 23 percent in 1934. Among the largest firms on the peninsula, the company held estimated assets in 1945 of nearly 500 million yen. A comparison of principal stockholders in 1931 and 1942 indicates early heavy investment of Japanese insurance companies, particularly Daiichi Life Insurance, joined later by the investment of state-affiliated finance institutions such as Chōsen Trust and the Chōsen Commercial Bank by 1942. Min Tae-sik served on the board of Keijō Electric from at least 1931 and possibly earlier. His prominence in both Chōsen Land Improvement and Keijō Electric and his ties with Ōhashi Shintarō were evidence of his stature and credibility among Japanese investors. Such credibility enhanced his claim for state support of the Tongil and his place in intercorporate Korean investments among an indigenous inner group of business leaders.

Between these outer levels of shareholding in joint investments and large Japanese firms, and a core group of family-owned and managed firms, Min Tae-sik and Kyu-sik concentrated their energies in ownership and executive duties at the Tongil. The forerunner of the Tongil, the Hanil Bank was founded by a group of Korean businessmen in 1906, though Paek In-gi of a wealthy Chŏnju landowning family soon joined the bank as executive director.[33] Paek's ouster as executive director nine years later roughly coincided with the renomination of a well-known former government official and Ch'ungch'ŏng Province landowner as president of the Hanil in July of 1915: Viscount Min Yŏng-hwi. The viscount tripled the paid-in capital to 750 thousand yen by 1919, and then to 1.625 million yen the next year. The patriarch made a bold move at the time to assert family control, replacing experienced administrators with his two sons, Tae-sik (thirty-eight years old) and Kyu-sik (thirty-two years old), and others of Tae-sik's Mining Company recently purchased by the bank.[34] Tae-sik succeeded his father as president of the Hanil Bank[35] in 1920.

Enthusiasm for expansion in the banking industry cooled with increased competition and further government regulations to insure solvency by the end of the decade. Frantic efforts for consolidation among the smaller local banks over the next few years can be traced to two factors: competition with the extensive financial base and networks of the Chōsen Commercial and Hansŏng banks, and a government ordinance of February 1928 directing commercial banks to raise their paid-in capital to the level of two million yen.[36] Although the ordinance did not directly affect the Hanil with its authorized capital of two million yen, it hastened efforts toward a larger capital base and branch network. Min Tae-sik succeeded in bringing about a merger with the Hosŏ Bank of South Ch'ungch'ŏng Province (1.15 million yen) in January of 1931.[37] The costs of the merger, the addition of Hosŏ shareholders critical of Min family leadership, and the sluggish economy in the early 1930s forced the Tongil into reorganization in March of 1933, although Min retained the presidency.[38] The Bank of Chōsen provided "direction" (*chido*) and the capital for reorganization. The Tongil gained permission from the government-general to write off delinquent loans, raise four million yen through sale of real estate holdings, and defer dividend payments "only after consultation with former Hosŏ Bank shareholders." Min reflected in a published interview that reorganization was possible only through the financial aid and advice of the Bank of Chōsen.[39]

Min now looked beyond the Hosŏ to a more formidable prize, the Kyŏng-sang Haptong Bank (1.33 million yen) of Chŏng Chae-hak in Taegu. The *Donga Ilbo* of April 8, 1932, reported a "Confrontation between Combines from the South and North." The Chŏng family of Taegu were described as millionaires, the Mins of Keijō as multimillionaires. Not only did the Mins have more capital, they also could call on kinship ties with Sŏ Sang-ho of the Kyŏngsang Haptong. The newspaper predicted victory for Min Tae-sik as both families maneuvered to gain a majority of the bank's stock, but surprisingly the Chŏngs beat the odds and retained control until their own merger with the Hansŏng in 1941. The failure to achieve further mergers, pressure from the government-general and shareholders over management improprieties, and weak bank performance led to major administrative changes at the Tongil in late July of 1936. Min Kyu-sik replaced his older brother as president while Japanese nationals received appointment as executive and managing directors.[40] Business conditions and a government ordinance of May 1942 forced further consolidation among surviving Korean banks, as the Tongil absorbed the Honam Bank and its nine branches,[41] and then itself was merged with the Hansŏng Bank in July of 1943 under state pressure.[42]

The log of daily bank transactions[43] offers a detailed picture of individual and corporate customers at the Tongil. One finds evidence here of the concentration of indigenous capital in agriculture, and on a more personal level, family interest in a credit facility for their investments. The bank cultivated ties with wealthy landowners and grain brokers of South Ch'ungch'ŏng, Kyŏnggi, and South Hamgyŏng provinces, as well as with grain brokers and others in commerce and real estate in the capital. Provincial landowners such as Pak P'il-byŏng of Ansŏng, Chang Yŏng-gyu, and a Mr. Nakaishi of Hansŏng, appear regularly in the ledgers, all with assets of one million yen or better. Seoul customers held similar assets, such as Cho Pyŏng-hak, a grain broker, and Wŏn Pong-su, specializing in fruit, marine products, and hides at Namdaemun market. The ledgers also tell a story of family credit transactions. Min Tae-sik's son, Pyŏng-do of Kyesŏng Agricultural Company, and his foster mother, Yi Min-ch'ŏn, were regular customers, both listing collateral of personal assets worth one million yen or better.

Among the joint-stock firms receiving loans from the Tongil, the Chosŏn

Silk Company of the Min family and the Sŏnil Paper Company of Pak Hŭng-sik were listed, as was the smaller Chosŏn Industrial Company, a Seoul finance company strongly supported by Tongil loans. But bank records suggest a general pattern of loans to mainly small-scale investors (i.e., net assets of less than 100,000 yen) and only a few large-scale investors. Most loans were related to agrarian investment, whether directed toward land purchase, grain brokerage, or finance agencies devoted to agriculture. Dealers in agricultural and marine products also received loans, as did small textile and transportation firms, and breweries. Although the majority of loan recipients were Korean, a few Japanese nationals received loans in 1934, and more in 1936, mostly small-scale investors. A picture emerges of a slow transition from agrarian capital into financial associations and commerce associated with agriculture, with some evidence of Tongil help for small industrial ventures. Lacking the capital resources for larger commercial or industrial enterprise, the Tongil found a niche among smaller-scale investors.

Investment in the Tongil Bank by the Mins was evidence of strong family interest. A few Japanese names can be found in the annual lists of major shareholders in the Hanil, but the members of Tae-sik's family and his brother, Kyu-sik, consistently held better than a quarter of the 40,000 shares, with no significant competitors among other shareholders.[44] Although only family members had been listed as the major shareholders of the Hanil, various outside investors held large numbers of shares in its successor, the Tongil. The family retained ownership of the bank through a set of foundations, holding companies, and direct holdings of family members. The patriarch Min Yŏng-hwi had founded and funded the Hwimun Middle School from 1906; the school foundation in turn held some 2,600 Tongil shares through 1942. Min Tae-sik is listed among the major shareholders only between 1931 and 1933, but his Kyesŏng Company emerged as the largest shareholder in 1936 as he relinquished the presidency, and soon increased its holdings to 14,583 shares of 18 percent of the total of 80,000 shares. Min Kyu-sik first appears with major shares in 1934, and by 1938 held 2,495 shares. His sons Pyŏng-ok and Pyŏng-sŏ and the family's Yŏngbo Company also appeared as major shareholders.

In 1940 Min family members and companies alone controlled some 26,500 shares, 33 percent of the total stock in the company. Included in this category of family members or family companies are the following names appearing on the list of major Tongil stockholders in CGKKY, 1931–42: Kyesŏng Company, Hwimun Foundation, Min Kyu-sik, Min Pyŏng-ok, Min Pyŏng-sŏ, Yŏngbo Company, and Yi Po-ŭng. Unlike the Hanil investment, the Min family at the Tongil Bank had to deal with a variety of powerful stockholders, including recalcitrant Hosŏ Bank investors. The experience of a joint-stock operation without a monopoly share proved difficult. The family hit upon the solution of friendly investment, seeking out associates among the local business elite such as Hyŏn Chun-ho of the Honam Bank and Pak Hŭng-sik of Hwasin. The tactic was supported by the interlocking directorates across a number of financial and industrial enterprises, as evident in both joint investment and joint participation on boards.

For instance, both Min Tae-sik and Kim Yŏn-su served as directors of the Chosŏn Trust Company (2.5 million yen), itself a major shareholder in the Tongil Bank. Although Chosŏn Trust was owned mainly by the Bank of Chōsen and the Chōsen Industrial Bank, the Tongil also held shares through 1935. The Tongil owned shares in the Chosŏn Life Insurance Company through 1940 as well. Pak Hŭng-sik and Hyŏn Chun-ho served as directors of the insurance company, and Hyŏn's Hakp'a Agricultural Estate held a major block of shares. There was also interpenetration evident in industry, especially in Kim Yŏn-su's foreign textile enterprise, South Manchurian Spinning, founded in 1939 with a paid-in capital of 5 million yen. Min Kyu-sik and Pak Hŭng-sik served as directors, and Hyŏn Chun-ho of the Honam Bank as an auditor.

The advent of joint-stock enterprises too large or too uncertain for massive investment by a single family stimulated intercorporate activity among the major local business elite. Similar to the function of wholly owned family agricultural and real estate companies such as Kyesŏng or Yŏngbo serving as holding companies in larger joint investments, a network of friendly investors helped secure a leadership role for family investment, though now without extensive liability. The holding companies and friendly investors permitted greater security and control in a competitive environment of sometimes uncooperative indigenous investors, market instability, and state-affiliated enterprises controlled by a colonial state oriented toward Japanese rather than indigenous interests.

The Min family proved more successful in maintaining their share in ownership than their part in management at the bank. First there were issues of internal control such as friction with former Hosŏ Bank stockholders critical of Min family management. Then there was intervention by the colonial state. Even though the family retained the presidency and their part in ownership through 1942, the prominent role of the Bank of Chōsen in Tongil reorganization in 1933, government intervention in Tongil management changes in 1936, and tighter controls on central bank funds for Korean banks from 1939 weakened indigenous control.[45] Lacking alternate sources of indigenous capital, the Tongil became increasingly dependent on central bank funds for loan capital. With wartime controls reducing the funds available, tighter government supervision and eventually consolidation with the Hansŏng Bank was the only means of survival.

The Bank of Chōsen made funds available to cover the Tongil's reorganization already in 1933, but a more ominous intracorporate intervention signaled fading indigenous control: the appointment of Japanese nationals as executive and managing directors. Ishikawa Shinjirō was appointed managing director in 1934, promoted to executive director in July of 1936, and was then succeeded by Kawaguchi Makoto in 1937. A protégé of President Katō Keizaburo of the Bank of Chōsen, Kawaguchi served as manager of the Bank of Chōsen's headquarters in Seoul. Adept at commercial banking activities, he was lauded by one author for later saving the faltering Tongil Bank.[46] The author emphasized Kawaguchi's tremendous political as well as economic contribution to the colony through his work at the Tongil. Curiously, Japanese investment did not follow with the addition of Japanese in top administrative positions,[47] but in finance where access to capital is so critical, control was evident on a more fundamental level: capital circulation through the central bank. A scene from the memoirs[48] of Min Tae-sik's son depicts central bank control at Tongil's Seoul headquarters from 1939. Min Pyŏng-do proceeded at the time hat-in-hand to the Finance Department of the government-general, hoping to receive deposits from the Bank of Chōsen to offset direct dependence on their funds for loans. A present of ten pounds of beef and a cogent plea won his Seoul branch a deposit of 1.8 million yen. Such occasional dramatic efforts and temporary funding were no solution for the Tongil's vulnerability to restrictive fiscal policies before and during the Pacific War.

Three stages in the bank's history unfold as we look to the adaptations of class and organization necessary for business survival among dependent local entrepreneurs in finance: (1) family control from 1920, (2) complexities of joint ownership in the initial years of the Tongil, and (3) fading control coupled with family reinvestment from 1936. Min Yŏng-hwi's dramatic effort to replace experienced bank administrators with his sons in 1920, the bank's purchase of Min Tae-sik's mining company, and the family's extensive financial commitment was possible in the less complex economy of the time with a smaller banking operation. Repeal of the Corporation Law in 1920 released demand for growth in industry, commerce, and even in indigenous banks. Moreover, Japanese investment in the Hansŏng and the Chōsen Commercial banks from the second decade of colonial rule had not yet come to play a dominant role in commercial banking.

Certainly there was government supervision in the banking industry at the time, but there was greater leeway for banks with Korean funding than would be possible in later years. The combination of ownership and management at the Hanil by Min Yŏng-hwi's sons continued through the end of the decade. Major direct investment by other Korean capitalists was not necessary, though Min family credibility among other landowners and business leaders was needed to draw customers. The commitment of family funds and family credibility can be appreciated more by contrast with the weak role of native capital and management at the Hansŏng Bank.[49]

Closer state controls on banking from 1928 and the growth of the Chōsen Commercial and Hansŏng banks forced consolidation among local banks in the 1930s. The takeover of the Hosŏ Bank doubled the authorized and paid-in capital of the newly named "Tongil" from 1931. Addition of unfriendly Hosŏ stockholders, the expanded scale of the operation, and the complexity of management in a difficult financial situation of the period all contributed to a diminished family role in bank management and ownership. The bank's problems led to reorganization two years later, clear evidence of a wider government role in direction and funding of the bank. The scale of investment and risk involved prior to 1936 apparently discouraged the Min family at the time from a larger financial commitment to maintain earlier levels of family. An interdependent group of friendly investors had not yet appeared among the Tongil's major shareholders, leaving the bank dependent on the continued investment of former Hosŏ bank shareholders.

Events of 1936 forced the Min family to reconsider their role in the Tongil Bank, even though the family retained the presidency in the person of Tae-sik's younger brother, Kyu-sik. Problems with management, confrontations with stockowners, and weak performance again brought on government intervention. As the addition of Japanese nationals with experience in colonial finance as executive and managing directors was seriously attenuating family control of the bank, the family invested heavily in bank stock to retain ownership. The latter trend of ownership despite fading authority continued with the addition of friendly Korean investors in the final years of colonial rule, consolidating the family's place in ownership of the bank. The trend indicated a shift also in business–state relations for the Min family, with state direction now internalized through the Japanese presence in the management of the Tongil. I would trace the capital support of friendly investors in the late colonial years to consolidation prompted by wartime controls and solidarity among an interdependent group of Korean investors, tied by pragmatic concerns of economic interest and mutual credibility with the state.

Events at the Tongil Bank unfolded within the context of multiple levels of Min family investments. The multileveled portfolio and intracorporate solidarity among the Korean business elite helped preserve the limited autonomy of ownership and management of indigenous enterprise. If the family's agricultural investment in the inner core of investments provided a reliable source of capital, contacts leading to mutual support with other prominent Korean and Japanese business leaders were one result of financial commitments in the third and fourth levels of investments. The wealth of the Kyesŏng and Yŏngbo companies reinforced the Min's credibility with other stockholders. Min Tae-sik's threats of departure and withdrawal of Min family backing gave him leverage in struggles with unfriendly Tongil investors. Even the colonial administration attempted at one point to link government aid for the bank with commitments of family capital.[50] Activity in the third level of medium-sized ventures without Min family management responsibilities cemented ties with friendly Korean investors like Pak Hŭng-sik, Kim Yŏn-su, Hyŏn Chun-ho of the Honam Bank, Ha Chun-sŏk, and Kim Sa-yŏn. The importance of such links and the resulting interdependence was especially evident in the constrained situation of the Pacific War years. Inner-group ties bolstered indigenous direction of major native enterprises in commerce and industry, but not ultimately in banking. Nonetheless, the third level of firms represented credible companies with strong growth potential, outlets for profits accrued in other Min family investments.

The participation of Min Kyu-sik and especially of his older brother, Min Tae-sik, in major Japanese ventures on the peninsula paralleled activities in the third level of smaller ventures. Here links with Japanese individual and corporate investors such as Ōhashi Shintarō, Daiichi Insurance, or Dainippon Beer reinforced Min family credibility as major business figures, and again provided profitable outlets for investment. Directorships at the Chōsen Land Improvement Company or the Chōsen Beer Company fit well with family investments in agriculture and brewing, providing contacts and knowledge useful for family enterprises. Min Tae-sik's role in Chōsen Trust and especially in the massive Keijō Electric helped set him apart among the leading Korean business elite, lending further credence to his leadership in banking.

The prominence of the Min family in banking was due to both family wealth and experience, and to a network of contacts that made productive financial relations possible with government-controlled banks and private investors. Agricultural and real estate ventures were the primary source of such wealth in the early colonial period. The skein of diversified investments in finance, industry, agriculture, and real estate earned the necessary capital for investment in the later colonial period. The family fostered contacts through education, ties with other aristocratic families, banking activities, and direct investment in other companies. The scale of Min family investment and even limited control at the Tongil would not have been possible without the pattern of financial and personal ties evident in the four levels of investments.

Conclusion

Dependent entrepreneurship demanded considerable agility in the fast-changing economy of the declining Japanese Empire. Rapid adaptations in finance to shifting state policy during the Pacific War forced change in both class relations and indigenous enterprise. Among significant policy changes, the Mins faced a redirection from external pressure through legislation and central bank control of load capital to the presence of Japanese managers within the Tongil itself. Such direct intervention left little room for Korean experience in management or development of financial institutions. The shift in modes of direction coincided with the more intrusive, militaristic controls of the government-general in the last decade of colonial rule. The changes spurred surprising adjustments in class ties among the leading segment of the local business elite. Competition between the Mins and the Hosŏ Bank leaders, or Pak Hŭng-sik and Ch'oe Nam marked both the expanding local economy of the second decade of colonial rule and the scramble for growth in the constrained economy early in the third decade. But wartime controls would dampen competitive expansion efforts in local markets and encourage solidarity among at least a small group of the local elite. No longer content simply with cooperative business transactions such as Pak's credit with the Tongil, the inner core opted rather for a growing interdependence evident in investment in one another's core enterprises and in joint ventures.

Policy changes also hastened the pace of structural reorganization in enterprise, as the local elite struggled to maintain at least ownership if not control. The de facto separation of ownership and management functions in the Tongil Bank from 1936, and aggressive family reinvestment to maintain ownership despite loss of actual management functions sharply distinguished the family's role in the late years of the Tongil from their earlier, comprehensive role in the family-owned and -managed Hanil Bank. Such extensive Korean investment in Japanese-manged firms was not common among large-scale dependent Korean investors who preferred ownership and control of their own enterprises. Dilution of family control at the Tongil gave notice of a more intense and comprehensive dependence, rather than a shift from dependent to comprador capitalism. The remarkable story of indigenous banking in colonial Korea concludes sadly with part owners like the Mins and Hyŏn Chun-ho deprived of management prerogatives. The new stage of alien control might have drastically affected the colonial experience in the long-term had not liberation brought this brief, confusing period of wartime business–state ties to an abrupt close.

The study of Min family enterprise across the breadth of the colonial years tells us more of enterprise, class, and state. Zeitlin looked to the concrete structure of ownership and intercorporate relations to clarify issues of control within large-scale enterprise.[51] In a colonial situation of local elites adjusting to the interventions of a strong state, however, the issue of intracorporate dynamics adds a further critical dimension to the analysis. Ishikawa Shinjirō and, later, Kawaguchi Makoto of the Bank of Chōsen assumed effective direction of the Tongil in the last years of colonial rule, although the Min family retained the top executive position. What amounted to assimilation of a private firm to the directions of the Bank of Chōsen would severely constrain the ability of the Min family to assure the bank's survival, much less realize more elaborate corporate objectives.

The problem was not simply the nationality of the managers. Growing ties with Japanese customers and suppliers and later pressure from the authorities led to appointment of Japanese nationals to management positions in large-scale native enterprises later in the colonial years. Ishikawa, Kawaguchi, and later Mitani helped direct the Tongil, while Yoneda Yasaburo and Chogō Eiji were active in management at Sŏnil and Hwasin, and Nakatomi Keita appeared as auditor on the board of Kyŏngsŏng Spinning and other Kim family investments. Japanese nationals could be assimilated to the wider purposes of the firm, enhancing the strength of the enterprise without diluting local control. But given the supervision of the Bank of Chōsen in Tongil affairs, and the subsequent Tongil merger with the state-owned Hansŏng, such high-level appointments did not bode well for the future of autonomous local enterprise at the Tongil. Developments in intercorporate relations at the same time among the Korean business elite offered some hope. We noted the adjustment of zaibatsu families to early expansion through a network of trusted associates. The circle of friendly local investors apparent in the late years of the Tongil was evidence of a similar dynamic in the turbulence of early capitalist development in the colony.

The colonial experience here tells more of class formation than simply friendly investors. Enjoying the advantages of prominent aristocratic status and close government ties, a few wealthy Korean families invested in banking at the end of the Chosŏn Dynasty. The historical record suggests continuity between early Min family enterprise in banking and the colonial enterprise of the Hanil/Tongil banks, and the importance of such continuity in colonial finance. Banking perhaps more than any other area of enterprise demands trust and reliability. The credibility afforded by status was more important for enterprise in finance than in other areas of enterprise, particularly in the early transition from agrarian to commercial–industrial capital. And certainly experience contributed toward effective management of such a complex enterprise as the Tongil. Yet the fact that entrepreneurs like Hyŏn Chun-ho of the Honam succeeded without the advantage of high status, and that few families with distinguished aristocratic backgrounds can be found among the leading colonial entrepreneurs makes one pause. Status coupled with wealth was no doubt an advantage, especially in finance in the early colonial years, but not sufficient in itself for successful enterprise.

The long prominence of the Mins in colonial finance and business also helped cement distinctive ties with the state. Min Tae-sik's association with such prestigious state-supported ventures as Keijō Electric and the Chōsen Land Improvement Company was evidence of high credibility with colonial authorities. His position in a Seoul-based bank such as the Hanil/Tongil would further contribute to close ties. Such contacts and whatever credibility he enjoyed would in turn support the Tongil's case for government support. But state support was linked with state direction. The Mins walked a tightrope in adaptation to state policy and the wartime economy in the late colonial years. The family could fall back on their agricultural holdings and smaller investments similar to many of the traditional elite, but banking remained the most prestigious sector for local enterprise and a potential area of growth. In comparison to other local bankers, the Mins did reasonably well to retain even limited control of a Seoul bank as long as they did. Dependent local capitalists would face no more severe challenge than in banking.

We began with the contrast between the comprador capitalism of Han Sang-yong at the Hansŏng and other Japanese investments, and the dependent capitalism of the Mins at the Hanil/Tongil. The records indicate both Han and Min Tae-sik held directorships in various prominent Japanese companies on the peninsula. The difference was the pattern of enterprise and investment among these two leading local figures in finance. The first two levels of family-owned firms remained the focus of Min family energies throughout the colonial years. With this core of native-owned and, for the most part, native-managed enterprise, the Mins accumulated indigenous capital, organized indigenous firms, and provided experience of relatively independent local enterprise in agriculture, real estate, and finance. I consider this dependent capitalism even in banking significantly different from Han's efforts mainly on behalf of foreign interests.

Min Tae-sik spoke of pragmatism in developing the Korean economy in a published interview of 1921.[52] Since Korea was a capital-poor agricultural society, he argued the challenge was not large-scale industry, but smaller, more feasible strategies to develop capital. While applauding investment in transportation and industrial plants, Min envisioned something more practical such as a silkworm industry to supplement agricultural production. He sounded again and again the themes of feasibility and effective implementation. Realism marked his efforts to adapt while keeping a family stake and usually control in a variety of enterprises. Korean society and Japanese colonial policy had changed dramatically between the 1920s and 1940s. The optimism of the Native Products Campaign faded by the close of colonial rule, while the indigenously owned assets of the Mins, Pak, and Kim grew. There is little doubt that ties with the state and major Japanese ventures on the peninsula tarnished the image of both Min brothers as native entrepreneurs working for the wider benefit of the populace. We are left with the strong impression of pragmatism and adaptability.

6

Pak and commerce

A few prominent Korean aristocrats turned to banking in the late nineteenth century. An established aristocratic and landowning family like the Kims led a few other of the landowning elite into industrial investment two decades later, again a considerable adjustment from the secure and lucrative investment in land common among the Korean aristocracy. But you find few aristocrats among leaders in commerce, for not only did the occupation of merchant rank lowest in the Confucian hierarchy of professions, but commerce itself was not sufficiently developed to attract large-scale capital in the self-sufficient, barter economy of agrarian Korean society. Both cultural and structural factors discouraged the growth of commerce critical in the transition from agrarian to commercial capital in the late Chosŏn Dynasty. The role of merchant took on a new importance with the rise of commercial agriculture stimulated by the expanding rice trade with Japan from the late nineteenth century,[1] though still few aristocrats were numbered among the leading merchants.

A domestic market on the peninsula quickly developed for cotton, wool, and silk textiles, paper products, ceramics, and oil during the colonial period. Imports[2] of cotton goods increased from 12 million yen to 36 million yen, woolen goods from less than 1 million to 10.5 million yen, and silk from 1 to 10 million yen between 1915 and 1935. The volume of imports indicated strong demand as evident in other light consumer goods as well, and expanding domestic production of such items as paper and rubber shoes. Large-scale production of consumer goods on the peninsula came to serve both local and foreign markets, particularly in textile production at Chōsen Spinning and Kim Yŏn-su's Kyŏngsŏng Spinning, and later at Kanegafuchi and Tōyō spinning plants. Traditional distribution networks such as periodic markets and local shops continued to operate with the growing demand; more innovative systems such as the Hwasin Chain Stores project from June of 1934 brought together a nationwide system of suppliers and distributors.

Commerce expanded dramatically through the colonial years, but it was clearly dominated by the capital and organization of the home islands. Nonetheless, the total paid-in capital of Korean-owned commercial firms jumped from 6.9 million yen in 1923 to 23.3 million yen in 1938. Pak's Hwasin and the Taech'ang Trade Company and Taech'angsa of the Paek Yun-su family led the way among local firms.[3] Seoul remained the commercial capital on the peninsula through the colonial period, and the Chongno district the bustling center of trade in grains, marine products, and textiles. Meanwhile a new type of large-scale commercial investment appeared a few blocks to the South: the department store. Leading Japanese stores such as Mitsukoshi, Chōjiya, Minakai, and Hirata dominated the Chungmu district, a symbol of Japanese preeminence in the colony's commerce.[4] But soon the Korean-owned Hwasin[5] and its competitor, the Donga Department Store, appeared on Chongno, the "Koreans' street."[6]

Hwasin matched the Japanese competition in distribution and organization with a main store in Seoul and network of chain stores across the peninsula. In contrast to the enterprise of the aristocratic Min family in finance, the record of entrepreneurship at Sŏnil Paper and the Hwasin reveal a commoner's colonial legacy of both experience and institutional continuity in trade, domestic and foreign. Pak was born in 1903 in Yongganggun in South P'yŏngan Province to a small landowning family. The deaths of his father and then his sole sibling, Pak Ch'ang-sik (1892–1910), left him with responsibility for his mother and his brother's son, Pak Pyŏnggyo. With only a local primary school education, Pak soon went into business first as a rice broker in Chinnamp'o, and then with the Sŏngwang Printing Company (paid-in capital in 1924 of 100,000 yen) in his hometown of Yonggang. He later prospered with Hwasin Department Store, Hwasin Chain Stores, and Hwasin Trade. If we sometimes find the rapid transition from agricultural to commercial capital among local merchants in a colonial situation puzzling, large-scale commercial enterprise by a local entrepreneur without even extensive agricultural capital is baffling. Commerce provides attractive opportunities for comprador capitalism, yet this merchant stubbornly retained locally owned and managed firms. How did he do it? The very success of Pak Hŭng-sik as a dependent capitalist raises questions of the nature and extent of his dependence on both the colonial state and alien enterprise.

Despite relatively little prior national experience in large-scale merchandising or in commerce across national borders, a number of Koreans developed successful commercial and trading firms in the later colonial years. These dealers proved "modern" insofar as they mastered contemporary methods of transportation, organization, and finance to profitably import and export, and to cultivate a reliable network of domestic suppliers. How did they acquire the capital and build their commercial organizations, develop effective networks for domestic and foreign trade, and nurture effective ties with the state and with Korean and Japanese business elites? A study of the enterprise of Pak Hŭng-sik, the most prominent of the indigenous commercial businessmen, will again draw our attention to issues of concentration in ownership and management, relations with the state, and class ties.

Enterprise

As with the Mins, so too we find with this commercial entrepreneur four levels[7] of enterprise by the late colonial years. Pak devoted his energies and capital to a closely held and managed core of interlocking companies, including Sŏnil Paper, Hwasin Department Store, and a construction and real estate firm, Taedong Industries. The absence of a major agricultural investment distinguished Pak's portfolio from the core investments of the Min family or of Kim Yŏn-su. Pak established the Sŏngwang Printing Company in his hometown of Yonggang in South P'yŏngyang Province already in 1920. Moving to Seoul by the middle of the decade, he risked a larger investment, the Sŏnil Paper Goods Company with an authorized capital of 250,000 yen. Pak and a few associates, such as Kim Ok-hyŏn of the Industrial Bank branch in Chinnamp'o, had put up equity capital of 62,500 yen, and with the help of loans from the Industrial Bank and the Commercial Bank began operations with headquarters in the Industrial Bank building on Ŭlchi Avenue in 1926. These paper dealers prospered in the late 1920s with imports of newsprint from Sweden and Canada for both Korean and Japanese customers on the peninsula, operating by 1931 with an annual budget of nearly one million yen and annual dividends of 10 percent. As president and owner, Pak raised the firm's paid-in capital to 125,000 yen by 1940 before absorbing the venture under Hwasin a year later.[8]

The early venture gave notice of Pak's unique blend of ambitious designs and bold entrepreneurship within and beyond the peninsula, and close state support gained through personal credibility and the ties of associates such as Kim Ok-hyŏn. Similarly, the concentration of ownership and continuity of direction under a small group of managers such as Kim Ok-hyŏn and Yi Kyu-jae at Sŏnil Paper would long characterize Pak's enterprises in this core level of investments. Early enterprise in paper and printing provided both capital and experience for a more ambitious venture, the Hwasin Department Store and affiliated chain stores project early in the 1930s. Both Sŏnil and Hwasin then served as a base of capital and personnel for diverse investments in similarly closely held and managed enterprises from the middle of the decade, such as the unsuccessful Chejudo Industrial for cattle ranching on the island of Cheju,[9] and a real estate and construction firm. Pak organized Taedong Industries (Taedong Hŭngŏp)[10] in September 1936 for urban real estate investment and agricultural development. Secured with assets in land and buildings of 1.25 million yen, the firm operated with an annual budget of 3.7 million yen. President Pak Hŭng-sik registered the firm at an authorized capital of 2 million yen with 500 thousand yen paid-in in 1940, under the familiar executive director Yi Kyu-jae and director Chogō Eiji. Pak, the Sōnil and Hwasin companies, and his nephew, Pak Pyŏng-gyo, held 94 percent of the shares available. We find here not only indigenous ownership and management, but closely held firms under a tight coterie of trusted executives.

Limited experience in joint enterprises with management responsibilities stood out as the major difference between the portfolios of Pak and his counterparts, Min Kyu-sik and Kim Yŏn-su. One can discover no parallel in Pak's portfolio to the Mins' Tongil or Kim's Kyŏngsŏng Spinning usually found in the second level of investments. Perhaps it was due to his humble origins and lack of contacts in Seoul, or to his relatively late emergence among leading local entrepreneurs. Perhaps Pak's financial and executive commitments in the complex ventures of his inner core of investments left no time for development of joint ventures with other investors under his management. Whatever the reason, the second level of joint enterprises under his direction included only one company, Hwasin Trade, organized in 1939. With an authorized capital of 2.75 million yen and 637,000 yen paid-in, Pak and executive directors Yi Kyu-jae and Chogō Eiji operated with an annual budget of 2.8 million yen.

Chogō's experience in government and trade fit well with Pak's plans for international trade first at Sŏnil Paper, and later in the trade venture. Born in 1896, Chogō[11] graduated from the Civil Engineering Department of Tokyo Imperial University in 1919 before joining the Ministry of Interior. He was dispatched to Korea in 1926 to supervise flood control projects and local railroad construction as chief of the Wŏnsan Civil Engineering Station. An advisor for the Manchuria and Chōsen Trade Association, Chogō later became involved in commerce. With headquarters in the Hwasin Department Store building on Chongno Avenue and branches in Tientsin and Osaka, Yi Kyu-jae and Chogō sought out markets in China and Manchuria, with exports of canvas shoes and marine products to Southeast Asia as well.

The firm reorganized after liberation into one of the leading trading ventures in the early years of the Republic. I find the firm significant not only as a major Korean venture in international trade, but also as Pak's only enterprise with a diversity of investors. Pak and his nephew held a dominant block of 27 percent of the shares, Kim Yŏn-su and Kyŏngsŏng Spinning 9 percent, and Hyŏn Chun-ho and his Honam Bank 5 percent of the shares. Other major shareholders included the Hansŏng and Tongil banks, and a Japanese store, Wakamoto Honten. One can only deduce from the familiar names on the list that only friendly principal investors were welcome.[12] Gaining support from the inner circle of Korean business elite for investment in the trading venture was an impressive achievement for the newcomer Pak, and further evidence of interdependence among the Korean business elite.

One can also find a third level of joint investments without executive commitments in medium-sized firms, quite similar to investment strategies of the Mins or Kim Yŏn-su. Pak invested heavily in local banks and finance firms such as the Tongil and Honam banks and Chosŏn Life Insurance. He was active with others of the inner circle in Ha Chun-sŏk's Chosŏn Engineering and Han Kyu-bok's real estate company, Chosŏn Industry and Management.[13] The Chosŏn Engineering Company (Chosŏn Kongjak)[14] was established in February of 1935 for manufacture of mining and military equipment. Chairman Han Sang-yong and president Ha Chun-sŏk registered the firm in 1941 at an authorized capital of 1 million yen with 250 thousand yen paid-in. The board included Min Kyu-sik, Kim Yŏn-su, and Pak Hŭng-sik. President Ha himself, Pak's colleague at Chejudo Industries, held nearly 50 percent of the twenty thousand shares available, with Min, Kim, and Pak also appearing among the principal stockholders. There were also more prestigious appointments evident in this third level of investments. Directorships in Kim Yŏn-su's major investments, the Kyŏngsŏng and South Manchurian Spinning companies, gave clear notice of Pak's place among major native entrepreneurs.

Pak took part in three larger joint investments under Japanese management:[15] Keijin Enterprise, Chōsen Wholesale Textile, and Daikō Trade. The former specialized in real estate and construction quite similar to Pak's own Taedong Industries. Pak served as a director of Keijin Enterprises (Keijin Kigyō)[16] and a principal shareholder together with Pang Ŭi-sŏk, the mining magnate Ch'oe Ch'ang-hak, and others. Founded only in July of 1940, the company listed an authorized capital of 2 million yen with 1 million yen paid-in, and estimated assets in 1945 of 28.9 million yen.[17] Other Japanese ventures such as Daikō Trade and Chōsen Wholesale Textile also complemented Pak's own investments in trade and retailing. Promoters of the wholesale venture had announced plans[18] for the company already in March of 1940, and formally established the Chōsen Wholesale Textile Company (Chōsen Seni Zakka Gensha)[19] in May of 1941 at an authorized capital of 2 million yen with 1.5 million yen paid-in, and estimated assets in 1945 of 15 million yen.[20] Japanese nationals managed and staffed the Seoul headquarters and P'yŏngyang branch, though both Pak and Ko Kwang-p'yo of Kim's Haedong Bank served on the board. I find it significant that despite the Japanese monopoly of wholesaling on the peninsula throughout the colonial years, Pak finally gained representation here on the board of one of the larger wholesalers.

The Daikō Trade Company represented Pak's most significant investment in medium-sized Japanese ventures. The state and the Chōsen Trade Association (Chōsen Bōeki Kyōkai) cultivated interest in trading firms among Japanese and Korean investors in the last decade of colonial rule. Koreans gained a place in at least three larger trading companies of the day: the Chōsen Trade Promotion Company (Chōsen Bōeki Shinkō), Chōsen Tōa Trade (Chōsen Tōa Bōeki), and Daikō Trade.[21] The key executive in these joint trade ventures with state-affiliated firms was a former Bank of Chōsen research director with wide knowledge of Manchuria and China: Shibuya Reiji.[22] Shibuya served as executive director of both Daikō and Chōsen Dōa Trade. Born in 1878, Shibuya graduated from Waseda University and served some years with the nationalist Genyōsha organization before joining the Bank of Chōsen. He helped organize and manage both trading ventures, and was prominent as well in trade policy associations. With a long resume in trade projects, the now senior Shibuya had reached his sixty-third year before founding Chōsen Tōa Trade in Seoul in the spring of 1941. As managing director he oversaw a company with an authorized capital of 5 million yen and 2.5 million yen paid-in, comparable to the capital base at Hwasin and Kyŏngsŏng Spinning. We find Kim Yŏn-su among the directors, and Shibuya himself, Chōsen Nitrogenous Fertilizers, Mitsui Commercial, and other Japanese interests among the major shareholders.[23]

Daikō's strategic location in the Chinese market, the scale of Pak's financial commitment in tandem with Kim Yŏn-su and the state, and the opportunity for contacts with other Japanese entrepreneurs set Daikō Trade apart in the third level of Pak investments. The Japanese-managed Daikō Trade (Daikō Bōeki)[24] stands out as the best example of a complementary investment, serving both state priorities and Pak's interest in foreign trade. With an authorized capital of one million yen and half of that paid-in, Daikō Trade was founded in the fall of 1939 with headquarters in Seoul and a branch in

Changchiak'on, Mongolia. Pak appeared as the sole Korean representative on the board, though Nakatomi Keita of Kyŏngsŏng Spinning also served as a director. Hwasin Trade, Kyŏngsŏng Spinning, and the Bank of Chōsen, Industrial Bank, and Japanese Imperial Household put up the capital for this joint venture between the colonial state and local capitalists.

Knowledge of Daikō trade with Mongolia no doubt proved valuable to someone developing his own trading company with interests in northern China. Contact with executive director Shibuya and with other directors such as Nakatomi Keita would have been important links for overseas trade. Daikō Trade in turn invested in two other companies involved in trade with China: the much larger Chōsen Dōa Trade already described, and Dōka Industrial. Dōka Industrial (Dōka Sangyō)[25] was established in May of 1940 at an authorized capital of 2 million yen with 500 thousand yen paid-in. Operating from headquarters in Tientsin and branches in Seoul and Tsingtao, the Korean-managed firm specialized in trade in agricultural goods between the peninsula and China. The prominent banker and financier Han Sang-yong served as chairman and Ha Chun-sŏk (under his Japanese name Kawamoto Toshimasu) as president, with only two Japanese on the entire board.

A fourth level in Pak's portfolio included directorships at strategic Japanese firms such as Chōsen Petroleum, North Korea Paper and Chemical Manufacturing, the Oriental Development Company,[26] and the presidency of the Chōsen Aircraft Manufacture from 1944. Activity here reinforced the joint investments and family investments of the inner levels. Even the resume of the well-established Min family did not match the prestigious directorships of the newcomer, Pak Hŭng-sik. Although Pak gained notoriety before and after liberation for his role at the aircraft company,[27] his decade of service in the earlier ventures merits more scrutiny. The prominent Ōji Paper Company of Japan founded North Korea Paper and Chemical Manufacture (Hokusen Seishi Kagaku Kōgyō)[28] with a plant in Kilchu, North Hamgyŏng Province, in April of 1935 at an authorized capital of 20 million yen with 10 million yen paid-in. The company operated with an annual budget of 23 million yen in 1941, and estimated assets by 1945 of 162.4 million yen. Among principal stockholders were Ōji Securities with 52 percent of the shares, Chōsen Trust (3 percent), the Oriental Development Company (1 percent), the Bank of Chōsen (1 percent), the Industrial Bank (1 percent), and Ch'oe Ch'ang-hak (1 percent). Pak won election to the board in 1935, and the ever-present Han Sang-yong as an auditor among a distinguished list of Japanese. How did Pak, the founder of a modest paper firm like the Sŏnil, get singled out for such a prestigious appointment? Pak himself recalled that none other than Governor-General Ugaki himself recommended Pak as an advisor to Ōji Paper.[29] Contact with Ōji executives would be useful for Pak's own paper manufacturing investment. Friendships on the board could also be useful. Akita Hideo, a major stockholder in North Korea Paper appeared in 1943 as a major investor in Hwasin.[30]

Hashimoto Keizaburō[31] of Japan Petroleum organized the massive Chōsen Petroleum Company[32] in June of 1935 in line with the government's new ordinance encouraging and subsidizing production of fuels on the peninsula itself. While Min Tae-sik attended board meetings at Keijō Electric under the eminent Ōhashi Shintarō, Pak Hŭng-sik mingled with the likes of Hashimoto Keizaburō in board meetings of Chōsen Petroleum. Hashimoto graduated from Tokyo Imperial University before entering the ministries of Finance, and later Agriculture and Commerce, rising to the level of vice-minister in both. He went on to the presidencies of Japan Petroleum and Chōsen Petroleum, directorships at numerous mining and industrial firms, and appointment to the House of Peers. Investors in Hashimotō's Chōsen Petroleum included Noguchi's Japan Nitrogenous Fertilizers (20 percent of the shares), Japan Petroleum (14 percent), the Oriental Development Company (19 percent), Chōsen Trust (5 percent), and Mitsui Trade (5 percent). A strategic investment supported by the alliance of colonial state and major zaibatsu, Chōsen Petroleum played a major role in the export of minerals and the import of paraffin, asphalt, coke, and oil, while returning a considerable profit.[33] A comparison of the initial investment with estimated assets ten years later indicate dramatic growth. The company initially registered an authorized capital of 30 million yen, and by 1942 operated with a paid-in capital of 22 million yen. Estimated assets in 1945 stood at 785.9 million yen, which earned Chōsen Petroleum a place among the ten largest Japanese investments on the peninsula.[34] Pak Hŭng-sik served on the board here of one of the more strategically important Japanese investments of the colonial period. The directorship afforded contacts with some of the most important state and zaibatsu interests on the peninsula, reinforcing Pak's credibility with the state and Japanese business figures.

Turning back to the core of Pak's portfolio, the Hwasin Company stood at the very center of these concentric levels of investments, based in the impressive department store building on Chongno avenue. A Korean-owned and -managed commercial investment, Pak registered Hwasin as a joint-stock venture[35] in September of 1931, and within a few years listed assets of 2.3 million yen. Rapid early growth has been attributed to large purchases of gold and silver stocks just prior to a gold embargo[36] of December 1931, together with currency inflation following the Manchurian Incident strengthening demand for precious metals. Pak himself attributed such early success as the absorption of a Korean competitor, the Donga Department Store,[37] to better organization and discipline. Certainly access to extensive amounts of capital earned in gold and silver sales played a role as well. Continuity in management under the familiar slate of President Pak Hŭng-sik, executive directors Yi Ki-yŏn and later Yi Kyu-jae, and managing directors Yun U-sik and Chogō Eiji marked the first decade at the store. Together with Chu Yo-han, the management team amounted to an interlocking directorate with nearly identical roles in Hwasin Chain Stores, the real estate company, Taedong Industries, and Hwasin Trade.

Pak reserved most of the twenty thousand shares of stock for himself or his companies. His nephew, Pak Pyŏng-gyo, and the tight band of executives held smaller blocks of shares. These joint-stock companies were distinguished on the whole by Pak's monopoly share among a very small number of shareholders, together with continuity in management. Although the salience of Pak's close band of executives faded somewhat at the very end of the colonial period, there was little dilution of ownership. The broader representation among stockholders in Hwasin Trade remained the exception. The flagship Hwasin firm absorbed Taedong Industries in 1941, raising the authorized capital to three million yen. Sŏnil Paper, Hwasin Chain Stores, and Hwasin Trade eventually became part of Hwasin in 1944, raising the capital to eight million yen, though with only sixty thousand shares and forty-five shareholders.[38]

A closer look at the Hwasin Chain Stores Company provides insight into both the growth of commerce on the peninsula and Pak's adjustment to state policy and economic conditions. The Hwasin Chain Stores Company (Hwasin Yŏnswaejŏm)[39] was established in March of 1936 at an authorized capital of 2 million yen with 500 thousand yen paid-in. The company moved into its own headquarters building two years later, built by Taedong Industrial in the western section of Seoul. Customers across the peninsula could find textiles, handicrafts, stationery, cosmetics, utensils, and various foreign goods at the stores. The network included 350 units with inventories worth from one thousand to four thousand yen. We meet again a familiar team at the helm, including President Pak Hŭng-sik, Managing Director Yi Kyu-jae, directors Chu Yo-han and Chogō Eiji. Among the total of forty thousand shares, Pak himself owned twenty-seven thousand, while Taedong Industrial and his nephew, Pak Pyŏng-gyo, each owned eight thousand.

Merchants in the provinces had little cash but could procure commodities such as locally produced items, and use real estate such as a storefront or larger property as collateral. Supplying the merchants with inventory on consignment would solve problems of capital circulation while hastening the transition to commercial capital. Hwasin found a way to supply merchandise on the security of the local merchants' property without charging interest, as long as the goods were sold in a relatively short time. The whole system depended on rapid transportation and access to a reliable line of credit, because Hwasin had to pay the manufacturers within two months of delivery, even though the local merchants could delay payment on inventories received up to four months from delivery. Sŏnil Paper and the Hwasin Department Store likewise depended on a mail-order system, reliable transportation, and credit facilities. Postal and transport systems were in place. Pak Hŭng-sik built the organization and developed ties with Japanese and Korean banks, and with Japanese suppliers and Korean merchants to make the system work. At the Sŏnil and Hwasin, Pak put the overdeveloped infrastructures of the colonial economy to work for the Korean population and made a profit. If the Mins were aristocratic financiers, Pak was a hard-driving businessman.

How did Pak maintain continuity of control across the core investments of Sŏnil Paper, Hwasin Department Store, and Hwasin Chain Stores? Allen[40] wrote of "interlocking directorates" among corporations sharing directors in common, and described their dual purpose: "an attempt by corporations to anticipate environmental contingencies and to control their relationships with other corporations." Looking to the colonial situation of dependence, I would not deny the importance of intercorporate relations, but Pak had to deal with contingencies like changing state policy and the constraints of the war economy. The Korean inner circle used interlocking directorates as one strategy to insure control in a very insecure environment of alien priorities and control. I find it necessary to distinguish in the colonial situation between interlocking directorates of company managers, and of corporate owners termed "friendly investors." The family companies of Pak Hŭng-sik and Kim Yŏn-su were characterized by both types of interlocking directorates, but only the latter were evident in the enterprises of the Mins.

Sŏnil Paper, Hwasin Chain Stores, and Hwasin Trade had been joined in 1941 to form Hwasin Commercial Company (Hwasin Sangsa). The board of directors in 1943 included President Pak and Executive Director Yi Kyu-jae, together with executive directors Hirata Shinpei and Mitani Toshihiro of the Tongil Bank.[41] Among the directors were Yoneda Yasaburo of Sŏnil Paper, Taguchi Sukeichi, and Hyŏn Chun-ho of the Honam Bank. Han Sang-yong of the Hansŏng Bank and Chosŏn Insurance served as an auditor together with the eminent Tagawa Tsunejirō, former president of the Keijō Chamber of Commerce and Industry.[42] Kim Yŏn-su appeared as a company director and Tsuda Shingo of Kanegafuchi Spinning as an advisor.[43] Tsuda[44] was a prominent Kobe businessman, a councillor for the Bank of Japan, and later a director of the Silk Yarn Control Company in the home islands during wartime. The final, preliberation character of Pak's board reflected a blend of the trusted Korean coterie of managers such as Yi Kyu-jae and Yoneda Yasaburo, Korean business leaders such as Kim, Hyŏn, and Han, and prominent Japanese such as Tagawa and Tsuda. Japanese investors appeared among minority shareholders, but Pak retained a controlling block of shares. Again Pak had adapted with consolidation and inclusion of prominent Japanese and Koreans to maintain the credibility of his own large firm with the state, Japanese business, and Korean business leaders.

Despite his nonaristocratic origins, lack of education or an agricultural base, Pak prospered as a dependent capitalist with Sŏnil and Hwasin, in joint ventures with other Koreans and Japanese, and as a director in large-scale Japanese industrial projects. Again we ask, how did he do it? The portfolio itself helped mightily. The joint investment in Hwasin Trade under Pak's management complemented the first level of Sŏnil and Hwasin investments, but this belated effort at joint investment with executive responsibility appeared the exception to the rule of an inner core of closely held companies. Nonetheless, the interlocking directorate of corporate owners was apparent in this second level of investments, and of course in the outer levels. Pak appeared more comfortable with the third level of joint investments, particularly in real estate, construction, and foreign trade, involving less of his time and capital while permitting useful ties with other Korean and Japanese entrepreneurs. The joint investments gave Pak a share in the profits and growth of projects too extensive or too uncertain to risk full ownership, yet at the same time tapped areas of interest to his own real estate and trade companies. The final level of participation in large-scale Japanese investments again proved complementary, facilitating contact with leading Japanese industrialists such as the eminent Hashimoto Keizaburō of Chōsen Petroleum.

Pak sought out capital commitments from other prominent Korean entrepreneurs only in Hwasin Trade. His limited efforts in this second level of business activity stand in stark contrast to the long-term Tongil commitment of the Mins and of Kim Yŏn-su's textile companies. It is clear that Pak was linked with other major Korean corporate owners and investors mainly through participation in finance, industry, real estate, and trade companies beyond both his first and second levels of interlocking companies. Ties with other major Korean entrepreneurs were crucial for investment and mutual support on boards and in joint enterprises, though not in Pak's core enterprises. Although Kim Yŏn-su served for a few years as a director of the Hwasin Company, and Min Kyu-sik was added as a director and Pang Ui-sŏk as an auditor of the Hwasin at the end of the colonial period, there appeared to be little room on the boards of Pak's own enterprises for those other than his close-knit group of administrators.

Strong in commerce, Pak later tried to diversify with investments in finance, real estate, and industry in the third level of his portfolio. As already noted, he held major shares in the Tongil Bank and Hyŏn Chun-ho's Honam Bank, and served as a director of Han Sang-yong's Chosŏn Life Insurance Company. Although he never developed his own industrial company, he served as a director for Kim Yŏn-su's Kyŏngsŏng Spinning and South Manchurian Spinning companies, and for Ha Chun-sŏk's Chosŏn Engineering Company. Parallel to his own investment in the Taedong Industries, Pak was listed on the boards and among the major shareholders in two real estate and construction firms, the Chosŏn Industry and Management Company and Keijin Enterprise. Nor were trade opportunities neglected. In addition to his own Hwasin Trade, he was represented in commerce with Mongolia as a director of Daikō Trade under Shibuya Reiji, and indirectly with Shibuya's larger venture, Chōsen Daikō Trade.

What can we conclude from this variety of investments in other Korean firms and medium-sized Japanese trading ventures by someone who had only recently joined the ranks of major Korean entrepreneurs? First of all, there was capital accrued from profits in his inner level of investments. Financially, Pak had arrived by 1935. Second, the military controls and mobilization priorities of the last decade of the colonial period were not conducive to extensive growth in retail trade in dry goods or printing. Recognizing the limitations on expansion of his own commercial ventures, he scrambled to gain a place among other investors in areas where he was unable to develop his own enterprises. Pak's entry here suggests also pragmatism on the part of other Korean investors, whether aristocrats or commoners. There was room among other entrepreneurs for this commoner from the north, given his capital and successful record of enterprise. The second and third levels of Pak's investments were evidence of his place among the inner group of colonial entrepreneurs.

The fourth level of Pak's investments reinforced the image of an ambitious, successful local entrepreneur with reliable government connections. He enjoyed neither long connections with major Japanese investments as did Min Tae-sik, nor the variety of connections typical of Kim Yŏn-su. Pak gained a place on the boards of Chōsen Petroleum and North Korea Paper and Chemical Manufacture in 1935 because of his prominence in the domestic paper industry and knowledge of northern Korea, and his high credibility with Governor-General Ugaki. Lacking Kim's knowledge and contacts in industry, and Min's high status from the early colonial period, Pak did not parlay these government-sponsored appointments into executive posts in other major Japanese firms until his ill-fated effort as president of the Chōsen Aircraft Manufacture. Nonetheless, the presence of a successful retailer without aristocratic background or strong industrial investment on the boards of these Japanese enterprises was remarkable.

Pak amassed a fortune by making foreign and domestic consumer goods available to the Korean population through effective domestic distribution networks. An ambitious salesman with excellent government relations, he took full advantage of the colonial railroad system, the postal system, of access to suppliers in Japan, and above all of the finance system making possible small and large-scale loans at reasonable rates. Distinct phases of enterprise through 1945 only highlight his adaptations to developing infrastructures, changing economic conditions, and state strategies.[45] The Sŏnil Paper Goods Company originally purchased newsprint from Canada, paper from Japan, and later developed its own paper manufacturing plant. The Hwasin Department Store later made a wide range of Japanese and Korean consumer goods available to the Seoul population in an attractive setting, making full use of improved transport and finance infrastructures. A chain stores project was organized within the Hwasin by 1934 to distribute merchandise directly from Japanese production centers to outlets across the peninsula. The latter two commercial investments did not run counter to administration policy for the assimilation of Korea and Japan. Hwasin Trade in the last years of colonial rule opened up new markets in the Yen Block for products from the domestic and Japanese networks cultivated through Hwasin Department Store and Hwasin Chain Stores. The fact that strong ties with the state and large-scale Japanese corporate investors lay at the heart of his enterprise raises questions of the nature and extent of his dependence.

A merchant buys cheap and sells dear. Nowhere was the state more critical than in providing the credit necessary for Pak to purchase in lot from domestic and Japanese suppliers, and sell at a profit. Pak gained the financial support of both Japanese and Korean banks throughout his entrepreneurial career. Loans from the Industrial Bank, the Chōsen Commercial Bank, and the Tongil supported his initial venture in Seoul in 1926, the Sŏnil Paper Goods Company.[46] But more than a merchant, Pak was an entrepreneur. He displayed considerable skills at designing and implementing new combinations of transport, suppliers, and customers in the chain stores project.

A loan of thirty million yen from the Industrial Bank in 1934 helped launch the chain stores project, and a special section of the bank was devoted to ongoing business with the branches.[47] Pak did well to have turned early on to merchandising. Unlike the problems of the Mins with close state scrutiny in finance, the Hwasin and associated commercial enterprises faced fewer state constraints until the economic controls of the Pacific War. Even then Pak hastened successfully to consolidate, maintain ownership, and adjust for a more prominent Japanese presence in management by promoting familiar Japanese colleagues such as Yoneda Yasaburo[48] of Sŏnil and Chogō Eiji of Hwasin. Few could equal Pak's agility at finding a place within state strategy and exploiting the business possibilities with his own core enterprises.

The question remains, How did Pak gain such generous state support so unlike most of his contemporaries? One could point to productive use of capital: Pak was a good risk. And the success of this effusive, hard-charging businessman served as further evidence for a restive local populace of what the state advertised as local economic growth. Supporting both arguments was the obvious fact of Pak's careful alignment with state policy. State direction, whether in policy or actual legislation, affected the Hwasin enterprises, though less so than financial institutions. Japan's expansion into Manchuria, development of Korea as an industrialized forward base, and the network of trading relationships termed the "Yen Block" all played a part in the growth of Pak's commercial investments. Pak organized Hwasin Trade in 1939 for foreign markets, an extension of Hwasin commerce abroad within a network of transport and markets established by the Japanese. The trade venture coincided with wider state efforts to integrate the Yen Block economies. He did not gain appointment as advisor to Chōsen Petroleum in 1935, or later as founder and president of the Chōsen Aircraft Industries Company by chance. As Pak himself later admitted, "I intended to use the Japanese but instead was used."[49]

Ties with Japanese business were likewise important. Hwasin had opened a purchasing bureau in Osaka already in January of 1932, evidence of the importance of contacts with Japanese suppliers for Hwasin merchandise. Among important suppliers, Pak maintained close relations with presidents Tsuda Shingo of Kanegafuchi Textile, Fujiyama Aiichirō of Japan Sugar Manufacture,[50] Arima of Meiji Confectionery, Suzuki Chūji of Ajinomoto,[51] and Masata of Japan Flour.[52] We already noted his ties with Hashimoto Keizaburō of Chōsen Petroleum. Pak also served on the board of Ōji Paper's affiliate, the North Korea Paper and Chemical Manufacture Company. The directorships in turn helped Pak's own enterprise, as participation in large-scale investments by Ōji Paper and Chōsen Petroleum supported by the government-general reinforced ties with the colonial state and enhanced his position as a business leader. How did Pak gain entree to the larger Japanese firms? I would point to prior credibility with the colonial state, reinforced by his own success as a merchant through ties with Japanese suppliers. The alliance of state and zaibatsu found the nominal representation of local business leaders useful, whether for local expertise regarding markets and labor, or simply as evidence of a benign capitalism. Recognized by the colonial state as reliable and adaptable to state policies, Pak went on to the boards of major Japanese investments on the peninsula.

Pak stands apart from the Mins and Kims among dependent capitalists. Despite similarities in portfolios, we must conclude that Pak was indeed unique. Lacking both the extended family relations of the Mins and the capital base of agricultural holdings, Pak drew about himself a coterie of trusted associates and a base of nearly wholly owned interlocking companies. Whereas the Mins could rely on the Kyesŏng or Yŏngbo agricultural companies for a capital base, and Kim Yŏn-su on the Samyang, Pak relied rather on extensive personal investment in tightly held joint-stock commercial ventures in paper, department stores, and later in real estate and construction. With no male siblings or relatives involved in large-scale commerce, he maintained something akin to family control through a close group of associates such as Kim Ok-hyŏn and Yoneda Yasaburo of Sŏnil, and Yi Kyu-jae and Chogō Eiji of Hwasin and other companies. The managers themselves formed an interlocking directorate evident in the Hwasin group of companies. The inner core of related companies formed around Sŏnil and Hwasin provided a base of capital and management expertise for expansion, and a shield against unfriendly Korean or Japanese investment. Yet even here Pak appeared insecure, unwilling to dilute the family share by permitting even his managers a larger stake.

Vulnerable to market dynamics in his commercial operations, and lacking a stable base of agricultural capital, Pak had reason to maintain the Hwasin and Sŏnil as nearly wholly owned and tightly managed ventures. Even with control, he still needed the contacts and outlets for diversified investment apparent in multiple levels of investment to maintain ownership and direction. The design of such a diverse portfolio is all the more remarkable given his northern roots, absence of a close circle of well-educated alumni, and a nonaristocratic background, leaving him without the network of prestigious personal contacts so important for large-scale enterprise. It was at once both more difficult for Pak to gain entry into this elite and more necessary than for his better established counterparts, Min Kyu-sik and Kim Yŏn-su.

Conclusion

Despite the dominance of Japanese firms in wholesaling, large-scale retailing, and trade, the number of local commercial firms and the amount of capital invested grew dramatically across the colonial period.[53] Korean and Japanese commercial enterprise prospered with early capitalist developments such as increased use of currency, of improved postal and transport networks for commercial purposes, and the transition from informal, family enterprise to registered partnerships and joint-stock companies. Sŏnil and Hwasin played a significant role in the origins of local enterprise, providing experience in large-scale retailing and foreign trade, and institutional continuity[54] in ownership, personnel, and management through 1945 and beyond. The story of Pak Hŭng-sik offers a chronicle of such developments in projects of an outsider among the Seoul business elite competing with large-scale Japanese firms. The story tells of both the growth of capitalism and the dynamics of the Korean inner circle of dependent capitalists. If the uniqueness of this native enterprise among Japanese competitors in Seoul lent a symbolic significance, the scale and extension of the Hwasin family of companies gave the effort a practical significance: organizational experience and confidence in retailing and foreign trade.

Pak pursued strategies of concentration, state relations, and class ties more intently than his peers, due to his relatively disadvantaged origins compared to the wealthy and aristocratic Mins, and the wealthy and well-respected Kims. Concentration of ownership and management compensated for the lack of a strong agricultural base of capital by assuring control in commercial enterprise in the initial years of Pak's entrepreneurship. The decade (1935–45) of Pak's prosperity were years of strong, state-led investment in industry and trade, in contrast to the early colonial years of strong government encouragement of agriculture. Agriculture was both an avenue for capital accumulation and a platform in efforts to gain social status through the end of the Chosŏn Dynasty. There were other means to status in the colonial years, but a shrewd investor such as Pak could hardly overlook lucrative agrarian investment. One wonders if in time he would have invested more in agricultural enterprise, and if the Cheju Island cattle-raising venture was not a start in that direction. Pak built his empire on the base of commercial capital, highly unusual in an agrarian society. One might conclude he led the local transition to commercial capital if it were not for the fact that he stood alone, and also succeeded only though credit financing from the Japanese. For all his success, the absence of a secure outside base of capital would leave Pak more reliant on state support and more vulnerable to state direction than his fellow dependent capitalists. If the Mins choice of finance rather than commerce left them more open to strong state supervision and direction, Pak's modest capital base deprived him of critical resources for greater autonomy in relations with the state.

Given his meager education and lack of experience in government, Pak proved remarkably adept in relations with the state. He gained government support without direct government investment and was ready later even for mandated participation of Japanese nationals in management with a corps of trusted Japanese such as Yoneda and Chogō. With neither the status nor capital for finance, nor the experience or capital for industry, Pak turned his energies to commerce. The path proved fortuitous, for commercial ventures were less scrutinized and controlled than industrial ventures, and of much less concern to state officials than banks. The state later made dramatic use of Pak's stature as a local entrepreneur, however, in the very area toward which his entrepreneurial instincts must have led – a major industrial venture. Pak showed himself less adept in government relations in taking on major responsibility for the Chōsen Aircraft Company. The state unleashed Pak's entrepreneurial ambitions at the helm of a lavishly funded war effort. Pak in turn lost all claim to enterprise for the benefit of the wider local populace.

Pak made his fortune by dint of talent and ambition, a coterie of competent managers, and by winning the respect and support of state authorities. Lacking the ties of the long-established Min family, or the backing of eminent Korean business figures such as Pak Yŏng-hyo or of his own family in the case of Kim Yŏn-su, Pak deserves credit as a self-made entrepreneur. His place among the inner group of local business leaders provides one compelling case for Imotani's argument[55] about the transition from hereditary aristocratic class to economic class in the colonial years. It was a painful transition. One wonders if the hard-won success on his own made him wary of taking on joint enterprises with a heavy financial and executive commitment. Perhaps, too, he was unsure about gaining the support of other major entrepreneurs. Whatever the reason, Pak appeared more ready to give than receive when it came to part ownership in joint enterprises. Interdependence was something of a one-way street. Certainly Pak could call on friendly investment and board participation from Min Kyu-sik and Kim Yŏn-su when necessary, but in a limited area of foreign trade and for a very short time. On the other hand, he invested heavily in the Tongil and Honam banks, and served on the boards of Kim's companies with apparently some investment as well.

I close with two images of this remarkable merchant from Chinnamp'o:

competitor and collaborator. In celebration of the chain stores project, Pak placed an advertisement[56] in the vernacular *Chosŏn Ilbo*. With candor, pride, and as much enthusiasm as ever, Pak announced his role in establishing a "commercial Korea" by improving service in rural areas and promoting currency circulation. I can think of few individuals, Korean or Japanese, who competed more successfully or contributed more through local merchandising in the transition to commercial capital on the peninsula. The contribution came at the considerable cost of dependence. If local business leaders faced the daunting task of being both Korean and successful within a colonial economy, Pak achieved commercial success only through close cooperation with the state. He accepted appointment to the prestigious Commission on the Japanese Industrial Economy (Nihon Sangyo Keizai Iinkai) and attended their meeting in Tokyo on December 15, 1942. When confronted about this by prosecutors in an antinationalist trial after liberation, Pak explained that it was an invitation from the emperor and a chance to meet "three thousand members of the Tokyo Chamber of Commerce."[57]

7

Kim and industry

Cho Ki-jun[1] has held up Kim Yŏn-su and his Kyŏngsŏng Spinning as the preeminent example of national enterprise, a colonial venture representing more than just local ownership and management. Only local industrial entrepreneurship and the career of Kim remain to complete our story of dependent capitalism on the peninsula through 1945, and bring us to a conclusion about benign capitalism. One would hope local accumulation in a colony might provide capital for commercial or industrial reinvestment and a start toward indigenous development despite economic reliance on the metropole. But the task of attracting capital to local industrial and commercial ventures demands both organizations and symbols, structures and precedents, a "demonstration effect"[2] of productive local enterprise: that is, indigenous banks, retailers, wholesalers, and light industries, plus confidence in their long-term viability. Consumers had been exposed to the quality and utility of Japanese manufactures flooding local markets. Now local consumers would be exposed to reliable, productive Korean manufacturers, retailers, and financiers. Such was the hope of the Native Products Campaign.

The Mins and Pak organized corporate structures and established precedents for productive local enterprise, but always by way of exception in a dependent situation. We can conclude this was "indigenous capital" insofar as they maintained local ownership and management for the most part. Was it for the wider benefit of the Korean nation? They did provide organizations and symbols but certainly not in defiance or even mild opposition to the colonial state or the state–zaibatsu alliance. For instance, we noted the overwhelming dominance of the Bank of Chōsen and the Chōsen Industrial Bank in Korean finance, and the growing Japanese presence and control even in surviving Korean commercial banks such as the Hansŏng and Tongil. The failure of the Min family to maintain direction of the sole surviving local bank in the last decade of colonial rule has been contrasted with continuity of local direction at Pak's Hwasin commercial enterprises. Even here Pak's success in local commerce stands as the exception to the rule of Japanese dominance in foreign trade, wholesaling, and large-scale domestic commercial operations on the peninsula.

How did local businessmen fare in industry? Statistics on industrial investment again suggest a strong foreign presence. The Japanese owned 94 percent of the equity in industry by 1940 among companies with a capital of a million yen or more.[3] But what can be said of the locally owned minority share of this rapidly expanding base of industrial investment, particularly in the textile industry, a critical sector of initial industrial growth in both colonial and postcolonial Korea? Although the familiar pattern of extensive Japanese investment again looms large, even the minor presence of native capital in textile production would be significant for early capitalist development in Korea. Korean-owned firms held 24 percent (10.2 million yen) of the capital invested in large-scale textile firms in 1938. Strong Japanese investment over the next two years reduced the total share of Korean capital in the industry to only 15 percent in 1940, although now the Korean-owned capital of large-scale textile firms on the peninsula amounted to fourteen million yen.[4]

The Kyŏngsŏng Spinning and Weaving Company (Kyŏngsŏng Pangjik) of the Kim family was the largest of the indigenously owned and managed industrial investments during the colonial period. Kim Yŏn-su (pen name, Sudang 1896–1979)[5] completed his secondary and college education in Japan, graduating from Kyoto Imperial University in 1921. He served as managing director and later president (1935–45) of Kyŏngsŏng Spinning, and from 1936 as president of the Chung'ang Commercial and Industrial Company. He organized, managed, and owned the Samyang Company, one of the largest indigenous agricultural corporations of the period, and also served as chief executive officer of the Haedong Bank from 1927 until 1938. Unlike Pak Hŭng-sik, Kim Yŏn-su began his career with the advantages of wealth. The Kim family had acquired considerable capital at the turn of the century.[6]

The family's fortunes prospered from the mid-nineteenth century under Yŏn-su's grandfather Kim Yo-hyŏp (pen name, Akche, 1833–1909). His marriage into the Chŏng family with extensive agricultural properties in Kobugun in southern Chŏlla Province provided a broader base for extending his own property holdings. Akche moved the family home to the village of Inch'on in Puanmyŏn, Kobugun, near the port of Chulp'o on the Yellow Sea. Here he was active in overseeing both his inherited holdings and helping with the holdings of the Chŏng family. Akche held government posts from 1872, culminating in positions on the Emperor's Advisory Council (Chungch'uwŏn) in 1898 and on the Royal Secretariat (Pisŏwŏn). Akche's two sons were likewise politically active while carefully expanding their agricultural venture. Kim Ki-jung (pen names, Wŏnp'a and Tongbok, 1859–1933) was a district (gun) official from 1900 to 1907, and Kim Kyŏng-jung (pen name, Chisan, 1863–1945) was active in the Royal Secretariat and as a district official. The legacy of political experience in the Kim family from the end of the Chosŏn Dynasty would serve their descendants well in the colonial era where cooperation with the state appeared a necessary condition for large-scale entrepreneurship.

Government service did not lure the sons away from the family business. Akche's sons moved their administrative center and warehouses to the seaside of Chulp'o in 1909 for easy access to the bustling port of Kunsan, an expanding center for the rice trade with Japan. Yŏn-su and his older brother, Kim Sŏng-su of the *Donga Ilbo* and Posŏng College, improved the family's fortunes with investments in agriculture and industry in Korea and Manchuria, and also in finance and the mass media. Although not as prominent in finance as the Min family and frustrated by the loss of the Haedong Bank, Kim Yŏn-su successfully retained ownership and management in a large-scale industrial enterprise. The continuity of family ownership and administration by a small coterie of colleagues distinguishing the enterprises of Pak Hŭng-sik was apparent also in the projects of Kim Yŏn-su, but there was no parallel with the remarkable scale and diversity of Kim family enterprises. The significance of his entrepreneurship lay in both the scale and continuity of personnel and experience, ownership and control in his enterprises through the end of the colonial period.

The issue of indigenous ownership and direction has been examined thus far in large-scale financial and commercial investments, with special concern for continuity through 1945. The Japanese role in finance so overshadowed the local role of Korean capital that one can hardly speak of competition. Pak Hŭng-sik was one of the few indigenous commercial elite to develop a retail enterprise comparable to the Japanese department store investments on the peninsula, but could hardly compete in the lucrative and expanding areas of wholesaling or foreign trade. Yet in the capital-intensive and technology-intensive area of textile production, one Korean-owned firm emerged with a capital base comparable to the middle range of Japanese textile investments on the peninsula.

Again questions come to mind of how Kim accumulated capital and maintained control in such a competitive area of industrial investment. Like Pak and the Mins, Kim survived and prospered only through close cooperation with the colonial authorities. We must look to the nature and extent of his dependence, and the distinctiveness of his adjustment. The answers will be framed with attention to concentration in ownership and management, relations with the colonial state, and ties with the Korean and Japanese business elite. If Min Tae-sik leaves the impression of pragmatism, and Pak of competition and collaboration, what can be said of this preeminent colonial capitalist?

Enterprise

The portfolio[7] of Kim Yŏn-su differed significantly from that of the Mins and Pak Hŭng-sik. Among the earlier of Kim's ventures, an inner core of family-owned and managed ventures such as the Samyang or Chung'ang Commerce and Industry certainly resemble the original agricultural and industrial investments of the Mins. But the core firms of Kim Yŏn-su represented larger and more diverse investments in land development in Korea and Manchuria rather than in urban real estate, and in rubber production rather than textiles. Kim devoted the Chung'ang Commerce and Industry Company[8] to industrial concerns within this core level of family-held ventures. The history of the Chung'ang reflects the organization, planning, and ambitions characterizing Kim family enterprise. The older brother, Kim Sŏng-su, had purchased one of the earliest indigenous industrial ventures, Kyŏngsŏng Weaving Company (Kyŏngsŏng Chigyu) in 1917. The weaving machinery of the company soon reverted to Kyŏngsŏng Spinning, though the company was maintained separately. The family registered the earlier acquisition under the title of Chung'ang Commerce and Industry (Chung'ang Sanggong) in 1926 with a reorientation toward marketing and rubber production. A tanning plant was added in 1939. This core-level investment registered a paid-in capital of one million yen in 1943, with only Kim family members and close associates as major shareholders.[9]

Kim organized the family landholdings into an agricultural company in 1924, and reorganized it in 1931 as an unlimited partnership of family members with headquarters in Seoul. The Samyang managed the family's original capital base of land, providing funds and a network of managers for other ventures. An earlier, private company named "Samsu" served as Kim's organizational base as he integrated his father's holdings into five agricultural estates in the Chŏlla area through 1931. The enterprise was reorganized again as a limited partnership in 1934 titled "Samyang," with Kim and his sons contributing the entire paid-in capital or 1.2 million yen.

The family more than doubled the paid-in capital of the company of 3 million yen in just six years.[10]

If expansion and integration of estates within the Chŏlla area was the focus in the 1920s, reclamation efforts along the tidal flats of the province seacoast marked the next decade of Samyang enterprise. By 1940 the company was busy recruiting farmers and developing land for estates in Manchuria. The family aggressively set about acquisition of high-quality paddy land in the fertile Chŏlla area. Samyang's predecessor, the Samsu company, had nearly doubled the original family holdings by 1931 through reinvestment of harvest profits for land acquisition, often from neighboring farms in debt.[11] Samyang's total holdings nearly doubled again by 1938, though now mainly through reclamation projects. Land acquired in Manchuria better than doubled the company's total acreage once more by the 1940s.[12] The Samyang was one example of continuity in agrarian capital accumulation from the late nineteenth century through 1945. And while Kim Yŏn-su's methods of organization, reclamation, and expansion abroad differed significantly from the agricultural enterprise of earlier generations, it was the traditional investment in land that provided a capital base for more modern industrial ventures.

The second level of Kim family investments paralleled the firms of the Mins in structure but, again, not in scale. Kim Yŏn-su assumed executive responsibilities and committed extensive family capital to retain major blocks of shares in three limited-liability joint-stock firms: Kyŏngsŏng Spinning, South Manchurian Spinning, and the Haedong Bank. The twenty-six years (1919–45) of Kyŏngsŏng development represented one of the longest, continuous indigenous investments in the colony; the five years (1940–5) of the Manchurian spinning venture one of the shortest; and Kim's eleven years at the Haedong Bank (1927–38) fit in between, coinciding with a critical decade of fundamental changes in banking on the peninsula. The Haedong Bank[13] was originally founded in 1919 with an authorized capital of two million yen. Cho Kye-hyŏn, a board member of Kyŏngsŏng Spinning, took over as managing director at the Haedong in 1925. Kim Yŏn-su consolidated control with 42 percent of the Haedong shares by 1927 and assumed the presidency for the next decade until the bank's merger with the Hansŏng in 1938. Despite hopes to develop the bank as a source for major industrial investment, Kim was only able to increase the paid-in capital of 300 thousand yen to 800 thousand yen. But if family ownership and control faded at the Min's Tongil and Kim's Haedong banks, there was continuity in Korean ownership and management at the Kim's spinning companies through 1945.

A third level of joint investments in medium-sized ventures without major administrative responsibility was apparent as well. The Samyang and Kyŏngsŏng eventually purchased most of the stock of Ko Wŏn-dong's Tonggwang Raw Silk Company,[14] though Ko, Pak Hŭng-sik, and Min Kyu-sik and his Yŏngbo Company retained shares. Kim Yŏn-su participated with Pak and Min in the Chosŏn Engineering Company, and together with Pak's Hwasin Trade, Kyŏngsŏng Spinning was a major shareholder in the Japanese firm active in Mongolia, Daikō Trade. The largest investment in this group was neither in industry nor commerce, however, but rather in gold mining. The Samyang[15] had purchased the Okkye gold mine in Kangwŏn Province, and the Kyeryong gold mine near Kongju in South Ch'ungch'ŏng Province in June of 1934. The assets were later developed in a joint investment, Okkye Gold,[16] with Japan Gold Mining[17] the majority partner and Kim a director with a minority share (20 percent). Japan Gold Mining, a joint investment of the Japanese government, Mitsui, Mitsubishi, and others, registered a paid-in capital of thirty million yen. Kim's links with such a large corporate investor made possible the heavy capital investment of productive gold mining. Japanese participation included both capital and control: that is, the entire board apart from Kim himself.

President Abe Sen'ichi organized Okkye Gold only in 1940, with a paid-in capital of one million yen.[18] A prominent figure in the alliance between colonial state and zaibatsu investment, Abe's record of government service and high posts in private enterprise gave considerable prestige to the mining venture. Abe served as secretary for the government-general in Seoul just after graduation from Tokyo University in 1919. He was later appointed mayor of P'yŏngyang and then governor of South Kyŏngsŏng Province before turning to industry. A board member of the Chōsen Gold Industry Company (Chōsen Sankin Shinkō), Abe managed their Korean operations with a capital in 1941 of 10 million yen. Chōsen Gold Industry estimated assets on the peninsula in 1945 of 97.5 million yen.[19] Abe later held the post of president at the government's control agency, the Chōsen Gold Sales and Purchase Company during the war years. The presence of such a prominent mining executive to direct the new Okkye venture was evidence of strong Japanese interest in the Samyang's mine, and Kim's acceptance of a joint venture in mining reflected adjustment to legislation regarding strategic resources. Still there is a striking contrast between joint investment in a separate mining venture with strong Japanese participation in this third level of Kim's investments, and the absence of Japanese corporate or individual names among the major stockholders in the second group of companies that Kim himself administered.

Kim was also active in a fourth level of larger Japanese investments on the peninsula, ranging from the printing company of the government-general, Chōsen Books and Printing, to Chōsen Tōa Trade, and even to the huge Chōsen Petroleum Company. Here one sees also investments in Japanese finance, railway, and utility companies[20] on the peninsula considerably larger than firms under Kim's management. He served on the board with the familiar Nakatomi Keita at two major Japanese firms: Chōsen Tōa Trade and Chōsen Refining. Nakatomi held 5 percent of the shares in the trade company, in tandem with Noguchi Jun's Chōsen Nitrogenous Fertilizers (5 percent), Mitsui Commerce (4 percent), and other prominent Japanese investors. The total Korean assets of Chōsen Tōa Trade in 1945 were estimated at about 25 million yen.[21] The close ties of both Nakatomi and Kim with the Chōsen Industrial Bank were apparent in their directorships at Chōsen Refining. The total Korean assets of Chōsen Refining (Chōsen Seiren) in 1945 were estimated at 108 million yen.[22] The bank held 25 percent of the shares available, and the bank's long-tenured president, Ariga Mitsutoyo appeared as both chair of the board and a major shareholder.

At the same time Min Tae-sik gained a place on the board of the venerable Keijō Electric, Kim Yŏn-su took part as a director and major investor in a leading utility, Kankō Hydroelectric. Organized only in 1939, the Kankō Hydroelectric Company (Kankō Suiryoku Denki) registered and authorized capital of 35 million yen and 12.5 million yen paid-in three years later. The Keishun Railway Company (16 percent), the Chōsen Industrial Bank (16 percent), and Japan High Frequency Heavy Industries (Nippon Kōshū Jugyō) (16 percent) were among the largest shareholders, and the Samyang owned 1.7 percent of the five hundred thousand shares. None other than Ariga Mitsutoyo organized the venture,[23] with Hayashi Shigeki as executive director.[24] Hayashi worked as a director of the Industrial Bank from 1933 to 1936, and later served as Ariga's executive director at the hydroelectric company. Ariga also served as president of Japan High Frequency Heavy Industries, while Hayashi headed up the Keishun Railway.

Looking to the railways, we meet the Japanese with whom Kim worked in ventures beyond the ken of his inner-level firms. He appeared as the largest individual shareholder in the Keishun Railway Company[25] with 2 percent of the shares. Corporate shareholders like Chōsen Trust held 18 percent, the Industrial Bank 15 percent, and the Chōsen Savings Bank nearly 4 percent. Organized in Seoul in 1936, the Keishun Railway Company (Keishun Tetsudo) listed an authorized capital in 1942 of 10 million yen with 5 million yen paid-in. The firm estimated assets on the peninsula in 1945 of 186 million yen.[26] One of the earlier private railways, the line served cities on its main trunk between Seoul and Ch'unch'ŏn in Kangwŏn Province. Prestigious appointments to the administration of the Keishun were evidence of the company's economic and military importance. Shiokawa Tōruyoshi of the Industrial Bank held the post of executive director under President Ushijima Shōzō. The former governor of Ibarakiken in the Kantō region of Japan, Ushijima came to the peninsula to serve as director of the Bureau of Education, and then of the Bureau of the Interior within the government-general.[27] Ushijima was succeeded at the railroad by Hayashi Shigeki, a former president of the Chōsen Industrial Bank and executive director of Kankō Hydroelectric. Hayashi Shigeki had also served as director of the Education Bureau and a governor of North Chŏlla Province before becoming active in finance and other business concerns.[28]

There were other railways in Kim's portfolio. He served as a director of the West Chōsen Central Railway Company (Seisen Chūo Tetsudo) in P'yŏngyang, owned mainly by Mitsubishi Mining (33 percent) and Chōsen Anthracite Coal (Chōsen Muentan) (37 percent) in 1942. The railway firm listed an authorized capital of 15 million yen in 1942, with 6 million paid-in.[29] Total Korean assets of the company in 1945 were estimated at 60 million yen.[30] Established only in 1938 by Mitsubishi and affiliates, the company quickly laid rail in the central west section of northern Korea to ship minerals to ports and industrial centers. The company transported coal domestically directly to the Mitsubishi Iron Works at Ch'ŏngjin, and linked the Sinch'ang and Changsŏng coal mines of a Mitsubishi subsidiary, Chōsen Anthracite Coal Company. Whereas one might expect export of the colony's raw materials to industry in the metropole, the colonial state in harness with zaibatsu chose rather to integrate industrial projects on the peninsula itself. The strategy still did not demand compradors, but did present excellent investment opportunities for local dependent industrialists. The prominence of railroad investments in Kim's portfolio was clear evidence of his place in zaibatsu transport ventures on the peninsula. Joint investment to gain a small place in the zaibatsu alliance with the colonial state represented one adjustment to state controls and incentives for infrastructural projects. The scale of the utility investments suggests a transfer of industrial capital to further industrial investment, rather than simply from agriculture or commerce to industry. Kim could draw on a larger and more fluid capital base than the Mins or Pak.

Kim's investment in this interconnected set of large-scale Japanese ventures was due in large part to ties with the Industrial Bank, but also to the wealth and prominence of the Kyŏngsŏng and South Manchurian Spinning, his most important ventures of the second level of core investments. Kim Sŏng-su and Marquis Pak Yŏng-hyo organized a number of Korean investors to form Kyŏngsŏng Spinning in October of 1919 with an authorized capital of 1 million yen, supported by nearly two hundred shareholders[31] paying in a total of 250 thousand yen. Pak Yŏng-hyo (1861–1939)[32] had gained prominence as a government official in the late Chosŏn Dynasty, as a strong advocate of liberal modernization strategies, and later, as a cabinet member in the short-lived (1894–5) reform government of Kim Hong-jip. He received both the title of marquis and an annual stipend from the government-general from 1910. Pak served as a director of the Chōsen Industrial Bank from 1918 to 1930, and then as an advisor until 1938. He was appointed to the Central Advisory Council in 1921, serving as vice-chairman, but later received the ultimate recognition for a Korean businessman in Japanese circles: appointment to the Japanese House of Peers.[33] The seventy-three-year-old Pak finally retired after sixteen years as president of Kyŏngsŏng Spinning in 1935.

Growing concentration of ownership and slow but steady plant expansion marked the first fifteen years at the company's factory in Yŏngdŭngp'o outside of Seoul. The total number of weaving machines grew from some two hundred in 1922 to better than five hundred in 1931, and nearly a thousand by May of 1936, together with 21,600 spinning machines.[34] Annual deficits through the first four years were replaced with marginal annual profits from 1924 through the early 1930s. The profits were made possible in part by annual subsidies from the government-general from 1924 through 1935 totalling about 250,000 yen. Even then the dividends represented an average annual return on capital invested of only 3 percent through 1931. The return[35] increased to between 4 and 6 percent annually through 1937. The paid-in capital of the firm had been raised to 400,000 yen by 1927, with only eighty-nine shareholders and the Kim family retaining 61 percent of the shares. The company listed a paid-in capital of one million yen by 1935 with sixty-nine shareholders and the Kim family and a few close associates retaining three-quarters of the shares. Continued concentration in ownership and continuity in management, coupled with rapid expansion and annual profits would mark the next decade of Kyŏngsŏng growth under President Kim Yŏn-su. He served as managing director of the company from 1922 until his appointment to a similar role at the Haedong Bank in 1927. Kim continued as a Kyŏngsŏng director until appointment as president in 1935.

Continuity in administration across the first decades was assured through a network of associates, including Kim Chae-su, Ch'oe Tu-sŏn, and Yi Kang-hyŏn, an experienced executive from the predecessor Kyŏngsŏng Weaving Company (Kyŏngsŏng Chigyu). Born in Seoul in 1888, Yi studied weaving technology at the Tokyo Higher Industrial School (Tokyo Kōtō Kōgyō

Gakko), and quickly became involved in the textile industry upon returning to Korea in 1911. He served as managing director through much of the first two decades of Kyŏngsŏng growth.[36] A contemporary of Kim Yŏn-su, Ch'oe Tu-sŏn[37] graduated from Waseda University in Tokyo. After further study abroad in Germany, he returned to Korea and a position as principal at the Chungyŏng Middle School of Kim Sŏng-su. Both Ch'oe and Kim served as directors of Kyŏngsŏng and of South Manchurian Spinning, of Chung'ang Commerce and Industry, and also of other Kim family investments such as Haedong Heungop (Haedong Hŭngŏp) with a paid-in capital of one million yen.[38] Interlocking directorates among the inner circle of Korean business leaders complemented the familiar set of managers serving on the boards of various family firms. Prominent capitalists such as Pak Hŭng-sik, Hyŏn Chun-ho, Min Kyu-sik, and Ch'oe Ch'ang-hak served as directors at Kyŏngsŏng, while Mun Sang-u of the Haedong Bank and Nakatomi Keita appeared as auditors.

Toward the end of colonial rule, the merger of various Kim family investments with Kyŏngsŏng Spinning helped expand the company's capital base without drastically diluting family ownership. For instance, the demise of the Haedong Bank only added to the strength of the textile company. When the Hansŏng Bank took over the banking operations of the Haedong in January of 1938, Kim formed the Haedong Finance Company as a holding company for the assets of the Haedong Bank. Kyŏngsŏng in turn purchased the finance company, absorbing its capital of 800 thousand yen. Kyŏngsŏng also purchased the Chung'ang Commerce and Industry Company in July of 1944, adding a further one million yen to its capital base.[39] The company also invested heavily in Tonggwang Raw Silk before absorbing the firm in July of 1944, adding two million yen to its capital base. Meanwhile newly published shares were absorbed by Samyang executives such as Sin Ki-ch'ang and Chu Pyŏng-p'yo, and former Haedong investors such as Ko Kwang-p'yo and Pak Hyo.[40] The paid-in capital had been raised to 7.5 million yen by 1942 and 10.5 million yen by 1944.[41] The company had made a strong bid to join the Japanese textile companies in the newly opened Manchurian market with a station in Mukden from 1934. Encouraged by the popularity of its white cotton broadcloth, the station was expanded into a branch office in July of 1938. An affiliate, South Manchurian Spinning, was organized in the same city six months earlier.

The South Manchurian Spinning and Weaving Company (Namman Pangjik) listed an authorized capital in 1940 of 10 million yen with 2.5 million yen paid-in. Kim Yŏn-su served as president with board members nearly identical to the Kyŏngsŏng board: Min Kyu-sik, Pak Hŭng-sik, Ch'oe Tu-sŏn, and Hyŏn Chun-ho. Only company associates recognized by the state or inner circle members were welcome. Among new names not appearing on the Kyŏngsŏng board, Ko Wôn-hun[42] had served as a principal at Posŏng School and a Central Advisory Council member from 1938. Kim Sa-yŏn[43] served as an auditor. The latter had been active in the Hanil Bank, and later served as president of Chosŏn Yeast (Chosŏn Kokja), a director of the Tongil Bank, and member of the Central Advisory Council from April of 1934. The company listed a paid-in capital of five million yen by 1941, with Kyŏng-sŏng holding 95 percent of the shares,[44] and a capital of ten million yen by 1944.

Investment in a new venture with a capital nearly equalling that of the mother company indicated commitment to foreign expansion, a surplus of funds for outside investment, and confident ties with the colonial state. Although the firm began operations at a plant near Mukden[45] only in December of 1941, South Manchurian Spinning listed total estimated assets in Mukden of 78.7 million yen in 1945, including 42.6 million yen worth of immovable assets.[46] Expansion abroad, expanded production with the addition of Kyŏngsŏng plants at Shihŭng near Seoul and Tanryul in Hwanghae Province, and favorable market conditions spurred dramatic growth in profits at Kyŏngsŏng Spinning during Kim Yŏn-su's tenure as president. The annual rate of return (i.e., net profits/paid-in capital) on capital invested[47] jumped to 33 percent in 1938, 45 percent and 48 percent in the next two years, and to 32 percent in 1941, before declining to about 20 percent from 1942 through 1944. Strong profits at the company help explain Kim's extensive investments in Japanese-owned utilities, railroads, and mining concerns, and in Manchurian projects from the late 1930s. The Kyŏngsŏng and Samyang provided a capital base. A multilevel portfolio then provided opportunities for profitable investment between inner- and outer-level ventures.

Concentration in ownership and continuity in administration linked the earlier and later decades of Kyŏngsŏng growth. Ownership was maintained in the earlier years through investments of individual family members, and friendly investment induced from Samyang and Haedong bank managers and investors. Rapid capital expansion in later years demanded institutional investment, bringing the Samyang Company to the fore among shareholders, and also prompting absorption of family-affiliated concerns. The size and strength of family investments in the Samyang and in Chung'ang Commerce and Industry helped make this continued family presence feasible in the Kyŏngsŏng even in the late years of the colonial period. The contrast with the Chosŏn Silk Spinning Company of the Min family is striking.[48] Founded in 1923, the Mins maintained control through 1935 but without raising the paid-in capital of only 175 thousand yen.[49] The family had raised the paid-in capital to only 200 thousand yen by 1941. Control and ownership soon faded as the firm listed a paid-in capital of 500 thousand yen in 1943 with a board of mainly Japanese nationals and Min Kyu-sik alone as representative director.[50] One major difference between the Kyŏngsŏng and Chosŏn Silk was in the product itself: Markets for cotton-made textiles were growing faster than outlets for silk products. Differences in procurement of raw materials was a further difference. I would highlight also differences in the commitment of capital from the outset. The Kims proved more aggressive in the scale of their industrial enterprise.

One could cite other reasons for the success of Kim's enterprises, such as Kim's diversification into profitable Japanese companies on the peninsula like Okkye Gold, Kankō Hydroelectric, and the Keishun Railway that strengthened his ability to keep pace with the capital investment necessary for continued growth in domestic and foreign textile production. Continuity in management coincided with Kim's financial and administrative commitment to the company, but was strengthened by the careers of executives like Ch'oe Tu-sŏn, Kim Chae-su, and Mun Sang-u in Kim family investments. Participation in the ventures of the third level with the likes of Pak Hŭng-sik, Min Kyu-sik, and Ch'oe Ch'ang-hak, and in second-level joint ventures helped bring together an interdependent band of investors. Their part in Kim's enterprises insured friendly Korean support and knowledge about commerce and finance markets. Family capital, a group of Samyang, Haedong Bank, and Kyŏngsŏng associates, and this set of major Korean investors made possible concentration in ownership and continuity of control.

The state's role in large-scale industry on the peninsula and in Manchuria was almost as extensive as its role in finance. The state not only set directions for industrial growth, it insured compliance through loans, subsidies, strict requirements on plant expansion, and other controls. The Kyŏngsŏng and other Kim family investments were supported by state-controlled subsidies and loans. Kim Yŏn-su's ability to procure such support and find a niche in the state's development plans on the peninsula and abroad was a key ingredient in his entrepreneurial success. Kim achieved in industry what both he and the Min family failed to achieve in finance: state support without state control. The record of state-controlled support through the Chōsen Industrial Bank for Kyŏngsŏng Spinning was impressive. An initial loan of 80 thousand yen saved the company from foreclosure[51] in 1920. I find the size of the loan remarkable, given the company had a paid-in capital of only 250 thousand yen. Annual government subsidies of about 20,000 yen helped reduce deficits through 1924, and then supported weak profits through the early 1930s.[52] We noted how the stature and influence of Marquis Pak Yŏng-hyo would have strengthened the Kyŏngsŏng request for help.

A similar pattern was evident at the Samyang, recipient of 825,000 yen in subsidies for reclamation of tidal basin tracts in North Chŏlla Province.[53] The recommendation of Pak Yŏng-ch'ŏl of the Chōsen Commercial Bank supported Samyang's petition for a land reclamation subsidy.[54] Pak had graduated from the Officers School of the Japanese Army in 1904 and served with the Japanese military until his return to Korean in 1912. He then held posts of county magistrate and later province governor. Retiring from public office in 1927, he soon became active in finance as president of the Samnam Bank. His strong credibility with the colonial administration led to appointment as an auditor of the Oriental Development Company, and as president of the Chōsen Commercial Bank, serving from 1932 through 1939. Keep in mind that the Samyang and Kyŏngsŏng were largely domestic ventures at the time; government support for these few Korean companies coincided with infrastructure development in the colony, and gave further evidence of state investment in local firms. But there was also support for investment beyond Korea. State subsidies and loans for foreign investment by a few Koreans coincided with the colonial strategy of Korea as a forward base for expansion. Kim's success in gaining government support for Korean industrial investment abroad[55] deserves further examination.

Japanese expansion into Manchuria in the 1930s provided Japanese firms with additional opportunities for overseas investment. The Japanese government planned to stabilize the territory of Manchukuo with development projects in agriculture and industry in tandem with the colonial state, particularly the Bank of Chōsen. Kim Yŏn-su was not about to miss the opportunity. Eager to move into new markets and frustrated by the administration in efforts to build a new facility at Shihŭng near Seoul, Kim quickly opened negotiations with the Japanese military in Manchukuo.[56] Whereas Kim had earlier needed the intervention of elder, eminent Korean business figures such as Pak Yŏng-hyo and Pak Yŏng-ch'ol, now Kim himself emerged as a leading Korean industrialist promoting expansion abroad. He succeeded Pak Yŏng-ch'ŏl as honorary Korean Consul-General for Manchukuo in June of 1939. Six months later he organized South Manchurian Spinning with a capital investment of 2.4 million yen and a loan from the Chōsen Industrial Bank of 2.6 million yen. Although Kim wrote of difficulties procuring labor for the new company, the dramatic increase in paid-in capital from 2.5 million yen in 1940 to 10 million yen in 1943 suggests the strong growth of the company's role in Manchurian markets. How did Kim gain such bank support? His success in procuring state support and finding a place in the wider development aims of the colonial state within and beyond the peninsula can be attributed to an extensive capital base, his record of productivity, his network of relationships with Korean and Japanese entrepreneurs, and to close ties with the Industrial Bank and colonial state. Like Pak, Kim used loans and subsidies productively; unlike Pak, Kim's industrial base permitted much more extensive indigenous enterprise.

Kim Yŏn-su and his brother, Kim Sŏng-su, gained considerable notoriety in the later decades of colonial rule. Sŏng-su's role in the prominent vernacular daily, the *Donga Ilbo*, and in the Posŏng School certainly played a part here, as did the success of Yŏn-su's Kyŏngsŏng and other enterprises. The salience of Yŏn-su in the emerging inner group of leading Korean capitalists was due not simply to the scale and wealth of his firms, but more importantly, to the network of colleagues he was able to mobilize in support of their Korean-owned and -managed ventures. Family, older and younger wealthy Korean investors, Japanese business and government officials were all a part of this network. Yŏn-su's father, Chisan Kim Kyŏng-jun, was the largest shareholder in the Kyŏngsŏng in 1919, and Sŏng-su's foster father, Wŏnp'a Kim Ki-jung put up his landholdings as collateral for the Kyŏngsŏng's initial loan of 80,000 yen from the Chōsen Industrial Bank.[57] This earlier generation provided Yŏn-su and Sŏng-su with capital, an education in Japan, and initial credibility among other major landowning families in the first years of the colonial period.

A Korean network of colleagues included older investors and administrators with close government ties such as Pak Yŏng-hyo and Pak Yŏng-ch'ŏl. Pak Hŭng-sik, Min Kyu-sik, and Hyŏn Chun-ho were prominent among the next generation of investors serving the boards of Kim Yŏn-su's enterprises.[58] The interdependent links among such major investors as Pak, Min, and Hyŏn strengthened indigenous ownership and direction. Major friendly investment was important, especially in the case of the Tongil Bank, the Hwasin Trading Company, and probably South Manchurian Spinning as well. The interlocking network of participation on boards was crucial in efforts to maintain friendly Korean direction in the face of increasing Japanese constraints on investments in the last decade of the colonial period.[59]

Direct and indirect ties with Japanese business leaders reinforced Kim's credibility with the colonial administration, and opened up investment opportunities for profits from the Samyang and Kyŏngsŏng companies. Very few Japanese served on the boards of Kim's companies even when legislation requiring Japanese participation was put in force in the waning years of the colonial period. At that time one Japanese with strong government ties did take part: Nakatomi Keita.[60] Born in 1888, Nakatomi was initially associated with Kobe Commerce (Kobe Shōgyō). An auditor of the Chōsen Industrial Bank, he served on the board of three trading companies: Chōsen Trade Promotion (Chōsen Bōeki Shinkō), Chōsen Tōa Trade (Chōsen Tōa Bōeki), and Daikō Trade (Daikō Bōeki). Kim and Nakatomi grew well acquainted through Kim's extensive dealings with the Industrial Bank. Nakatomi took part as an auditor of both the Kyŏngsŏng and the South Manchurian Spinning ventures, though he was not listed among the major investors.

Kim also could count among his associates one of the most eminent Japanese entrepreneurs on the peninsula, Sakoma Fusatarō, a business leader in Pusan. Among the earliest and most prominent Japanese business leaders on the peninsula, Sakoma helped organize the Japanese businessmen's association in Pusan, predecessor of the Pusan Chamber of Commerce. He then helped lead the chamber, and served the state as a vice-chairman of the South Kyŏngsang Province Council.[61] He was listed as the representative of the Pusan Marine Products (Fuzan Suisan) in 1937 with an authorized capital of 2 million yen and 1.01 million yen paid-in.[62] Sakoma was also a major shareholder in the Chōsen Spinning Company of Pusan, a major competitor of the Kyŏngsŏng. A protégé of Sakoma, Mun Sang-u had worked for the Sakoma Trading Company in Pusan before turning to finance in Pusan, and later in Seoul serving as managing director of the Haedong under Kim from 1927, and still later as an auditor for both Kyŏngsŏng and South Manchurian Spinning in Kim's network of close associates.[63] Kim had more direct contact with Sakoma as well. Both served as directors of the Chōsen Savings Bank from its founding in 1929 through the early 1940s. Sakoma was also a fellow board member with Nakatomi and Kim at Chōsen Refining and Keishun Railway.

The role of the well-connected Nakatomi Keita within Kim's own enterprises and ties with eminent entrepreneurs like Sakoma Fusatarō, and of former administration officials like Ariga and Hayashi indicate Kim's prominence among local government and business leaders in the colonial years. Such prominence was common among the leading members of the Korean inner group of business leaders. But there was more to the entrepreneurship of Kim Yŏn-su. His investment and participation in utility companies and private railways signaled a distinct role among leading Japanese zaibatsu ventures on the peninsula in the last decade of the colonial period. It was clear that Kim developed close ties with individual Japanese investors and with public and private Japanese corporate investors, but to what purpose? These relationships took him well beyond the network of Korean associates and friendly investors to profitable investments and at least to a part in the direction of larger Japanese ventures on the peninsula at the end of the colonial period. Class ties with Japanese corporate and individual interests did not dilute his links with Korean investors, and no doubt reinforced his credibility with state-affiliated institutions.

The pattern of business activity among interrelated levels emanating from the family-owned Samyang and Chung'ang companies insured stability, security, and outlets with growth potential for productive use of profits. Agricultural investment was balanced with textile production, investment in Korean-owned and -administrated firms with stock in Japanese firms, and later, Korean factories and agricultural estates with similar facilities in Manchuria. The pattern first appeared in the late 1920s with the Samsu and Kyŏngsŏng companies and Chōsen Savings developing rapidly with Kim's diversification of investments from 1935 through 1940. It was this pattern of investments and personal contacts that loomed so large in Kim's accumulation of indigenous capital, together with networks of Korean managers and associates, and positive relations with the state and Japanese business figures that made indigenous direction possible. The fact of a network of investments in family, joint Korean, and joint Japanese ventures must temper conventional perceptions of the fierce independence of the Kyŏngsŏng as a nationalistic enterprise. The company's success as a Korean-owned and -managed enterprise depended on a set of interconnected investments and certainly on a network of contacts with both the Japanese and Korean business elite alike, necessary for large-scale enterprise in a dependent capitalist economy under alien rule.

The genius of Kim Yŏn-su lay not so much in his fierce independence as in his clever and credible diversification of investments. His varied yet well-integrated portfolio represents a remarkable adaptation of a local entrepreneur to the demands of being both Korean and successful as an entrepreneur. He found a niche in the development plans of public and private Japanese corporate interests on the peninsula.[64] It was a distinctly Korean role in view of his central commitment to Kyŏngsŏng and Samyang, but nonetheless played out in tandem with the colonial administration and major Japanese investors.

Conclusion

Kim Yŏn-su resigned as president of Kyŏngsŏng in December of 1945, four months after liberation. The textile venture continued after 1945 under Kim Yong-wan, his brother-in-law, and a leading manager in the late colonial years. The firm prospered in the First Republic with the strong support of Samyang investment. The Samyang Company likewise continued, though land reform forced the company to redirect investment into trade and light industrial production of items such as sugar and salt. But if the companies played important roles in competition with other indigenous firms in the postcolonial economy of the south, their roles in the colonial environment as native firms in a Japanese-dominated economy were critical. The survival and growth of the Kyŏngsŏng through two and one-half decades of colonial rule established patterns of enterprise that persist in Korean industrial organization today.

Kim's investments on the peninsula have been termed the "Honam chaebŏl," and indeed many of the salient characteristics of today's chaebŏl were evident in Kim's colonial enterprises, especially the concentration in ownership and management, and the salience of relations with the state. But such features could be seen in smaller colonial ventures as well, and in larger industrial colonial enterprises that did not survive through 1945 under indigenous ownership and management. I emphasize the continuity of Kim's textile venture as evidence of dependent versus comprador capitalism, and because of its symbolic value in the history of early capitalism on the peninsula. The Kyŏngsŏng was a major industrial venture that survived and prospered under indigenous direction and ownership. Despite limited capital and little experience in large-scale industrial enterprise, here Korean entrepreneurs did compete successfully with medium-sized Japanese colonial firms.

The symbolic significance of Kim's enterprise has been widely recognized. My contribution has been to probe the dynamics by which Kim was able to maintain ownership and direction of this enterprise. Concentration, ties with the state, and other business leaders characterized large-scale entrepreneurship in colonial Korea. Varieties of investment stretching out from a base of wholly owned ventures was typical of the more successful of the Korean colonial entrepreneurs. By examining dynamics of concentration and ties with state and other prominent business figures within the framework of these levels of investments, rather than solely with regard to the Kyŏngsŏng itself, I have tried to sort out Kim's place and function among leading Japanese and Korean capitalists in colonial society. Without these wider networks and a diversified portfolio, he could not have maintained continued growth and indigenous ownership and direction of his large-scale enterprises.

The review of Kim's enterprise raises a number of issues regarding capitalist development. The interplay of agriculture and industrial investment between the Samyang and Kyŏngsŏng companies represents a curious blend of old and new in the process of socioeconomic development. Agricultural investment by large landowners in the colonial period has often been cited as exploitive and anything but modern, contributing little to long-term development of agricultural lands or technological improvements. Did Kim employ semifeudal methods in agriculture, particularly high tenant rents and high-interest loans, to accumulate the capital necessary for continued growth of the more modern industrial enterprise at the Kyŏngsŏng? Or did the growth in acreage at the Samyang reflect more modern methods of cultivation, agricultural management, and land reclamation? We also see in Kim's portfolio a further transition to reinvestment of industrial capital, rather than simply turning agricultural profits into commerce or industry. Here scale and sector distinguished Kim from the Mins and Pak. Finance and commerce could be profitable within limits, but neither could compete in the later colonial years with the profitability of Kim's expanding industrial ventures. As a sector of the economy, industrial activity brought Kim into the center of leading corporate and private investors on the peninsula, as evident in the fourth level of his portfolio.

Regarding class, I find curious Kim's relatively exclusive ties with a few Korean entrepreneurs and a few Japanese entrepreneurs. The close network of managers can be explained in terms of enterprise solidarity and consistent direction. But why the focus on Pak Hŭng-sik, Min Kyu-sik, Hyŏn Chun-ho, and a very few others? Certainly the pool of knowledgeable and successful Korean entrepreneurs was not that small. Did the insecurity of the colonial situation encourage such limited numbers, or, again, was it the need for friendly investors in public corporations that feared massive outside investment? Similarly, one notes the web of relations with Sakoma Fusatarō, Nakatomi Keita, and Ariga Mitsutoyo and Hayashi. There was concentration in class ties as well as in ownership and management.

The pattern of Kim's relations with the colonial state raises a further question. The prominence of his brother, Kim Sŏng-su, in nationalist political activity, education, and especially in the vernacular daily *Donga Ilbo* reinforced the reputation of the Kyŏngsŏng as an indigenous enterprise with a strong nationalist commitment. On the other hand, some ties with the colonial government were necessary for any large-scale enterprise. Such ties could be entrusted to Marquis Pak Yŏng-hyo as president of the company, especially in view of his prominent role at the Industrial Bank. This permitted Kim Yŏn-su himself to maintain some distance from the colonial administration in the 1920s, even as managing director of an enterprise receiving annual subsidies from the government. The argument for nationalist enterprise in this context would be supported by Kim's own distance from official positions tied with the state. Senior Korean colleagues such as Pak Yŏng-hyo and Pak Yŏng-ch'ŏl mediated this earlier dependence.

Expansion of his enterprises into Manchuria in the late 1930s brought Kim into more direct contact with the state, and a quite different type of dependence. Close ties with former Industrial Bank executives such as Ariga Mitsutoyo of Nakatomi Keita proved necessary now in major investments. Were Kim's closer ties simply a result of his prominence among Korean business leaders, a result of a commitment to ever greater capital accumulation, or did Kim find Korea's future to be so intertwined with Japanese investment on the peninsula that greater cooperation was seen now as inevitable? This latter phase of dependence brought Kim into cooperation with both the state and state–zaibatsu alliance, evident in official positions such as consul to Manchukuo and investments with Mitsubishi, Mitsui, and Japan Gold Mining. Such dependence meant further adjustments to colonial strategic policies as a price for dramatic growth in Kim's own industrial investments. His locally owned and managed firms prospered, but did they serve the wider interest of the Korean nation in the last decade of colonial rule?

Kim provided the most salient symbol of national enterprise and the most sophisticated and extensive organizations of indigenously owned and managed firms within and beyond the peninsula. Although accurately labeled as a collaborator and brought to trial following liberation, his structural and symbolic contribution to subsequent forms of capitalism in South Korea distinguishes him from Han Sang-yong and other compradors investing mainly in Japanese enterprise. Both sides in the debate over "national capital" must recognize such precedents and structures, and carefully gauge their effect on subsequent postcolonial industrialization processes. At the same time, one cannot ignore the fact that Kim garnered success as a businessman at the expense of his nationalist image. South Manchurian Spinning may not have shocked proponents of nationalist enterprise as much as Pak's Chōsen Aircraft Manufacturing, but Kim and Pak risked identification with the Japanese cause in both enterprises. Their very success as businessmen and intense search for new markets and products brought them ever closer to assimilation to the economic goals and methods of the state and cooperative zaibatsu. If the aristocratic financier Min Tae-sik leaves the impression of pragmatism, Pak of competition and collaboration, Kim conveys the image simply of dependence, cooperating when necessary and never confronting, but at the same time careful to maintain direction and a major share in his remarkably extensive and complex industrial ventures.

Apart from questions, the failures as well as successes of Kim's colonial enterprise spark thoughts of what might have been. He succeeded in agriculture and industry but failed in banking. The role of a strong indigenous bank with industrial priorities might have alleviated the need of Korean entrepreneurs for constant government support for new ventures, and provided an outlet for investment in other indigenous enterprises. Capital was ultimately the crucial issue in the colonial period. Even a wealthy, successful entrepreneur like Kim Yŏn-su remained dependent on the colonial state for large amounts of credit necessary in major ventures. One wonders how success at the Haedong would have affected the nature and extent of colonial dependence, but also subsequent patterns of Korean industrial finance. Japanese zaibatsu had developed their own financial facilities in the early part of the century to moderate their dependence on government funding. The postcolonial chaebŏl never gained such independence. The state in South Korea maintained the colonial pattern of public control of finance to nurture and then direct chaebŏl growth toward national priorities.

8

Legacies

Min Tae-sik, Pak Hung-sik, and Kim Yŏn-su confronted the awesome task of being both Korean and successful within the colonial economy. They took up the challenge with their own blend of ideology, enterprise, and portfolio management in the shadow of a strong colonial state and extensive zaibatsu investment on the peninsula. Sustained ownership and management of core ventures represented a legacy of both structure and precedent for post-colonial capitalism in Korea. And if patterns of concentration, state relations, and class ties among a Korean inner circle distinguish dependent capitalism in large-scale enterprise through 1945, intriguing questions of causes, continuity, and concepts remain. I conclude with possible causal factors behind these patterns, continuities in the postcolonial economy, and the theoretical significance of the colonial experience of large-scale enterprise.

Attention to portfolios with interrelated levels of investment puts the issue of concentration in a different light than is evident in case studies of simply the major enterprise of one or another native entrepreneur. Ownership and control characterized the first two concentric levels of investment, director-ships and smaller blocks of shares distinguished the outer two levels. The Mins, Pak, and Kim concentrated capital in core ventures of the first two levels, balancing their portfolios with more diversified holdings on the third and fourth levels. As executives they dedicated their administrative energies and managerial teams to enterprises of the first two levels with distinctive local patterns of family ownership and a kinshiplike group of managers. In contrast, efforts at the outer levels in the medium-sized joint ventures and in massive Japanese firms resembled the diversified participation in joint-stock ventures characteristic of business leaders in contemporary Western capitalist societies. Diversity of investment permitted multiple ties with leading local and foreign business leaders, and multiple outlets for profitable redirection of capital. The portfolio itself was one key to maintaining the capital base and access to information necessary for indigenous large-scale enterprise in the colony.

Reliance on state credit and controls demanded continuing adjustments in private enterprise, but why the concentration of capital, ownership, and control in family-held companies? One could point to precedents in the late Chosŏn Dynasty when large landowners prospered with concentration of capital, though usually without direct administrative responsibility or centralized management. One could point also to various insecurities endemic to both the colonial context and early capitalist development on the peninsula, such as unfriendly fellow Korean investors, unstable markets, and the penetration of Japanese capital. The strength of the latter and uncertainty over the role of indigenous capital in the early decades of the colonial economy contributed to a sense of insecurity. Constraints and anxieties at the time of the Pacific War prompted further consolidation among major native enterprises, again doing little to allay fears or engender trust among major investors. The Mins, Pak, and Kim hedged their extensive investments in family companies and a second level of family-affiliated joint-stock ventures with a variety of investments in the outer circles, but kept their major commitment of capital and administrative energies at home.[1]

The demands of adaptation evident in business dealings with the colonial state strongly colored the format of business–state relations for the Korean business elite. One scholar[2] of Western capitalism observed, "Self-interest as ultimately the servant of society, the minimumization of the role of the state, and the institution of private property constituted the essence of capitalism in the nineteenth and early twentieth centuries." The strength of state-affiliated enterprise, for instance, and the investment of these institutions in the private sector of Japanese zaibatsu ventures on the peninsula blurred the distinction between "public" and "private" common in autonomous, Western capitalist societies. Indirect investment through the subsidies and credit of state-affiliated banks further eroded the distinction, as did the prominence of former state officials such as Ariga and Shibuya in private enterprise. The Chōsen Industrial Bank under Ariga and his successors served as a focal point for state support of major private enterprise.

I have cited multiple joint investments between the bank and major zaibatsu as evidence of an alliance for industrial development of the peninsula, serving state strategic aims while bringing profit to the zaibatsu. Business policy associations such as the Chambers of Commerce and Industry carefully aligned the interest of their members with the colonial state to assure some place for Japanese and Korean capitalists apart from the zaibatsu. Further evidence of adjustment to the strong state was evident in honorary positions for private entrepreneurs such as Kim Yŏn-su's appointment as Honorary Korean Consul to Manchukuo, a stepping stone to extensive investment. The Mins, Pak, and Kim faced the challenges of nationalism and capitalism simultaneously. They could not look back to any viable earlier format for distinctions between public and private in a capitalist market economy. Nor could they rely on local precedents for ties between state and private enterprise in a complex market economy across regions and national borders. The state–zaibatsu alliance represented one viable pattern for business–state relations within a capitalist economy. Koreans with ambitions of large-scale enterprise yet local loyalties could not ignore the pattern.

The causes behind the strong state intervention of the Japanese colonial state in Korea and Taiwan, and the implications of such intervention on the shape of Korean capitalism have been discussed elsewhere.[3] Here again the Korean colonial experience of dependence needs to be distinguished from the Latin American experience, as do the contrasting set of constraints and opportunities faced by local entrepreneurs. Cumings cited the unbalanced growth resulting from such Japanese intervention: the "overdevelopment" of economic infrastructures on the peninsula through 1945 such as transportation and finance, and the underdevelopment of human resources.[4] Mitsubishi's West Chōsen Central Railway in P'yŏngyang transported local coal not to Japanese markets, nor to Korean consumers or Korean plants, but mainly to the foundries of Mitsubishi and its affiliates in the area. The state in harness with the zaibatsu invested heavily in industrial projects on the peninsula as a forward base for further expansion and in wartime, a secure area distant from the vulnerable main Japanese islands.

The investments and directorships of Kim Yŏn-su in the West Chōsen Central and Keishun Railways and in Okkye Gold indicate the curious blend of constraint and opportunity for a local entrepreneur. Kim lacked the extensive capital base to undertake on his own a capital-intensive, leading strategic industry such as steel or petrochemicals or even a more sophisticated gold mining effort. But he did parlay profits from his agricultural and textile investments into shares in strategic transport ventures. Capital accruing from part ownership in the latter in turn made possible continued ownership and expansion of core ventures. One common feature to colonialism in Latin America and Asia, however, was the colonizers' primary interest in their own economic and military priorities rather than in the prosperity and balanced growth of the local economy. This was the legacy of a strong colonial state with near absolute autonomy vis-à-vis local leadership.

Of special interest here are the means by which the native business elite found access to state support. Subsidies and loans for domestic enterprises, and especially support for ventures abroad, suggest a coincidence of interests between the state and native business leaders. The Korean business leaders won at least a consultative role in policy-making in the peninsula's economy through participation on the boards of larger Japanese firms, prominence in business-policy associations, and their position in the local economy as corporate owners. Pak Yŏng-hyo and Pak Yŏng-ch'ŏl played more prominent roles in the middle decades of rule as advisors and consultants. Min Tae-sik's position as president of the Hanil/Tongil and Kim Yŏn-su's status as president of the Haedong Bank permitted some consultative role in policy regarding commercial banking. Kim's position as honorary Korean Consul for Manchukuo and Pak's presidency of the Chōsen Aircraft Manufacturing Company certainly afforded them some small voice in policy-making on the peninsula regarding Korean investment in Manchuria and state support for strategic industries. Dependent but not invisible, a few Korean business figures found ways to affect economic policies of even the strong colonial state.

Local solidarity in relations with a powerful state and the massive presence of the zaibatsu, together with the common economic interest of a rising group of major local capitalists helped forge bonds among Korean business leaders. I have looked briefly to the interdependence apparent among a small group of the Korean business elite by the end of the colonial period. Interlocking corporate directorates of family members and close associates within family firms have been cited as an example of concentration of management and control in the enterprises of the Mins, Pak, and Kim. Apart from managing their own businesses, the Mins, Pak, and Kim also served on the boards of one another's enterprises, and joined with Han Sang-yong, Ch'oe Ch'ang-hak, Ha Chun-sŏk, Kim Sa-yŏn, and others on the boards of joint investments. Interlocking corporate directorates of major native business figures were evidence of differentiation along an inner group axis, by which major corporate owners assured friendly investment and control of their own boards.

Allen concluded that the primary function of "corporate interlocking" in the United States was the exchange of expertise and information between corporations.[5] Such exchanges were important in colonial Korea as well, but the record of investment and administrative commitment in the native enterprises suggests a more pressing issue of control in an unstable and unfriendly business environment. The insecurities prompting concentration can be cited as factors encouraging interlocking directorates as well. Insofar as relations with the state and the massive presence of major Japanese zaibatsu in the domestic economy helped the Korean business elite to pull together in this inner circle, the legacy of colonial business–state relations would foster common interests among an elite of major indigenous business leaders.

If insecurities in a very competitive situation and the exigencies of dealing with a strong, interventionist colonial state encouraged concentration and group solidarity, one result was a small core of indigenous "dependent capitalists," in company but not competition with major Japanese business figures on the peninsula such as Ariga Mitusutoyo, Abe Sen'ichi, and Ōhashi Shintarō. A closer look at the patriotism and enterprise of the colonial entrepreneurs offers some insight into this basic but divisive issue of large-scale private enterprise and national development. Kajimura described the nationalist aims of a dependent capitalist "to gradually foster the real strength of indigenous capital within the colonial framework by enlisting the help of the government-general on the basis of confronting labor in cooperation with the government-general."[6] The emphasis in our study on indigenous ownership and internal control of native enterprises provides further evidence for Kajimura's conclusion of dependent rather than comprador capital. I have argued that structure and precedent represent the wider contribution to national development among the core enterprises of the Mins, Pak, and Kim.

But given the alternatives of comprador efforts in alien firms, or simply small-scale enterprise, why do we find this third alternative of dependent capitalism in major local enterprise in the Korean colonial experience? Maunier[7] looked to the colonial situation through the interaction of the colonized and colonizers. On the Korean side, nationalism affected the choice for dependent versus comprador capitalism, as evident in the consistent praise for colonial rule in the writings and speeches of Han Sang-yong from annexation to the Pacific War, versus the more subdued and locally sensitive rhetoric of the Mins and Kim Yŏn-su across the breadth of the colonial years. A material base also made possible the choice for independent ventures, as did a record of productivity. The local business elite would not have been able to sustain ownership and control of large-scale local enterprise without a base of agrarian or later commercial and industrial capital. On the other side, the Japanese colonizers, unlike their Western counterparts in distant and alien dependencies, found less use for compradors given the proximity, similarity of climate and terrain, and Asian cultural similarities in the life-styles of Japan and Korea. The Japanese moved onto the peninsula in force, particularly in managerial slots and positions of technological expertise, leaving less opportunity for a comprador population in upper-level posts. I have also noted the Japanese colonial state found some advantage in successful local enterprise as evidence of the benefits of colonial rule for the wider local population, as long as local enterprise fit state economic priorities and did not challenge state economic control.

Continuities

The colonial experience had much to do with the origins of the Korean chaebŏl. I find postcolonial continuities most striking in patterns of concentration, continued prominence of the family in large-scale enterprise, and persistence of close business–state ties. Bureaucratic control of critical economic resources by a state with at least the ambitions for comprehensive direction remained a part of economic life in postcolonial capitalism on the peninsula. Hagen Koo has summarized this structural continuity:

Before colonialism the state in both Korea and China was relatively weak vis-à-vis the agrarian upper class. But during the colonial period the state bureaucracy emerged as a force paramount over the class structure and over society as a whole. This pattern persisted into the postcolonial period.[8]

Whereas agrarian concentration and state efforts to control grain production and distribution provided precedent in the Chosŏn Dynasty, the modern shape of Korean major enterprise and the aggressive role of state bureaucracies in a capitalist economy stand as precedents from the colonial experience. Concentration and the need for close state ties during the First Republic resulted again in an "inner circle" of major business leaders, including familiar figures such as Kim Yŏn-su and his sons, Kim's brother-in-law Kim Yong-wan, Pak Hŭng-sik, Min Kyu-sik and Taesik's son, Min Pyŏng-do, together with a host of rising new entrepreneurs such as Lee Byung-chull and others.[9] Land reform depriving the colonial agrarian elite of a capital base discouraged land-based class ties from the 1950s, and although many of the colonial dependent capitalists regained prominence with investment in trade and light manufactures, it was not a smooth transition.

Events of the immediate postcolonial years left the leading colonial period Korean economic elite in disarray. Cool relations with Japan and hostility with Communist regimes deprived the earlier business leaders of familiar Japanese suppliers and funding sources, and markets in Japan, North Korea, Manchuria, and northern China. Domestic unrest in the south slowed production in the remaining textile and food-processing plants, and a new

Western ally, the United States, became the dominant focus of foreign trade. Aggressive land reform programs of both the American Military Government and the early Rhee administration unraveled large-scale investments in agriculture.[10] Three years (1950–3) of war with the north destroyed much of the industrial plant and transportation network in the Republic. Apart from dislocation, reconstruction, and the salient role of the United States in the economy, the colonial elite also found themselves struggling to find a political identity and a positive reception for private enterprise within the early Republic. The double challenge of nationalism and capitalism continued. Kim Yŏn-su and Pak Hŭng-sik were charged and jailed in 1948 for "antinationalist crimes" during the colonial period, and the firms of both prosecuted again in 1961.[11]

Although both gained acquittal in the earlier trials and other less prominent colonial period entrepreneurs were never brought to trial, the group could hardly dominate political directions of the Rhee administration in such an atmosphere. In time, however, the colonial experience of business management and investment, and a base of capital would permit a few of the earlier elite such as Kim and Pak to take advantage of new market situations in competition with a larger group of local entrepreneurs. If they had learned of enterprise, they had also learned much of state relations. They had survived and prospered under an alien regime; they now found ways to adjust to the ambitions, controls and ambiguous economic direction of the Rhee state. If concentration had been encouraged by state subsidies and loans through 1945, the Rhee state made little effort to break the pattern.

For instance, a variety of state resources helped foster concentration in the textile industry, the leading sector of postcolonial industrial growth. The constitution of the Republic armed the state with extraordinary legal powers to intervene in private firms.[12] U.S. intelligence officers reacted to "very strong tendencies toward state socialism" in the Republic's constitution of 1948, and found Article 88 particularly alarming: "Private enterprises shall be transferred to state or public ownership or their management shall be placed under control or supervision of the state or juridical persons of public law, when it is deemed urgently necessary in accordance with provision of the law."[13] Amendments in the fall of 1954 to the economic provisions still fell far short of U.S expectations of a market economy. An analyst for the U.N. Office of Economic Coordinator (OEC) pointed out that "private enterprise will still be subject to expropriation or control when it is necessary to meet urgent necessities of national defense or national life."[14] State intervention in the economy again gained legal recognition in the post-colonial capitalism on the peninsula.

The Rhee state intervened in the market with production, tax, and trade controls to promote local industries and protect against foreign competition. Ministry of Trade and Industry directives of December 1954 and July 1955 closed the door on foreign imports of finished cotton goods.[15] An "autarkic policy of total exclusion of foreign goods held to compete with domestic products" drew the ire of U.S. officials, as did complex procedures, taxes, and other means of "harassment of foreign businessmen."[16] The government removed wartime ration controls on textile sales in January of 1954 for domestic producers, and reduced various taxes on raw materials and textile products.[17] State controls on trade assured access to raw cotton for the licensed importers while restraining foreign competitors.[18]

In addition to legal controls, the Rhee state also commanded extensive material resources of technology, capital, and even raw materials. Much of the manufacturing sector in South Korea in 1945, formerly owned by Japanese, was "vested" in the government of the First Republic for eventual transfer to private ownership.[19] Among the most important assets were the former Japanese textile plants, maintained temporarily as large state firms and then sold off to private interests. The very scale of the plants in South Korea's primitive industrial structure after the war gave these properties a salient role in production of the growing textile market on the peninsula. The result was a small number of very large textile firms by the mid-1950s.[20]

Although transferring this technological base to the private sector, the state also fostered concentration in textile manufacturing through access to local credit and foreign aid. Following liberation in 1945 the state invested in maintaining the machinery of earlier Japanese firms while temporarily operating the plants under state protection and later helped fund reconstruction following the war.[21] Local funding was channeled through the Korean Reconstruction Bank and local commercial banks. Reconstruction Bank credits for textile manufacturing accounted annually for 30 percent of its total funds for manufacturing in 1957, and 20 percent for the next two years. The bank had committed about 9.7 billion hwan to the industry in 1957, 13.2 billion hwan the next year, and 17.4 billion hwan in 1959. Commercial banks under government control and often with state owner-ship, also devoted a major share of manufacturing funding to textiles. Loans to textile firms by commercial banks amounted to about 11 billion hwan in 1957, 13 billion in the next year, and 15.9 billion hwan in 1959, ranging between 27 and 34 percent of all loans for manufacturing in those three years.[22]

Direct foreign aid represented a further source of support for textile manufacturers.[23] Initial grants for operation of vested properties in the state's care that were later sold to private interests were one example, as was United Nations' assistance for war damage from the U.N. Korean Reconstruction Agency. One could also cite U.S. loans from the Foreign Operations Administration (FOA) and the International Cooperation Administration (ICA), predecessors of the Agency for International Development. Commercial procurement of dollar funds was controlled jointly by the U.N. Office of Economic Coordinator (OEC) and the Korean Ministry of Reconstruction.[24] State-controlled access to American foreign currency coupled with official exchange rates far below the actual market value of U.S. dollars provided a further source for external financing.[25] ICA aid and supplies for plants and technology in manufacturing alone amounted to $57.1 million between 1955 and 1959. Supplies and aid for purchase of raw cotton amounted to $138 million between 1953 and 1959.[26] The Rhee state commanded an extensive legal, technological, and capital base for fostering concentration in the First Republic.[27]

Postwar development at Samsung's Cheil Wool and Cheil Sugar, and Kim Sŏng-gon's Kŭmsŏng Textile and subsequent Ssangyong chaebŏl provide ample evidence of concentration of ownership and control, and close state ties.[28] We see the influence of the earlier patterns not only in the new chaebŏl, but also in persisting organizations of the colonial entrepreneurs. How did the dependent capitalists of the colonial years respond to both the indigenous state and new market opportunities? Trade and light industrial production in sugar, flour, and textiles drew off the lion's share of native investment capital through 1960. Pak Hŭng-sik had reorganized his earlier trading venture into Hwasin Trade in December of 1946 with a capital of forty million won under the direction of his nephew, Pak Pyŏng-gyo.[29] With the severing of links with China from late 1946, Hwasin redirected exports of ginseng, vegetable gelatin, and marine products to Hong Kong and Macao, opening a branch office in Hong Kong in February of 1948. The trading company was integrated into the larger holding company, Hwasin Industrial (Hwasin Sanŏp), in January of 1950 with a capital of three hundred million wŏn.[30]

A truce of 1953 brought the hostilities of the Korean War (1950–3) to a close and peace to the Republic of Korea. The state turned its attention to reconstruction and local production of consumer goods. Major private entrepreneurs recognized at the same time the need for effective ties with the government to insure necessary authorizations and access to credit funding and foreign currency.[31] Pak Hŭng-sik and Kim Yŏn-su were among those developing trade and consumer industries with help from the Rhee administration and foreign aid through 1960. Pak Hŭng-sik wrote of Hwasin's close ties with the state-operated tungsten company,[32] with the Office of Monopoly, and with the National Federation of Irrigation Associations, enabling Hwasin to export tungsten while importing fertilizers and grains.

Pak gained control of the Inch'ŏn plant of the Teikoku Hemp Spinning Company (Teikoku Seima), a vested enterprise, and established the Heung Han Spinning Company in 1953, an investment in light industry to balance his commercial investments. He had purchased the spinning plant from a group of investors, establishing the Heung Han with a capital of 50 million hwan. The firm procured a United Nations grant[33] of $850 thousand for purchase of equipment in June of 1955, and listed 10,300 spindles in operation by the end of that year.[34] Pak later benefited greatly from legislation in 1957 permitting a three-year grace period on debt repayments for company reorganization. Pak's appointment for company president, Yi Chong-hyŏn, was exposed in 1957 for profiting with such government loans secured for company development. The company was forced to pay penalties, but regained financial stability within the three-year grace period provided by the new law.[35]

The Honam chaebŏl fared better than Hwasin in the transition after 1945. Although division from the north and from Manchuria, together with land reform policies in the south after liberation deprived Kim Yŏn-su of much of his agricultural investment, he was able to reinvest in sugar refining and a trading company after the war. Kim's efforts to redirect resources toward sugar manufacture reveal much about the new pattern of constraints and opportunities evident in the First Republic. He began planning for Samyang's Wisan Sugar Refinery during the Korean War. The company first searched in vain for Korean technicians from the Dainihon Sugar Refining Company (Dai Nihon Seitō), a large Japanese-owned sugar company on the peninsula during the colonial period. Kim then dispatched his son, Kim Sang-ha, to Tokyo in February of 1952, where he procured the services of two Japanese knowledgeable about sugar and gelatin production in a newly opened Samyang office in Tokyo. A sugar-refining expert was hired to plan the refining plant budget, and a researcher from Tokyo Industrial College was hired to develop plans for the production of chemical gelatin.[36] The Rhee government soon thwarted plans for purchase of Japanese technology, however, stipulating that the necessary FOA loans could be spent only on

West German machinery. Accordingly the company purchased the German technology and brought over three West German technicians to help with construction and placement of the machinery.[37] The company raised capital through the sale of land bonds received for Samyang argricultural estate properties, while a total of $747,707 of FOA loans from the United States supported initial construction of the Wisan sugar refining plant, completed in January of 1956.[38] The sugar company quickly gained a large share of the domestic sugar market.[39]

And if Kyŏngsŏng Spinning had prospered in the colonial period under the direction of Kim Yŏn-su and his Samyang chaebŏl, reconstruction aid and further foreign aid permitted recovery following the Korean War. Kim relinquished the presidency of the textile venture in December of 1945 to his brother-in-law, Kim Yong-wan, while maintaining family investment in the firm through the late years of the First Republic. Renamed "Kyungbang" after liberation, the firm quickly reemerged as a leading textile producer, responsible for 8 percent of the nation's spindles in 1958. Kyungbang received ICA equipment support totaling $104,000 in 1957.[40] The firm procured smaller ICA grants for raw materials in October of 1958 of $50,000 (2.5 million hwan) and $28,800 in equipment support.[41] In 1959 the firm received ICA funding worth $98,292 (4.9 million hwan) for twenty special-ized spinning machines and a further $149,000 (7.45 million hwan) for related equipment, grants amounting to about 12 percent of its capital.[42]

A review of the postcolonial enterprises of Pak and Kim highlights two characteristics of business–state relations that would affect formation of a business elite in the subsequent years of Park Chung-hee's Third Republic (1963–79). On the one hand, continuity with their formative entrepreneurial experience under the Japanese colonial administration was evident in their organizational patterns of large family-owned companies, managed by family members and close associates. There was continuity as well in their reliance on state support for credit funding, and on state authorization for access to foreign technology and expertise. One can point also to their experience of international trade, and adjustments to transportation and finance difficulties in developing new areas for exports and imports. Their adaptation to a new political situation in the Rhee state further distinguished business–state ties. The prominent Korean economic historian Cho Ki-jun[43] faulted entrepreneurs of the day "for the shrewdness through which opportunity is grasped in collusion with government officials, selfishness in tramping on social justice in pursuit of profit, and by collaboration with foreign capitalists disregarding the interest of the national economy." He traced such negative adaptive capacities directly to "institutional deficiencies" persisting from the colonial period. It is interesting to note how quickly the Rhee administration and private enterprise found ways to cooperate once mutual dependence became apparent. Accustomed to dealing with the strong colonial state, leading private entrepreneurs from the colonial period adjusted to the Rhee interlude of a "weak state" direction and "strong state" economic ambitions.[44]

Cho had emphasized institutional continuities from the colonial years, but we can point to other factors promoting concentration in ownership and management, and close state ties evident in postwar chaebŏl development. For instance, the postwar state did not set about breaking up the assets of earlier chaebŏl or discouraging other firms from concentration. Indeed the record of distribution of vested properties would suggest just the opposite. Whether by design or default, the Rhee state fostered concentration in the textile industry by maintaining the earlier Japanese properties. If we look to private enterprise, collusion with bureaucratic officials to gain licenses and credit, domestic market insecurities, and the availability of large amounts of capital and raw materials through foreign aid certainly did not discourage concentration.

Local entrepreneurs would be challenged to adjust again with the advent of the clear, authoritarian direction of Park Chung-hee's administration from 1963, a radical departure from the Rhee state. Leaders of major private enterprises were charged and convicted in 1961 of unfair practices in gaining access to foreign exchange, favorable loan rates, and other advantages during the Rhee years. Rather than simply remitting heavy fines to the government, the coup leaders under Park Chung-hee used the penalties as leverage to gain the close cooperation of major private enterprise in long-term investment in industrial projects of clear benefit to the national economy. The government's successful effort to investigate and prosecute collusion in business–state relations of the previous administration was an early sign of the "strong state" policies that would characterize the disciplined economic direction of the Park administration through 1979. Effective government controls on access to foreign technology, foreign markets, and especially on credit financing would serve as a pattern of opportunities and constraints for private enterprise.

But if private enterprise would need government support, so also would the government need private enterprise, as indicated by the resolution in 1961 of directed investment rather than simply fines and lengthy prison sentences. The Park state needed the base of private enterprise for economic development on the peninsula. The Rhee administration came to recognize the private sector as a source for political funding and leadership in trade and light industry, a far cry from the near absolute autonomy of the Japanese colonial state. The emphasis of the Park government on economic growth gave the major combines an even greater role in the economy of the South Korean state, though under careful government supervision.

Enterprise, class, and state

This review of the origins of capitalist enterprise would not be complete without returning to the original concepts of entrepreneurship, dynamics of initial capitalist class formation in a colonial society, and the economic role of the Japanese colonial state. If there is a distinctive model of Korean capitalism and lessons to be learned from the colonial experience, it is here we must begin. For instance, the study highlights a number of issues that must be considered in developing a theory of state and major private enterprise pertinent to Korean capitalism. I would emphasize continuities in patterns of concentration and state relations, as well as the phenomenon of interdependence in postcolonial class ties among the major business leaders. We must also clarify the more specific issue of Korean entrepreneurship, a convergence of dynamics of concentration, state relations, and class formation.

If the characteristics of "innovation" and "risk" delimit the Western concept of *entrepreneur* within a capitalist economy, the case studies here reflect a distinctive Korean style of entrepreneurship. The Japanese colonial administration and subsequent Korean administrations guaranteed the rights of private property, although the institutional practices of both the colonial and postcolonial governments did not promote the free and open economy most conducive to widespread Korean entrepreneurship. The three early Korean entrepreneurs cited here displayed considerable innovative skills in organization, development of markets, and application of technology. One could point to Pak's chain stores project in the 1930s and the land reclamation projects of Kim's Samyang Company during the colonial years. Their development of trading companies, and of sugar and textile production through 1960 also demanded innovative skills, and in the Korean context cooperative skills as well.

The basic resources of capitalist development such as land, labor, capital, and entrepreneurs were available on the peninsula from at least the 1930s. The scarcity of these resources coupled with government constraints on their use forced prospective Korean entrepreneurs to emphasize cooperative as well as innovative skills. Why cooperation as well as innovation? Hirschman pointed to structural constraints on entrepreneurs in the late-developing societies of Latin America, necessitating cooperation with foreign capital and domestic state administrations. I would point to cultural adaptations in Korea affecting cooperation as well, adjusting the individualist aspects of the entrepreneurial role to fit a more group-oriented society. But the issue is not simply a distinction between individualist and more group-oriented societies.

Hirschmeier and Yui distinguished between "merchants of fortune" like Iwasaki Yatarō of Mitsubishi, and "government protégés" like Minomura Rizaemon and Shibusawa Eiichi among Meiji period Japanese entrepreneurs.[45] The former owed their success to determination in pursuit of their own profits, the latter to government contacts, and usually enterprise on behalf of wider national goals. Korean entrepreneurs under foreign colonial domination were loathe to be considered "government protégés," but close identification with the Rhee administration subsequently proved embarrassing and anything but "patriotic." The record of government charges against Pak and Kim in 1948 and again in 1961 would suggest their cooperative talents were for personal (i.e., selfish, unpatriotic) gain rather than the good of the wider society.[46] Yet their subsequent major roles in commerce and industry during both the Rhee and Park administrations would indicate the state found some benefit in supporting them.

The contribution of the Mins, Pak, and Kim to Korea's capitalist development process in the colonial and postcolonial periods remains a moot point, but certainly the structural dynamics of initial entrepreneurial experience in an alien "strong state" regime, and then adjustment to the less cohesive economic direction of the Rhee "weak state" and adaptation to a political role with either the government or opposition party deserve greater attention. Mainly "merchants of fortune" or at best entrepreneurs with nationalist sentiments under colonial rule, Pak, Kim, and the Mins had to cooperate with the state yet maintain distance from the goals of the colonial administration and the practices of the Rhee administration. The continuity between private enterprise and the state in Japan promoted by Shibusawa was absent in Korean society. Innovation and cooperation appeared critical for Korean entrepreneurs, given both the structural constraints of a developing economy and cultural constraints in a more group-oriented society. Yet even though cooperative and adaptable to government direction, the Korean entrepreneurs under an alien and later a collusive local state were necessarily more individualistic than their Japanese colleagues. Networks among kin and close associates became even more critical given unstable and at times hostile relations with the state.

"Risk" across these five decades (1910–60) on the peninsula also helps to distinguish Korean entrepreneurship. Landed aristocrats and other potential investors in an agrarian economy do not easily turn to even commercial investments until the development of cash-crop agriculture, markets, and financial structures to support and possibly insure their investment are in place. Enterprises of the colonial administration and later of private Japanese firms developed on the peninsula in commercial agriculture, commerce, trade, and industry. Market and finance structures developed, encouraging the transfer of capital from land to commerce and industry, though not necessarily for local investors. The very small minority of Korean investments on the peninsula through 1945 reflects the difficulty for indigenous entrepreneurs in the face of strong Japanese competition. The small number of colonial entrepreneurs who survived and succeeded indicates the uncertainties and difficulties of major private enterprise on the peninsula. Unlike their Japanese counterparts, the Korean entrepreneurs in general were unable to develop financial institutions within their business groups that might moderate losses and provide loan capital for innovative ventures.

Pak and Kim limited the uncertainty with state subsidies and loans to initiate large-scale enterprises. More importantly, however, they developed close family control or control through close associates to insure continuity and some security of investment capital and direction of the enterprises. In the postcolonial years loss of plants due to division and war, as well as to the instability of the Rhee administration further contributed to the uncertainties of investment. Again family and a close circle of associates proved necessary to delimit the risk, insuring some continuity of investment and direction. The role of the family in both ownership and management deserves close scrutiny, as do issues of intergenerational continuity in the Korean chaebŏl. A closer look at the concentration of investment capital, particularly the circulation of capital and credit among affiliates, and at methods of control through rotation of a corps of managers and executives suggests distinctive organizational strategies. We also need to better understand the distinction between internal control of a private enterprise, and adaptation to the wider economic policies and direction of a strong state.

The study also tells us much of the Japanese colonial state and of the intriguing issue of even limited autonomy among local economic elites in a tightly controlled dependent situation. I find interesting the variety of controls exercised by the state and its affiliated institutions, including legislation, the blend of direct and indirect investment, and particularly the "governmentalized" business associations. The fact that a few local elites gained some consultative voice within this system, and were able to consolidate and foster enterprises should not divert attention from the wider context of minimal Korean investment and massive Japanese investment. There was little opportunity for large-scale Korean enterprise within the highly competitive environment of strong alien investment initially in agriculture and commerce and later in industry.

Apart from effective controls, the study also highlights the custom of prominent Japanese bureaucrats moving into leadership positions in private industry. The phenomenon is perhaps clearer in colonial situations where government ties were so critical in the development of private enterprise. Within the context of Japanese business practice, one can understand the entry of former Industrial Bank president Ariga Mitsutoyo into heavy industries on the peninsula, of Abe Senichi into mining, and of lower level officials such as Shibuya Reiji of the Bank of Chosen into trade. But one is impressed with their contact and continued ties with prominent Korean businessmen. Witness Kim Yŏn-su's directorship in Ariga's Chōsen Refining and Kankō Hydroelectric, his joint investment in Okkye Gold Mining with such a prominent mining executive as Abe, and the trade investment of Kim and Pak in Shibuya's Daikō Trade. Businessmen can be very pragmatic, and obviously there were benefits to be gained for both sides. Kim and Pak were able to gain entry into a tight circle of major Japanese investors on the peninsula, though never able to compete at that level. Such was the character of dependence for even the most prominent of the Korean businessmen.

The history of business–state relations in colonial and postcolonial Korea provides an important case of adjustment from the strong state economic direction of the colonial administration to the weak state economic policies and strategies of the Rhee administration, and from little effective political participation to prominence as at least government party financial supporters or opposition political leaders in the First Republic (1948–60). Contrasts and comparisons of the role of business leaders in educational, cultural, and political institutions between the colonial and postcolonial years would help clarify both business–state relations and processes of class formation.

And, finally, the concept of an inner circle among the colonial business elite has proved useful in defining the composition and function of an emerging class of corporate leaders through 1945. Although the notion of a "politicized leading edge" may appear contradictory in a dependent colonial situation, the colonial administration's dual policy of political repression and economic productivity left a few select Korean businessmen an opportunity to gain state support for locally owned enterprise. Each of the inner circle examined here took a somewhat different approach to state relations and state appointments, often based on their own resources and, no doubt, own advantages. I find Han Sang-yong best fits the term "comprador," but Kim Yŏn-su's extensive wealth and political identification with the nationalist aspirations of the family-associated *Donga Ilbo* newspaper and Posŏng College permitted the limited independence more characteristic of the "dependent capitalist." Others fit somewhere in between as each found ways to promote enterprise and deal with the alien objectives of the colonial government.

The dynamic of interdependence among an inner group of the Korean business elite could be better specified with studies of the ideology of postcolonial business leaders, and of their ties in business policy associations and joint political efforts. If indeed we could better distinguish this inner group as a "class segment," then comparisons of the ideology and enterprise of the inner group with the larger class of corporate owners in medium and small industry and commerce would contribute to a much broader understanding of the capitalist class in South Korea. What we do know is that the colonial elite developed an initial business ideology of benign capitalism, a pattern of concentration in corporate ownership and management, and a format for relations with a strong state. The same elite proved to be the exception rather than the norm in a transition of local capital from agrarian to commercial and industrial purposes, and at the very end of the colonial period, of reinvestment of commercial and industrial capital into industry. But if the experience of the Mins, Pak, and Kim sheds light on the colonial roots of Korean enterprise, we still must look to origins in the late Chosŏn Dynasty, as well as to postcolonial developments.

Notes

Chapter 1. Origins

1. Karl Moskowitz made this argument in his review of studies on Korean development: "Korean Development and Korean Studies–A Review Article," *Journal of Asian Studies* 42, 1 (Nov. 1982): 63–90

2. Kang Man-gil, "The Modernization of Korea from the Historical Point of View," *Asiatic Research Bulletin* 6, 1 (March 1963): 6.

3. Zenkoku Keizai Chōsa Kikan Rengōkai, Chōsen Shibu, *Chōsen keizai nempō 1941–1942* [Annual of the Korean economy, 1941–1942] (Tokyo: Kaizōsha, 1943), 488–9 (cited hereafter as CKN); Kim Kwang-tiek, "Industrialization of Korea under Japanese Rule: A Case Study" (Ph.D. diss., University of Maryland, 1974), 237, Table III. A Korean resident at the turn of the century, Homer Hulbert described his impressions in "The New Century," *The Korea Review* 1, 1 (1901): 3–16, while Yi Kyu-tae looked back to the same period in *The Modern Transformation of Korea* (Seoul: Sejong Publishers, 1970). Descriptions of major Korean cities during the colonial period can be found in an extensive report by the Joint Army–Navy Intelligence Studies Publishing Board, titled *JANIS Korea (including Tsushima and Quelpart)*, April, 1945, abbreviated here simply as *JANIS*.

4. Terms and personal names from Asian languages have been romanized according to the following systems. Korean words have been transliterated according to the McCune-Reischauer System, as explained in Korea Branch of the Royal Asiatic Society, "Tables of the McCune-Reischauer System for the Romanization of Korean," *Transactions of the Korea Branch of the Royal Asiatic Society* 38 (Oct. 1961): 121–8.

Japanese words have been transliterated according to the modified Hepburn System as used in Koh Masuda, ed., *New Japanese–English Dictionary* (Tokyo: Kenkyūsha, 1974), and names for the most part according to P.G. O'Neill, *Japanese Names* (New York: Weatherhill, 1972). I have relied on the annual volumes of Kamesaka Tsunesaburo, ed., *Who's Who in Japan, with Manchoukuo and China* (Tokyo: Who's Who in Japan Publishing Office, annual) whenever possible for transliteration of Japanese names. (Volumes of *Who's Who in Japan* hereafter will be cited as *WWJ*.)

Exceptions to both systems were made for place names in common Western usage under different spellings, such as "Tokyo" and "Seoul," though not for the less familiar "Keijō," the official Japanese name for Seoul during the colonial period. The names of firms in which Japanese nationals held a majority of the shares are cited in Japanese, and in Korean when Korean nationals held the majority of shares. Since I am interested in publicly registered large-scale investments, I cite mainly joint-stock enterprises in this study. For easier reading of company names, I will omit the formal term *joint-stock* firm (*chusik hoesa*; or *kabushiki kaisha*).

5. The totals represent the net value of commodity product at 1936 constant prices, based on statistics provided in the *Chōsen tōkei nempō*, and the statistical appendices of CKN. The data have been collated by Suh Sang-chul in Table A-12, "Net Value of Commodity Product at 1936 Constant Prices," pp. 170–1 in *Growth and Structural Changes in the Korean Economy, 1910–1940* (Cambridge: Harvard University Press, 1978). Similar figures can be found in the Industrial Bank's *Chōsen Shokusan Ginkō nijūnen shi* [A twenty-year history of the Chōsen Industrial Bank] (Keijō: Industrial Bank, 1938), 55, cited in Takasugi Tōgō, *Chōsen kinyū kikan hattatsushi* [A history of the development of financial institutions in Korea] (Keijō: Jitsugyō Taimususha, 1940), 630.

6. Total paid-in capital amounted to 360 million yen in finance, 325 million in commerce, and 563 million yen in manufacturing. The total paid-in capital for various areas of the economy, and relative shares of Japan-based versus peninsula-based firms has been compiled from data in two reports. See "Chōsen tōka naichi shihon go kore ni yoru jigyō" [The enterprises of Japanese capital invested in Korea], *Shokugin Chōsa Geppō*, no. 65 (June 1940): 41. See also "Chōsen ni okeru hantōjin shihaika no kaisha jōsei" [The condition of companies under native management in Korea], *Shokugin Chōsa Geppō* (Jan. 1940): 26–27.

7. Tōyō Keizai Shinpōsha, *Chōsen nenkan, 1942* [Korea annual, 1942] (Tokyo: Tōa Keizai Shinposha, 1942), 26–7; Kim Tu-yong, *Chōsen kindai keizaishi wa* [Reflections on the recent history of the economy in Korea] (Tokyo: Kyōdo Shōbo, 1947), 234.

8. Firms with headquarters on the peninsula accounted for a total capital of 87 million yen in finance in 1938, 89 million yen in commerce, and 245 million yen in industry. Korean-owned firms represented only 10 million yen in finance, 23 million yen in commerce, and 30 million yen in industry.

9. Kim Tu-yong, *Chōsen kindai keizaishi wa*, 235.

10. See Reinhard Bendiz, "Industrialization, Ideologies, and Social Structure," *American Sociological Review* 24, 5(Oct. 1959): 618–19.

11. Clifford Geertz, "Ideology as a Cultural System," in his *The Interpretation of Culture* (New York: Basic, 1973), 47–56.

12. I have examined both conservative and liberal Korean ideologies of change in my dissertation, "Imperial Expansion and Nationalist Resistance: Japan in Korea, 1876–1910" (Ph.D. diss., Harvard University, 1983), 150–213.

13. Theontonio Dos Santos, "The Structure of Dependence," *The American Economic Review* 60, 2(1970): 231. For a discussion of classical dependency in Korea through 1945, see my "Korea and Brazil at the Turn of the Century: Trade, Elites and Foreign Ties," in Kyong-dong Kim, ed., *Dependency Issues in Korean Development: Comparative Perspectives* (Seoul: Seoul National University Press, 1987), 496–511.

14. F. H. Cardoso and E. Faletto, *Dependency and Development in Latin America* (Berkeley: University of California Press, 1979); Peter Evans, *Dependent Development* (Princeton: Princeton University Press, 1979).

15. The *zaibatsu* (literally, *financial clique*) has been described as "a conglomerate of horizontally and vertically related enterprises in mining, industry, finance and commerce under a single family's ownership and control." See Hugh Patrick, "Japan 1868–1914," in Rondo Cameron et al., eds., *Banking in the Early Stages of Modernization* (London: Oxford, 1967), 241. The Japanese term *zaibatsu* and Korean term *chaebŏl* are different pronunciations of the same two Chinese characters. I will omit italics from this point on for easier reading of the two terms.

The distinctive features of the Korean combines or *chaebŏl* are described in Chu

Chong-hwan, *Chaebŏl kyŏngje non: sanŏp chojik nonjŏk chŏpkŭn* [An economic study of the chaebŏl, from the perspective of industrial organization] (Seoul: Chŏngŭm Munhwasa, 1985). See also Hong Sŏng-yu, *Han'guk kyŏngje ŭi chabon ch'ukchŏk ŭi kwajŏng* [The process of capital accumulation in the Korean economy] (Seoul: Korea University Press, 1965); Kang Tong-jin, "Han'guk chaebŏl ŭi hyŏngsŏng kwajŏng kwa kyebo" [Background and development of Korean conglomerates], *Chŏnggyŏng Yŏn'gu* 2, 11(Nov. 1966): 121–8; Kim Sŏng-du, "Han'guk tokchŏm chaebŏl hyŏngsŏng ŭi t'ŭgisŏng [Unique characteristics in the formation of Korean conglomerates: the inefficient and uneconomical nature of Korean conglomerates], *Sasanggye* (Sept. 1968): 108–22. For a review of the ties between large firms and the state from 1961, see Leroy Jones and Il Sakong, *Government, Business, and Entrepreneurship in Economic development: The Korean Case* (Cambridge: Harvard University Press, 1980).

16. Joseph Schumpeter, *The Theory of Economic Development* (New Brunswick, NJ: Transaction, 1983), 132; see also Paul Wilken, *Entrepreneurship. A Comparative and Historical Study* (Norwood, NJ: Ablex, 1979), 57.

17. Albert Hirschman, *The Strategy of Economic Development* (New Haven: Yale University Press, 1958), 17.

18. The official yen exchange rate in 1940 for U.S. currency was twenty-three cents for one yen. See table for *Japan Statistical Yearbook 1949* reprinted in Keizo Seki, *The Cotton Industry of Japan* (Tokyo: Maruzen, 1956), 408. According to the official rate, an investment in 1940 of 500 thousand yen amounted to $115 thousand, one million yen to $230 thousand, 10 million yen to $2.3 million, and 100 million yen to $23 million.

19. Maurice Zeitlin, "Corporate Ownership and Control: the Large Corporation and the Capitalist Class," *American Journal of Sociology* 79, 5(1974): 1091.

20. Johannes Hirschmeier, "Shibusawa Eiichi: Industrial Pioneer," in William W. Lockwood, ed., *The State and Economic Enterprise in Japan* (Princeton: Princeton University Press, 1965), 209–47; Hirschmeier and Tsunehiko Yui, *The Development of Japanese Business* (Cambridge: Harvard University Press, 1975); Yasuzō Horie, "Modern Entrepreneurship in Meiji Japan," in Lockwood, ed., op. cit., 183–208; Byron K. Marshall, *Capitalism and Nationalism in Prewar Japan. The Ideology of the Business Elite, 1868–1941* (Stanford: Stanford University Press, 1967).

21. Ishida Takeshi, "The Development of Interest Groups and the Pattern of Political Modernization in Japan," in Robert E. Ward, ed., *Political Development in Modern Japan* (Princeton: Princeton University Press, 1968), 293–336; Arthur E. Tiedemann, "Big Business and Politics in Prewar Japan," in James William Morley, ed., *Dilemmas of Growth in Prewar Japan* (Princeton: Princeton University Press, 1971), 267–316; Arnold J. Heidenheimer and Frank C. Langdon, *Business Associations and the Financing of Political Parties* (The Hague: Martinus Nijhoff, 1968).

22. Ikeshima Hiroyuki, "Nihon ni okeru kigyōhō no keisei to tenkai" [The formation and development of enterprise legislation in Japan], in Takayanagi Shinichi and Fujita, *Shihonshugihō no keisei to tenkai* [The formation and development of capitalist law] (Tokyo: University of Tokyo Press, 1973), 205–58; Nakagawa Keiichiro, ed., *Strategy and Structure of Big Business* (Tokyo: University of Tokyo Press, 1976).

23. Stephen Krasner, *Defending the National Interest: Raw Materials Investments and U.S. Foreign Policy* (Princeton: Princeton University Press, 1978); Peter B. Evans, Dietrich Rueschemeyer, and Theda Skocpol, eds., *Bringing the State Back In* (Cambridge, Eng.: Cambridge University Press, 1985).

24. Alexander Gerschenkron, "Economic Backwardness in Historical Perspective," in his *A Book of Essays* (Cambridge: Harvard Belknap, 1966), 5–30; Henry Rosovsky, *Capital Formation in Japan, 1868–1940* (New York: Free Press, 1961).

See also Chalmers Johnson, "Political Institutions and Economic Performance: The Government–Business Relationship in Japan, South Korea, and Taiwan," in Frederic C. Deyo, ed., *The Political Economy of the New Asian Industrialism* (Ithaca: Cornell University Press, 1987), 136–64; Stephen Haggard and Chung-In Moon, "The South Korean State in the International Economy: Liberal, Dependent, or Mercantile," in John Gerald Ruggie, ed., *The Antinomies of Interdependence: National Welfare and the International Division of Labor* (New York: Columbia University, 1983), 13–89; Thomas B. Gold, *State and Society in the Taiwan Miracle* (New York: Sharpe, 1986); Frederic C. Deyo, *Dependent Development and Industrial Order: an Asian Case Study* (New York: Praeger, 1981).

25. Gunnar Myrdal, *Asian Drama* (London: Penguin, 1968), 66, 896.

26. Mark R. Peattie, "Introduction," in Ramon H. Myers and Mark R. Peattie, *The Japanese Colonial Empire, 1895–1945* (Princeton: Princeton University Press, 1984), 3–26; James I. Nakamura, "Incentives, Productivity Gaps, and Agricultural Growth Rates in Prewar Japan, Taiwan, and Korea," in Bernard S. Silberman and H.D. Harootunian, eds., *Japan in Crisis, Essays in Taishō Democracy* (Princeton: Princeton University Press, 1974), 329–73.

27. Peter B. Evans and Dietrich Rueschemeyer, "The State and Economic Transformation: Toward an Analysis of the Conditions Underlying Effective Intervention," in Evans, Rueschemeyer, and Skocpol, *Bringing the State Back In*, 44–77; also Michael Mann, "The Autonomous Power of the State: Its Origins, Mechanisms and Results," *Archievs Européennes de Sociologie* 25 (1984): 185–213.

28. Edward I-te Chen, "The Attempt to Integrate the Empire: Legal Perspectives," in Myers and Peattie, *The Japanese Colonial Empire*, 264.

29. G. Balandier, "The Colonial situation: A Theoretical Approach," in Immanuel Wallerstein, ed., *Social Change: The Colonial Situation* (New York: John Wiley, 1966), 53.

30. See Michael Useem, "The Social Organization of the American Business Elite and Participation of Corporation Directors in the Governance of American Institutions," *American Sociological Review* 44 (Aug. 1979): 554.

31. Ibid., 556.

32. Michael Patrick Allen, "The Structure of Interorganizational Elite Cooptation: Interlocking Corporate Directorates," *American Sociological Review* 39 (1974): 393–406; Useem, "Social Organization and Participation."

33. Useem, "Social Organization and Participation," 555.

34. Michael Useem, *The Inner Circle* (New York: Oxford, 1984), 3.

35. See, for instance, Yen-P'ing Hao, *The Comprador in Nineteenth Century China: Bridge between East and West* (Cambridge: Harvard University Press, 1970).

36. Kang Tong-jin, *Ilche ŭi Han'guk ch'imnyak chŏngch'aeksa: 1920 nyŏndae rŭl chungsim ŭro* [The political policy of penetration in Korea under Japanese rule: the 1920s] (Seoul: Hangilsa, 1980), 202–16.

37. Kajimura Hideki, "Minjok chabon kwa yesok chabon" [National capital and dependent capital], in Kajimura Hideki et al., *Han'guk kŭndae kyŏngjesa yŏn'gu* [Studies of modern Korean history] (Seoul: Sagyechŏl, 1983), 523. The article is a Korean translation of a section of Kajimura's *Chōsen ni okeru shihon shugi no keisei to tenkai* [The structure and development of capitalism in Korea] (Tokyo: Ryūkei Shosha, 1977), 213–42. Hagen Koo has noted the absence of a "viable comprador class" in colonial Korea, despite accumulation of native fortunes through close ties with the colonialists. See "The Interplay of State, Social Class, and World System in

East Asian Development: the Cases of South Korea and Taiwan," in Deyo, *Political Economy*, 170–1.

38. Cho Ki-jun, *Han'guk kiŏpkasa* [A history of Korean entrepreneurs] (Seoul: Pagyŏngsa, 1973); Kang Man-gil, "Reflections on the Centenary of the Opening of Korea," *Korea Journal* 16, 2(Feb. 1976): 16.

39. See, for instance, Park Soon Won, "The Emergence of a Factory Labor Force in Colonial Korea: A Case Study of the Onoda Cement Factory" (Ph.D. diss., Harvard University, 1985).

40. See, for instance, Karl Moskowitz, "Current Assets: The Employees of Japanese Banks in Colonial Korea" (Ph.D. diss., Harvard University, 1979).

41. See Abe Kaoru, *Chōsen kōrōsha meikan* [A list of eminent figures in Korea] (Keijō: Minshū Jironsha, 1935), 59–60. He was active in a family mining company from 1911 before joining the administration of the Hanil in 1920. Apart from directing the family-owned Kyesŏng Company, he also served as a director of the Chōsen Trust Company, of the Chosŏn Beer Company, and as representative director of the Chosŏn Brewery (Chosŏn Yanjo). See his resume in Teikoku Kōshinjo, *Teikoku ginkō kaisha yōroku* [A list of banks and corporations in the empire] (Tokyo: Teikoku Kōshinjo, 1940), 29: 159, Executive Section. (This annual listing will be cited hereafter by TGKY, the year, and volume number.); also Koh Seung-jae, *Han'guk kumyungsa yon'gu* [Studies in the history of Korean finance] (Seoul: Ilchogak, 1970), 40–42.

42. TGKY (1940), 29:159, Executive Section. Biographical details can also be found in U.S. Adjutant General's Office, "Names and Biographies of Members of Central Advisory Council of Koreans," 1945, Adjutant General's Office, Target No. 61, Min Kyu-sik, RG 407, National Archives. Further biographical materials can be found in the archives of the Choheung Bank, Seoul, Korea.

43. Hanil Unhaeng, *Hanil Unhaeng osipnyŏnsa* [A fifty year history of the Hanil Bank] (Seoul: Samsŏng, 1982), 96–101, 125–32, 804.

44. See Pak Hŭng-sik, "Pak Hŭng-sik," in Wŏllo Kiŏbin, eds., *Chaegye hoego* [Memoirs of the financial world] (Seoul: Han'guk Ilbosa, 1981), 171–257; Abe Kaoru, *Chōsen kōrōsha meikan*, 828–9; TGKY (1940), 29: 180, Executive Section.

45. See Inch'on Kinyŏmhoe, *Inch'on Kim Sŏng-su chŏn* [A biography of Inch'on Kim Sŏng-su] (Seoul: Inch'on Kinyŏmhoe, 1976) (cited hereafter as *In'chon*). Since Sŏng-su was adopted by his father's older brother and raised separately from Yŏn-su, the brothers by birth are sometimes referred to as cousins.

46. TGKY (1940): 185, Executive Section; Kim Sang-hong, *Sudang Kim Yŏn-su* [Sudang Kim Yŏn-su] (Seoul: Sudang Kinyŏm Saŏphoe, 1971) (cited hereafter as *Sudang*).

47. I am indebted to two Korean scholars in particular for their pioneering studies of colonial enterprise, Professors Cho Ki-jun and Koh Seung-jae. See Cho Ki-jun, *Han'guk chabonjuŭi sŏngnipsa non* [A study of the development of capitalism in Korea] (Seoul: Taegwangsa, 1977), *Han'guk kiŏpkasa* [A history of Korean entrepreneurs] (Seoul: Pagyŏngsa, 1973), *Han'guk kyŏngjesa* [An economic history of Korea] (Seoul: Ilsinsa, 1985), and a recent paper, "Han'guk chabonjuŭi hyŏngsŏnggi ŭi kiŏbin yŏn'gu" [Studies of entrepreneurs in the formation of Korean capitalism], *Haksulwŏn nonmunjip* (1987): 80–125. See also Koh Seung-Jae (Ko Sŭng-je) *Han'guk kŭmyungsa yŏn'gu* [Studies in the history of Korean finance] (Seoul: Ilchogak, 1970), and *Han'guk kyŏngsŏngsa yŏn'gu* [Studies in the history of business management in Korea] (Seoul: Samwha, 1975). Hwang Myŏng-su provides a useful discussion of the pertinence of Western entrepreneurial theory in his *Kiŏpkasa yŏn'gu* [Studies in entrepreneurship] (Seoul: Ch'ŏndae Publishing, 1983).

Chapter 2. Benign capitalism

1. Ko Wŏn-sŏp, *Panminja choesanggi* [A record of charges against the antination-alists] (Seoul: Paegyŏp Munhwasa, 1949), 17.

2. Byron Marshall, *Capitalism and Nationalism in Prewar Japan. The Ideology of the Business Elite, 1868–1941* (Stanford: Stanford University Press, 1967), 4.

3 See Han Pae-ho, "Samil undong chikhu ŭi Chosŏn singminchi chŏngch'aek" [Colonial policy in Korea immediately after the March First Movement], in Ch'a Ki-byŏk, ed., *Ilche ŭi Han'guk singmin t'ongch'i* [Colonial administration in Korea under Japanese imperial rule] (Seoul: Chŏngŭmsa, 1985), 78–107; Yamabe Kentarō, *Nihon tōchika no Chōsen* [Korea under Japanese rule] (Tokyo: Iwanami Shoten, 1971); David Brudnoy, "Japan's Experiment in Korea," *Monumenta Nipponica* 25 (1970): 155–96; Chang Yunshik, "Colonization as Planned Change: The Korean Case," *Modern Asian Studies* 5, 2 (1971): 161–86; Kim Han-kyo, "The Japanese Colonial Administration in Korea: An Overview," in Andrew C. Nahm, ed., *Korea under Japanese Colonial Rule* (Kalamazoo Center for Korean Studies, Western Michigan University, 1973), 41–53.

4. Baldwin concurs with the smaller figure, noting that one million male demonstrators would represent about one-sixth of adult Korean males at the time. See Frank Baldwin, "The March First Movement: Korean Challenge and Japanese Response" (Ph.D. diss., Columbia University, 1969), Appendix 2, 228–31. Regarding casualties, Baldwin noted the figure of 7,645 Korean deaths was closer to the truth than lower Japanese administration figures. See his Appendix 3, p. 234. The total Korean population in 1919 was estimated at 16.8 million. See Government-General of Chōsen, *Chōsen in Pictures* (Keijo: Government-General, 1921), Table 1.

5. For a study of Korean political response to colonial rule, see my "Comparative Colonial Response: Korea and Taiwan, 1895–1919," *Korean Studies* 10 (1986): 54–68.

6. The text of the declaration can be found in Sin Sŏk-ho, ed., "Samil undong ŭi chŏngae" [The unfolding of the March First Movement], in Donga Ilbo, ed., *Samil undong osipchunyŏn kinyŏmjip* [A fifty-year memorial volume of the March First Movement] (Seoul: Donga Ilbosa, 1963), 166–8. An English translation of the document can be found in Baldwin, "The March First Movement," 224.

7. See Michael Robinson, "Colonial Publication Policy and the Korean Nationalist Movement," in Ramon Meyers and Mark Peattie, eds., *The Japanese Colonial Empire* (Princeton: Princeton University Press, 1983), 326. The *Chosŏn Ilbo* had a daily circulation of 24,000 in 1929, the *Donga Ilbo* close to 38,000.

8. For a listing of the more prominent nationalist groups in the early 1920s, see Kim Chun-yŏp and Kim Ch'ang-sun, *Han'guk kongsanjuŭi undongsa* [A history of the Korean Communist Movement] (Seoul: Korea University Press, 1969) 2: 9–10.

9. See especially Suh, *The Korean Communist Movement, 1918–1948* (Princeton: Princeton University Press, 1967), 59–65.

10. See Chin Tŏk-su, "1920 nyŏndae kungnae minjok undong e kwanhan koch'al" [Reflections on domestic national movements in the 1920s], in Song Kŏn-ho and Kang Man-gil, eds., *Han'guk minjujuŭi ron* [A study of democracy in Korea] (Seoul: Ch'angjak kwa Pip'yŏngsa, 1982), 140–59; K. M. Wells, "The Rationale of Korean Economic Nationalism under Japanese Colonial Rule, 1922–1932: The Case of Cho Man-sik's Products Promotion Society," *Modern Asian Studies* 19, 4 (1985): 823–59; Michael Robinson, *Cultural Nationalism in Colonial Korea, 1920–1925* (Seattle: University of Washington Press, 1988).

11. Kim Chun-yŏp and Kim Ch'ang-sun, *Han'guk kongsanjuŭi undongsa* 2:177.

12. Strong Japanese investment had already diluted indigenous ownership in the

Hansŏng Bank.
13. The initial public discussion took place early in the careers of these entrepreneurs: Pak Hŭng-sik was only twenty-two years old in 1925, Kim Yŏn-su twenty-nine, and Min Kyu-sik thirty-seven.
14. Wells, "Rationale of Economic Nationalism," 828.
15. The society published a journal, *Sanŏpkye* (The Industrial World), later renamed *Chosŏn Mulsan Changyohoe Hoebo* (Journal of the Korean Products Promotion Society) from November of 1923 until 1932. Although various activities were promoted through 1932, the society flourished for only eight months or so from early 1923 through the beginning of 1924. Chin Tŏk-su, "1920 nyŏndae kungnae minjok undong e kwanhan koch'al," 148.
16. See his *Han'guk chabonjuŭi sŏngnipsa ron*, 546–7.
17. The newspaper was founded in April of 1920 through the efforts of Kim Sŏng-su and Pak Yŏng-hyo. Pak served briefly as the company's first president, and Kim Sŏng-su and Song Chin-u led the company thereafter as presidents or leading advisors. See Kim Sang-man, ed., *Donga Ilbosa sa* [A history of the Donga Ilbo Company] (Seoul: Donga Ilbosa, 1975), 411. For the wider role of the *Donga Ilbo* in the nationalist movement in the 1920s, see Song Kŏn-ho, *Han'guk minjujuŭi ŭi t'amgu* [A study of democracy in Korea] (Seoul: Hangilsa, 1978), 115–57; also Michael Robinson, "Colonial Publication Policy."
18. "Kongŏp ipkuk ŭl nonhanora" [A discussion of industrialized nations], *Donga Ilbo*, May 15–17, 1921. Reprinted in Donga Ilbo Sasŏl P'yŏnch'an Wiwŏnhoe, ed., *Donga Ilbo sasŏl nonjip* I (1920–1940) [Collection of editorials from the *Donga Ilbo*, 1920–1940] (Seoul: Donga Ilbosa, 1977), 154–60. (This volume will be cited hereafter as DISN.)
19. May 15, 1921, DISN, 155.
20. "Sanŏp ŭl chaech'ang hanora" [Promotion of an industrial campaign], May 17, 1922, DISN, 225–6. Similar themes are presented in editorials of February 15, May 23, and May 27, 1923.
21. Yu Tu-ch'an, "Nonggongŏp sanguro pon pando kyŏngjegye" [The economic situation on the peninsula: agriculture and industry], *Kaebyŏk* 4(Sept. 1920): 91–5.
22. Kim Ki-sae, "Nongch'on kaešon ŭi kin'gŭp tongŭi" [An urgent proposal for agricultural reform], *Kaebyŏk* 6(Nov. 1920): 16–21; "Sin Chosŏn ŭi unmyŏng kwa nongmin ŭi chiwi" [The position of the agricultural population and the fate of the new Korea], *Kaebyŏk* 41(Nov. 1923): 2–10; "Chabonjŏk kyŏngnyak ŭi hogi" [An opportunity for the administration of capital], *Kaebyŏk* 52 (Oct. 1924): 1–3.
23. "Chosŏnin ponwi sanŏp chŏngch'aek ŭi ŭiŭi" [Ideas for a government industrial policy regarding the position of Koreans], September 20, 1921, DISN, 164. See also "Ilbon chabon kwa Chosŏn puwŏn" [Japanese capital and Korean resources], May 29, 1925, DISN, 514–16.
24. May 17, 1922, DISN, 225.
25. May 15–17, 1921, DISN, 154–60.
26. "Ch'ŏlchŏhan kago wa chigujŏk silko" [Thorough understanding and persistent application], *Donga Ilbo*, January 8, 1923, reprinted in Pak Kwŏn-sang, ed., *Donga Ilbo nonsŏl yugsimnyŏn* [Sixty years of editorials in the *Donga Ilbo*] (Seoul: Donga Ilbosa, 1980), 91–3. (This source will be cited hereafter as DINY.) See also "Chosŏnin ŭi kyŏngjejŏk unmyŏng" [The economic fate of Koreans], May 28, 1923, DISN, 302–3.
27. January 8, 1923, DINY, 91–3.
28. September 20, 1921, DISN, 164. See also "Chosŏnin ŭi kyŏngjejŏk unmyŏng," 302–3.
29. May 17, 1922, DISN, 226–7; January 8, 1923, DINY, 92; see also "Mulsan

changryo ŭi haengryul kŭmji" [Prohibition of the products promotion parade], February 15, 1923, DISN, 277–8; May 28, 1923, DISN, 302–3.

30. May 17, 1922, DISN, 226.

31. "Minjokchŏk kyŏngnon" [A national economic argument: part three], January 4, 1924, DISN, 363–4.

32. May 17, 1922, DISN, 226–7; January 8, 1923, DINY, 91–3; May 28, 1923, DISN, 302–3.

33. "Kyŏngje chosa kigwan ŭi p'iryo" [The need for an economic research organization], January 17, 1923, DINY, 88–91.

34. "Chungsan kyegŭp ŭi iikchŏk undong" [A self-interested campaign of the middle class], *Donga Ilbo*, March 20, 1923; reprinted in Kim Chun-yŏp and Kim Ch'ang-sun, *Han'guk kongsanjuŭi undongsa* 2:18–19.

35. "Kŭndae sahoe sasangsa" [A history of modern social thought], *Kaebyŏk* 51 (Sept. 1924):10–11, 14.

36. "Onjŏng juŭi ŭi open gwa sahoejuŭi ŭi open" [Owen's kindliness and Owen's socialism], *Kaebyŏk* 54 (Dec. 1924):60.

37. "Chayukwŏn gwa saengiŏn kwon" [The right to be free and the right to exist]. DISN, 483–8.

38. Suh, *Korean Communist Movement*, 140.

39. Han'guk Inmyŏng Taesajŏn P'yŏnch'an Wiwŏnhoe, ed., *Han'guk inmyŏng taesajŏn* [A dictionary of eminent Koreans] (Seoul: Singu Munhwasa, 1967), 599.

40. "Minjokchŏk kyŏngnon [An economic argument for the nation]," January 2–6, 1924, DISN, 359–67.

41. K. M. Wells noted a similar view among many of the Korean Products Society leaders, as well as the continuity here with earlier enlightenment reformers such as Yu Kil-jun, Sŏ Chae-p'il, and Yun Ch'i-ho. See his "Rationale of Economic Nationalism," 852.

42. *Donga Ilbo*, February 28, 1923, p. 3.

43. *Donga Ilbo*, January 1, 1922, p. 5.

44. *Donga Ilbo*, January 1, 1926, part 3, p. 1.

45. *Donga Ilbo*, January 3, 1933, p. 1.

46. *Donga Ilbo*, January 1, 1933, p. 9.

47. Pak In-hwan, ed., *Kyŏngbang yuksimnyŏn* [Sixty years of the Kyŏngsŏng Spinning and Weaving Company] (Seoul: Samhwa Publishing, 1980), 63–4 (cited hereafter as *Kyŏngbang); Kim Sang-hong, ed., Sudang Kim Yŏn-su* [Sudang Kim Yŏn-su] (Seoul: Sudang Kinyŏm Saŏphoe, 1971), 95–6 (cited hereafter as *Sudang*).

48. *Donga Ilbo*, November 27, 1924.

49. *Donga Ilbo*, January 3, 1933, p. 6.

50. The estimates are derived from company statistics on landholdings, together with their policy of allotting at least two chŏngbo (i.e., about five acres) of land per family.

51. Kim Sang-hong, ed., *Samyang yuksimnyŏn* [Sixty years of the Samyang] (Seoul: Chusik Hoesa Samyangsa, 1984), 87, 94 (cited hereafter as *Samyang*).

52. *Donga Ilbo*, January 3, 1933, p. 4.

53. *Donga Ilbo*, June 15, 1934; also Kim Wŏn-tae, ed., *Fifty Years of Whashin* (Seoul: Whashin Industrial Company, 1977), 124–5 (cited hereafter as *Fifty Years*).

54. *Donga Ilbo*, March 26, 1933.

55. *Donga Ilbo*, April 8, 1932.

56. *Samyang*, 96.

57. *Fifty Years*, 114–16. The Donga rented space in a building owned by Min Kyu-sik.

58. *Fifty Years*, 118–19; also *Donga Ilbo*, August 22, 1932.

59. *Han'guk inmyŏng taesajŏn*, 255.

60. *Samyang*, 77–8, 118–19; *Sudang*, 227–9.

61. *Fifty Years*, 193–9.

62. *Maeil Sinpo*, September 12, 1941, p. 2; October 9, p. 2.

63. *Fifty Years*, 210–19; Civil Property Custodian, External Assets Division, General Headquarters, Supreme Commander of Allied Forces in the Pacific, *Japanese External Assets as of August, 1945*, vol. 1, "Korea," RG 59, National Archives, p. 149. (This title will be cited hereafter as JEA, along with the appropriate volume number.)

Chapter 3. Colonial state

1. The government-general was preceded by a Japanese residency-general in Korea during the Protectorate period from 1905 until annexation on August 29, 1910, with former premier Itō Hirobumi serving as resident-general (1906–9). The governor-generals were selected from among Japan's top military leaders. The following served in the post of governor-generals (*sōtoku*) in the colony of Korea (Chōsen): Gen. Terauchi Masatake (10/1/1910–10/9/1916); Gen. Hasegawa Yoshimichi (10/16/1916–8/12/1919); Adm. Saitō Makoto (8/12/1919–12/10/1927); Gen. Ugaki Kazushige (4/14/1927–10/1/1927); Gen. Yamanashi Hanzō (12/10/1927–8/17/1929); Adm. Saitō Minoru (8/17/1929–6/17/1931); Gen. Ugaki Kazushige (6/17/1931–8/5/1936); Gen. Minami Jirō (8/5/1936–6/15/1942); Gen. Koiso Kuniaki (6/15/1942–7/24/1944); Gen. Abe Nobuyuki (7/25/1944–8/15/1945). Chōsen Sōtokufu, *Shisei sanjūnen shi* [A thiry-year history of administration] (Keijō: Chōsen Insatsu Kabushiki Kaisha, 1940), Appendix: "Nempyō" [A chronology]. (This reference will be cited hereafter as Chronology.) Andrew C. Nahm, ed., *Korea Under Japanese Colonial Rule* (Kalamazoo: Center for Korean Studies, Western Michigan University, 1973), Appendix 1.

Due to the prominence and independence of the governor-general in Korea, the term "colonial state" in this study refers to the Government-General of Chōsen. Regarding the independence of the colonial administration, see Edward I-te Chen, "The Attempt to Integrate the Empire: Legal Perspectives," 262.

2. Alfred Stepan, *The State and Society: Peru in Comparative Perspective* (Princeton: Princeton University Press, 1978), xii.

3. Peter B. Evans and Dietrich Rueschemeyer, "The State and Economic Transformation: Toward an Analysis of the Conditions Underlying Effective Intervention," 44–77.

4. Stephen Krasner, *Defending the National Interest*, 56–7.

5. Imotani Zenichi, *Chōsen keizaishi* [A history of the Korean economy] (Tokyo: Daitōkaku, 1955), 165–73.

6. Norman Jacobs, *The Korean Road to Modernization and Development* (Urbana: University of Illinois Press, 1985).

7. Shikata Hiroshi, *Chōsen ni okeru kindai shihonshugi no seiritsu katei* [The formation of a modern capitalism in Korea], in the series, *Chōsen Shakai Keizaishi Kenkyū* [Studies in the social and economic history of Korea] (Keijō: Keijō Daigaku Hōbun Gakkai, 1933), 207–8.

8. See Yamabe Kentarō, *Nihon tōchika no Chōsen* [Korea under Japanese rule] (Tokyo: Iwanami Shoten, 1971); Suh Sang-chul, *Growth and Structural Change in the Korean Economy, 1910–1940*; Suzuki Takeo, *Chōsen keizai no shin kōsō* [New ideas in the Korean economy] (Tokyo: Taikaido Insatsu Kabushiki Kaisha, 1942),

3–35; Lee Chong-sik, *The Patterns of Korean Nationalism* (Berkeley: University of California Press, 1963); David Brudnoy, "Japan's Experiment in Korea," 155–95; Military Intelligence Service, War Department General Staff, "Historical Sketch of Japanese Administration in Korea since 1910," in *Survey of Korea* (Washington, DC: War Department, June 15, 1943), Appendix 8.

9. For a description of the economic role of peninsula industries in the empire in the last decade of colonial rule, see CKN, 1941–1942, 305–26.

10. Yanihara Tadao, "The Problems of Japanese Administration in Korea," *Pacific Affairs* 11, 2 (June 1938): 207. However, Dong Wonmo concluded that assimilation policy directives regarding Korean names and the Korean language were beginning to affect the wider population by the end of the colonial period. See his dissertation, "Japanese Colonial Policy and Practice in Korea, 1905–1945: A Study in Assimilation," Georgetown University, 1965.

11. Michael Mann, "The Autonomous Power of the State," 189.

12. Government-General of Chōsen, *Annual Report on Reforms and Progress in Chōsen, 1918–1921* (Keijō: Government-General, 1921), 227. A bridge over the Yalu had been completed in 1911, linking the system in Korea with the South Manchurian Railroad and Chinese Eastern Railroad. An Imperial Ordinance of July 31, 1917, granted operation of the state-owned railways in Korea to the South Manchuria Railway Company for a period of twenty years. Ibid., 135.

13. Office of Strategic Services, Research and Analysis Branch, Department of State, *Korea: Economic Survey*, August 5, 1942, R&A 744, RG 59, National Archives, p. 78.

14. The aggressive role of the Japanese state from the late nineteenth century in promoting industrial development in the home islands has been widely noted. See Harold G. Moulton, *Japan: An Economic and Financial Appraisal* (Washington, DC: Brookings, 1931); William W. Lockwood, "The State and Economic Enterprise in Modern Japan, 1868–1939," in Simon Kuznets, Wilbert E. Moore, and Joseph J, Spengler, eds., *Economic Growth: Brazil, India, Japan* (Durham: Duke University Press, 1955), 537–602; Henry Rosovsky, *Capital Formation in Japan*.

15. "During the period 1905–10, Japan wielded sufficient power and influence over Korea to promulgate certain laws. From 1910 to August, 1945, when the Instrument of Surrender was executed, resulting in severance of Korea from Japanese sovereignty, several bodies of law were in force in Korea. These were: (1) laws promulgated by the Japanese between 1905 and 1910; (2) Japanese Codes; (3) some branches of Korean Customary Law and a few unrepealed Korean statutes; (4) Imperial Ordinances of the Japanese Government particularly directed to Korean affairs; (5) Ordinances, orders, regulations and other laws of the Japanese Government-General in Korea, and (6) a qualified application of the Japanese Constitution."

See American Advisory Staff, Department of Justice, "Draft of Study on the Administration of Justice in Korea under the Japanese and in South Korea under the United States Army Military Government in Korea to 15 August 1948," (Seoul: USAMGIK, 1948), RG 407, Box 2067, National Archives, p. 1; also Jōyaku Kyoku Hōkika, "Nihon tōchi jidai no Chōsen [Korea under Japanese rule]," *Gaichi Hōseishi* 4 (March, 1966): 61–98; Kang Tŏk-sang and Kajimura Hideki, "Nitteika Chōsen no hōritsu seido ni tsuite" [The legal system in Korea under the Japanese Empire], in Fukushima Masao, ed., *Nihonhō to Ajia. Niida Noboru Hakasei Tsuite Ronbunshū* [Japanese law and Asia: essays in memory of Dr. Niida Noboru], no. 3 (Tokyo: Keiso Shobo, 1974), 319–37; Edward I-te Chen, "Attempt to Integrate"; Edward J. Baker, "The Role of Legal Reforms in the Japanese Annexation and Rule of Korea, 1905–1919," in David McCann et al., eds., *Studies on Korea in Transition* (Honolulu: Center for Korean Studies, 1979), 17–42.

16. The subsequent government-general would undertake a cadastral survey with the same purpose. Residency-General of Korea, *Annual Report for 1907 on Reforms and Progress in Korea* (Keijō Residency-General, 1908). (These annual reports will be cited hereafter as *Annual Report* along with the appropriate year.)

One immediate problem was ambiguity in ownership of property, which led to the "Land and Building Certification Regulations" of October 31, 1906. "The fundamental object of this law is to guarantee to natives as well as to foreigners, legitimate rights of ownership of real estate."

17. The industrial policy from 1937 included legislation to control capital, natural resources, labor, land, and markets. See Hŏ Su-ryul, "1930 nyŏndae kunyo kongŏphwa chŏngch'aek kwa Ilbon tokchŏm chabon ŭi chinch'ul [The industrialization policy for military needs in the 1930s, and the advance of Japanese monopoly capital]," in Ch'a Ki-byŏk, ed., *Ilche ŭi Han'guk singmin t'ongchi* [The colonial administration of Korea under Japanese rule] (Seoul: Chŏngŭmsa, 1985), 228–88.

Nakamura Takafusa has described wartime controls in financial and commodity markets in his *Economic Growth in Prewar Japan* (New Haven: Yale University Press, 1983), 263–301; also Jerome Cohen, *Japan's Economy in War and Reconstruction* (Minneapolis: University of Minnesota, 1949).

18. Three types of registered business enterprises were permitted in colonial Korea. Most medium-sized and larger firms were incorporated as share or "joint-stock" corporations with limited liability (*kabushiki kaisha*; Korean, *chusik hoesa*). There were also two types of partnerships. In limited partnerships (*gōshi kaisha*; Korean, *hapcha hoesa*), one or more partners were liable only to the amount of their equity contribution. There were also unlimited partnerships (*gōmei kaisha*; Korean, *hammyŏng hoesa*) with unlimited liability. See Foreign Economic Administration, Enemy Branch, *Japanese Economic Penetration into Korea as of 1940 as Shown by an Analysis of Corporations Operating in Korea* (Washington, DC: State Department, October 23, 1945), 3–4; Lee Hoon K., *Land Utilization and Rural Economy in Korea* (New York: Greenwood, 1969), 33.

Some 86% of the 1,945 companies registered in Korea with an authorized capital of 100 thousand yen or more in 1940 were joint-stock corporations, as are almost all the companies of interest in this study. There were two prominent exceptions, both in agriculture: Kim Yŏn-su and his sons organized the Samyang as a limited partnership, and Min Kyu-sik and his sons maintained the Yŏngbo company as an unlimited partnership.

The joint-stock corporations were registered with an authorized capital, representing the total face value of all their individual shares. Shareholders were required to pay in at least 25% of the face value of each share, and these funds were called the "paid-in" or paid-up capital. The paid-in capital represents the funds actually invested, and the authorized capital represents the legal ceiling on funds that might be invested.

The joint-stock corporations were led by a president (*shachō*; Korean, *sajang*), who also served often as the representative director (*daihyō torishimariyaku*; Korean, *taep'yo ch'wich'eyŏk*), and sometimes in very large corporations by a chair of the board (*kaichō*; Korean, *hoejang*). A senior or executive director (*senmu torishimariyaku*; Korean, *chŏnmu ch'wich'eyŏk*) oversaw large units of the enterprise, and a managing director (*jōmu torishimariyaku*; Korean, *sangmu ch'wich'eyŏk*) supervised a number of departments or smaller divisions. The ordinary directors included both managers from within the company, and outside directors either from among major business leaders with investments in the company or special expertise or contacts, or from among a pool of retired civil servants. The board also included auditors (*kansayaku*; Korean, *kamsayŏk*). See Rodney Clark, *The Japanese Company* (New Haven: Yale

University Press, 1979), 100–1.

19. Chōsen Tōkanfu, *Kanbo* [Official Gazette], April 30, 1906, no. 3440, pp. 333–5. The regulations affected only Korean, not Japanese banks on the peninsula. Approval of the Minister of Finance was required "for establishment of a new bank, floating of debentures, and for establishment or abolition of a branch office or agency. He is further empowered to order investigations into the business conditions and property of a bank, whenever his judgment suggests such a course. At the end of each half year, every bank must prepare, and present to the Finance Ministry, a balance sheet and other reports, and must publish the balance sheet in the newspapers or by other means." *Annual Report*, 1907, 55.

20. Chōsen Sōtokufu, *Hōreishū* [Collection of laws] (Keijō: Chōsen Sōtokufu, 1936), 16–17. *Annual Report*, 1929, 50–1.

21. See Ikeshima Hiroyuki, "Nihon ni okeru kigyōhō no keisei to tenkai" [The formation and development of enterprise legislation in Japan], in Takayanagi Shinichi and Fujita, eds., *Shihonsugihō no keisei to tenkai* [The formation and development of capitalist law] (Tokyo: University of Tokyo Press, 1973), 233–4.

22. Chōsen Sōtokufu, *Chōsen Sōtokufu Kanbo* [Official Gazette of the Government-General], February 24, 1928, 1–3.

23. The administration argued such laws were originally necessary to stabilize commerce and prevent "establishment of illegal and bubble companies," but "as the progress of the times made the interference of the government unnecessary, these regulations were abolished in March, 1920." *Annual Report*, 1918–1921, 119.

24. The law was rescinded on April 1, 1920. Chronology, 10, 24. The text of the fourteen articles of the original law together with revisions can be found in Chōsen Sōtokufu, *Chōsen hōrei shūran* [A collection of legislation in Korea] (Tokyo: Teikoku Chihō Kyōsei Gakkai Chōsen Honbu, 1938), vol. 2, sec. 17, "Industry," pt. 2, "Companies," 158–60.

25. In 1910, 152 companies with headquarters on the peninsula were registered, and 571 in 1920. See "Chōsen tōka naichi shihon gokorei ni yoru jigyō" [The enterprises of Japanese capital invested in Korea], *Shokugin Chōsa Geppō*, no. 65(June 1940): 32. The number of factories increased from 252 in 1911 to 2,087 in 1920, employing 14,500 workers at the beginning of the decade and 55,000 by 1920, while capital invested in factories increased from 10 million to 160 million yen. "Chōsen no kōgyō go kōjō [Industrial factories in Korea] *Shokugin Chōsa Geppō*, no. 58 (Dec. 1939): 58.

26. Ikeshima Hiroyuki, "Nihon ni okeru kigyōhō no keisei to tenkai," 213–14. The Commercial and Civil Codes in Japan were made applicable to Korea on March 18, 1922, in the Chōsen Civil Affairs Ordinance. Chronology, 12; American Advisory Staff, "Draft of Study on the Administration of Justice," 1.

27. A list of the control laws can be found in Chronology.

28. Chronology, 8. The bureau was dissolved by an ordinance of November 5, 1918. Ibid., 21.

29. *Annual Report*, 1911, 13.

30. There was distinction between privately owned land (*sajŏn*) and publicly or "state-owned" land (*kongjŏn*), although government land grants to private interests and cultivation rights on public land were not always clear. See Pak Ki-hyuk et al., *A Study of Land Tenure System in Korea* (Seoul: Korea Land Economics Research Center, 1966). For a study of the process and results of the cadastral survey, see Miyajima Hiroshi, "Chosŏn t'oji chosa saŏp yŏn'gu sŏsŏl" [An introduction to studies on the land survey in Korea], in Kajimura Hideki, ed., *Han'guk kŭndae kyŏngje yŏn'gu* [Studies in the modern economic history of Korea] (Seoul: Sagyejŏl Printing, 1983), 299–330; Edwin Gragert, "Landownership Change in Korea under Japanese

Colonial Rule: 1900–1935" (Ph.D. diss., Columbia University, 1982); Kim Hyun-kil, "Land Use Policy in Korea with Special Reference to the Oriental Development Company" (Ph.D. diss., University of Washington, 1971).

31. Major Japanese and Korean agricultural companies and individuals are described in Ōhashi Seizaburō et al., eds., *Chōsen sangyō shishin* [A guide to industry in Korea] (Tokyo: Kawabata Kentarō, 1915).

32. Civil Property Custodian, External Assets Division, General Headquarters, Supreme Commander of Allied Forces in the Pacific, *Japanese External Assets as of August 1945*, Vol. 1, "Korea," revised September 30, 1948, RG 59, National Archives. (The materials will be cited hereafter as JEA 1).

33. See Karl Moskowitz, "The Creation of the Oriental Development Company: Japanese Illusion Meets Korean Reality," in James B. Palais, ed., *Occasional Papers on Korea*, No. 1 (Seattle: Joint Committee on Korean Studies of the American Council of Learned Societies and the Social Science Research Council, 1974), 73–109.

34. Data on total assets would provide a more useful indicator of the size of a financial or industrial investment than paid-in capital. Estimates of total assets of Japanese corporations on the Korean peninsula in 1945 were gathered by the U.S. Military command in Tokyo following the war. Officials then correlated totals submitted by the companies with earlier company reports and public records, as well as with on-site investigations on the southern half of the peninsula. The investigators were permitted only a limited inspection of certain factories in the northern section of the peninsula under Russian supervision, and since much of the Japanese industrial investment was located in the north, the lack of on-site reports somewhat diminishes the credibility of the project. A further difficulty for the investigators was the exchange rate between the U.S. dollar and the wartime Japanese yen. The estimates were published in dollars at an exchange rate of fifteen yen per dollar. The estimated assets of the ODC in Korea in 1945 amounted to 1.2 billion yen. JEA 1:157.

35. Tōa Keizai Shinpōsha (Nakamura Sukeryō, ed.), *Chōsen ginkō kaisha kumiai yōroku* [A list of banks, firms, and partnerships in Korea] (Keijō: Tōa Keizai Shinpōsha, annual). (The annual editions of this list will be cited hereafter as CGKKY.) CGKKY, 1941, 642–3; DKB, 1942, 75.

36. A list of ODC investments can be found in Foreign Economic Administration, *Japanese Economic Penetration*, 15.

37. The bank was originally chartered as the Bank of Korea in 1909 under legislation establishing a central bank, and organized as a joint-stock corporation by the end of October with one hundred thousand shares representing a capital of 10 million yen. The Korean government held thirty thousand shares, with the rest sold to Japanese and Korean interests. The name was changed to Bank of Chōsen in March 1911. Chronology, 7, 10. See also Koh Sung-jae, "The Role of the Bank of Chōsen (Korea) and the Japanese Expansion in Manchuria and China," *Journal of Social Sciences and Humanities* 32 (June 1970): 25–36.

The bank was registered with a paid-in capital of 25 million yen in 1927, and 30 million yen in 1941. The Bank of Chōsen was listed with estimated assets in 1945 of 96.4 million yen. See CGKKY; also JEA 1:149.

38. The bank listed a total of 5,824 shareholders with a total of 400,000 shares in 1941. Other corporate investors included the Itō Manufacturing Company, Chōsen Commercial Bank, the Tongil Bank, Chōsen Trust, and the Korean Royal Household.

39. See Chōsen Shokusan Ginkō, *Chōsen Shokusan Ginkō nijūnen shi* [A twenty-year history of the Chōsen Industrial Bank] (Keijō: Industrial Bank, 1938); Karl

Moskowitz, "Current Assets: The Employees of Japanese Banks in Colonial Korea" (Ph.D. diss., Harvard University, 1979), 32–8; Takasugi Tōgō, *Chōsen kinyū kikan hattatsu shi* [A history of the development of financial institutions in Korea] (Keijō: Jitsugyō Taimususha, 1940), 601–16.

A brief comparison of the Industrial Bank with commercial banks on the peninsula can be found in Pak Hŭng-sŏ, ed., *Hanil Unhaeng sasimnyŏnsa* [A history of forty years of the Hanil Bank] (Seoul: Samsŏng, 1972), 21–5. The legislation establishing the regional development banks in 1906, i.e., "Agriculture and Industry Banks" (Hōkō Ginkō), and the Industrial Bank in 1918 is briefly described in Chronology, 3, 21.

40. CGKKY, 1927, 3; 1941, 2. The Industrial Bank was listed with estimated assets in Korea in 1945 of 151 million yen. JEA 1:153.

41. Although the Chōsen Savings Bank (Chōsen Chochiku Ginkō) was spun off from the Industrial Bank in 1929, the Industrial Bank retained over 50% of the shares. CGKKY, 1941, 4–5.

42. The Chōsen Trust Company (Chōsen Shintaku) was founded in December of 1932 with headquarters in Seoul. By 1941 it was registered with an authorized capital of 10 million yen, with 2.5 million paid-in, and six branches across the peninsula. Han Sang-yong served as president, and Pak Yŏng-ch'ŏl (until his death in 1939), Min Tae-sik, and Kim Yŏn-su served on the board. The Bank of Chōsen and Industrial Bank held 30% each of the total shares available in 1934, and 37.5% each by 1941. CGKKY, 1934, 16; 1941, 17–18. The trust company held 5% of the shares available in the Chōsen Petroleum Company, 4% of the Keijō Electric Company shares, and 3% of the shares available in the North Korea Paper and Chemical Manufacture in 1941.

43. The Industrial Bank was listed as the sole major shareholder in this company, founded in 1931 with headquarters in Seoul for the purpose of real estate transactions and agricultural administration. The company was registered in 1941 with an authorized capital of two million yen, with five hundred thousand yen paid-in. CGKKY, 1941, 303. The company's estimated total assets in Korea in 1945 amounted to fifty-seven million yen. JEA 1:157.

44. The funding process is described in Lee Hoon K., *Land Utilization*, 124. A list of the major Japanese firms and their reclamation projects can be found in the *Chōsen Shokusan Ginkō nijūnen shi*, 118–120. The Hamp'yŏng and Haeri reclamation projects of the Samyang Company are described in *Samyang*.

45. See *Kyŏngbang*, 523, 107.

46. *Fifty Years*, 129.

47. *Fifty Years*, 127–8.

48. *Chōsen Shokusan Ginkō nijūnen shi*, 265–6.

49. See Yamakawa Chikashi, *Jigyō oyobi jinbutsu* [Enterprise and entrepreneurs] (Tokyo: Tokyo Dempō Tsūshinsha, 1941), 314; Abe Kaoru, *Chōsen kōrōsha meikan*, 50; WWJ, 1939, 50. The Industrial Bank and Keishun Railway Company each held 16% of the shares in the hydroelectric company, while Samyang held 1.7%.

50. Shibuya Reiji was listed as executive director, and the names of Pak Hŭng-sik and Nakatomi Kazuō of Kyŏngsŏng Spinning appeared as ordinary directors. The company in turn invested in Ha Chun-sŏk's Dōka Industries, and Dōa Trade in which Kim Yŏn-su was active. CGKKY, 1941, 532.

51. Chronology, 9.

52. *Annual Report*, 1918–21, 31.

53. *Annual Report*, 1929, 34. A list of the names can be found in Shakuo Shunjō, *Chōsen heigōshi: ichimei, Chōsen saikinshi* [Annexation of Korea: the first chapter, Korea's recent history] (Keijō: Chōsen oyobi Manshūsha, 1926), 606–8.

54. The Central Advisory Council (*chūsūin*; Korea, *chungch'uwŏn*), was described officially as an advisory group of the governor-general. "The *Central Council,* the highest Korean advisory organ, is consulted by the Governor-General. After amalgamation in 1910, the organic regulations for this Council were issued with the object of providing the Governor-General with a Consulting Organ on administrative measures. The officials of the Council are composed of the chairman, advisers, members, chief secretary, secretary and Interpreter Secretary. In 1921, revision was made in its organization by which treatment of its members was improved, restriction in their voting power withdrawn, their term of service fixed, etc. . . . It appoints standing Committees among its members, and conducts various investigations on questions of Economy, Industry, Arts, Science, Social and other Systems, in addition to those of administration, under the name of the Administrative Investigation Society, in compliance with the requests of the Governor-General, and on other questions deemed necessary by the Council itself. . . . The Central Council consists of 64 members, and 3 advisers under the Chairmanship of the Vice Governor-General (Civil Administrator), but with its own vice-chairman." *Annual Report,* 1937, 42–3.

U.S. intelligence officials were alert to the activities of the Central Advisory Council, putting together resumes at the end of the colonial period of Korean members called "targets." The design and activities of the Council were summarized in a report of April 1945.

"The Central Advisory Council is the only nation-wide body approaching legislative status, but as can be seen from its name, its function is purely advisory. Its 65 councilors are appointed by the Governor-General from the Korean *yangban* or wealthy class for a term of 3 years. The Civil Administrator, a Japanese, acts as the chairman of the council.

This body can offer advice only upon the request of the Governor-General and then upon a specific subject. The Governor is under no obligation to follow the advice given by the Council, and while its recommendations have sometimes been put into effect, in practice its advice has been asked only on matters of lesser importance. It has therefore, achieved very little in securing political advantages for the Korean and, in fact, its members have been chosen not because of their qualities of leadership, but because the Japanese wanted to give some semblance of "face" to the old ruling class of Korea. Those who have shown any anti-Japanese sentiments have never been chosen for the Council; the Council members are either elderly persons who helped sell out the old Korean regime to Japan or are new officers of companies which have as their purpose the consolidation of Japanese control over Korean assets." JANIS, X15.

55. I have examined the chamber in an article titled, "The Keishō and the Korean Business Elite," *Journal of Asian Studies* 48, 2 (May 1989): 310–23. The names of these associations in Korea and Japan were changed by government ordinace from "chamber of commerce" to "chamber of commerce and industry" in 1927.

56. Chōsen Shōkō Kaigisho, *Zensen shōkō kaigisho hattenshi* [A history of the development of chambers of commerce in Korea] (Pusan: Fuzan Nippōsha, 1935), 71–2.

57. Ibid., 4–8.

58. The Chambers of Commerce Law was promulgated on July 15, 1915. Chronology, 17. The administration provided its own explanation for the legislation. "In 1915 regulations for Chambers of Commerce were promulgated, as these had been established by Japanese and Korean separately and worked independently in one and the same locality. These regulations allowed only one Chamber of Commerce to exist in any one locality, to membership of which Japanese and Korean were equally eligible. The status of juridical persons were given them, and their system, competency and supervision were duly set forth." *Annual Report*, 1918–21, 119.

59. See Keijo Shōkō Kaigisho, *Keijō Shōkō Kaigisho nijūgo nenshi* [A twenty-five year history of the Keijō Chamber of Commerce and Industry] (Keijō: Keijō Shōkō Kaigisho, 1941). Ariga Mitsutoyo of the Chōsen Industrial Bank and Pak Yong-ch'ŏl of the Chōsen Commercial Bank participated as advisors. The annual budget of the organization grew from 4,000 yen in 1916 to 280,000 yen in 1940, while membership increased from 586 in 1916 to 5,056 in 1940. Ibid., 147.

60. Keijō Shōkō Kaigisho, *Tōkei nempō 1940* [Statistical annual, 1940] (Keijō: Keijō Shōkō Kaigisho), 138.

61. Abe Kaoru, *Chōsen kōrōsha meikan*, 86.

62. Ibid., 51.

63. Pak Hŭng-sik was president of the National Association of Department Stores (Zenkoku Hyakkaten Kumiai), established by department store owners on the peninsula on May 10, 1940. CKN, 1941–42; Chronology, 17. He was also a representative on the Japan Industrial Economy Commission (Nihon Sangyō Keizai Iinkai) during the Pacific War. Ko Wŏn-sŏp, *Panminja choesanggi*, 19.

64. For examples of publications by the association, see their *Chōsen kōjō meiran* [List of factories in Korea], (Keijō: Chōsen Kōgyō Kyōkai, 1932, 1936, 1940), or *Chōsen no kōgyō to sono shigen* [Industry and industrial resources in Korea] (Keijō: Chōsen Kōgyō Kyōkai, 1937).

65. *Chōsen kōrōsha meikan*, 37–8.

66. Shibuya Reiji, "Chōsen ni okeru kōgyō kankei shokikan oyobi shuppanbutsu" [Industry in Korea: related government agencies and publications], in *Chōsen no kōgyō to sono shigen*, 48–64.

67. Ibid., 52.

68. Useem, "Social Organization of American Business Elite," 557–8.

69. See "Chōsen tōka naichi shihon gokorei ni yoru jigyō," 20; U.S. Department of State, Office of Advisor to the Commanding General, U.S. Forces Korea, "A Review of Fiscal Operations of the U.S. Military Government in Korea," December 1, 1946, RG 407, Box 2058, National Archives, pp. 2–7.

70. Bruce Cumings, "The Legacy of Japanese Colonialism in Korea," in *The Japanese Colonial Empire*, 489; Hyman Kublin, "The Evolution of Japanese Colonialism," *Comparative Studies in Society and History* 2, 1(Oct. 1959): 81.

Chapter 4. Japanese investment

1. Early Japanese investors formulated their own ideology of altruism and national purpose in efforts on the Korean frontier. They argued investment on the peninsula was not only good business, it was also an effort at economic modernization to save Korean society from internal dissolution. See my article, "A Frontier Ideology: Meiji Japan and the Korean Frontier," *The Journal of International Studies* 12 (Jan. 1984): 43–64.

2. Nichitsu is an abbreviation for the Japanese name of the company, Nippon Chisso Hiryō (Japan Nitrogenous Fertilizers Company). The firm founded a Korean subsidiary (Chōsen Chisso Hiryō) in 1927, absorbed by the mother company in 1941. Other zaibatsu with interests in Korea included Asano, Manchuria Heavy Industry Development Corporation, Mori, Nippon Soda Company, Nippon Iron Manufacturing Company, Riken (Physico-Chemical Research Institute), Sumitomo, and Yasuda.

See Foreign Economic Administration, *Japanese Economic Penetration*, 19. This was a statistical study based on data available in TGKY, 1940. The review was limited to the 1,945 firms registered on the peninsula with an authorized capital of 100 thousand yen or more.

3. Yanihara Tadao, "Problems of Japanese Administration," 204.

4. Yasuoka Shigeaki, "Capital Ownership in Family Companies: Japanese Firms Compared with Those in Other Countries," in Akio Okochi and Yasuoka Shigeaki, eds., *Family Business in the Era of Industrial Growth: Its Ownership and Management* (Tokyo: University of Tokyo Press, 1983), 1.

5. Miyamoto Matao, "The Position and Role of Family Business in the Development of the Japanese Company System," in Okochi and Yasuoka, *Family Business*, 56–67.

6. The government soon rescinded the unfavorable rates for partnerships. "The tax reform of 1920 made the tax rate uniform for every type of corporation; the rate varied only with the amount of corporate income." Ibid., 63; see also Ikeshima Hiroyuki, "Nihon niokeru kigyōhō no keisei to tenkai," 208–9, 213–14, 231ff. Ikeshima described careful efforts of the Japanese government to foster and then control the "joint-stock company boom" from the time of World War I.

7. "Non-family subscribers who were offered stocks were not members of the general public, but rather were individuals who had personal connections with the companies, such as the managers and other employees of these firms." Ikeshima, 61.

8. Robert A. Scalapino, *Democracy and the Party Movement in Prewar Japan. The Failure of the First Attempt* (Berkeley: University of California Press, 1953), 266–73.

9. Ishida Takeshi, "The Development of Interest Groups," 297; Arnold Heidenheimer and Frank Langdon, *Business Associations and the Financing of Political Parties*, 140–69; Yanaga Chitoshi, *Big Business in Japanese Politics* (New Haven: Yale University Press, 1968).

10. Ishida Takeshi, "The Development of Interest Groups," 297.

11. "Chōsen tōka naichi shihon gokorei ni yoru jigyō," 32.

12. *Japanese Economic Penetration*, v, 9–10. The term "production establishment" refers to facilities of "production, extraction, or processing of any commodity or article including minerals, fish, and agricultural products, for generation of electric power, and for railway transportation."

13. Corwin D. Edwards, et al., *Report of Mission on Japanese Combines*, March, 1946, General Headquarters, Supreme Commander for the Allied Powers, RG 407, National Archives, 1:51 (hereafter cited as *Japanese Combines*).

14. Ibid., 51–2.

15. T. A. Bisson, *Zaibatsu Dissolution in Japan* (Westport, CT: Greenwood Press, 1976), Appendix. See also, *Japanese Economic Penetration*, 12–13.

16. JEA 1:155. Mitsui Bussan was listed with a paid-in capital of 204.7 million yen in 1941, prior to the war and loss of assets in Korea, Manchuria, and China. CGKKY, 1941, 654.

17. Chronology, 25.

18. Ibid., 158–9.

19. *Annual Report*, 1936, 56. See also Statistical Research Division of the Office of Administration, "Ginseng," in *Summation of U.S. Army Military Government Activities in Korea*, vol. 2, June 1946, 150–9, Box 2105, RG 407, National Archives.

20. Pak was organizing the Chōsen Aircraft Industry Company at the time.

21. Tōyō Silk Manufacture (Tōyō Seishi) was listed with an authorized and paid-in capital of 2.4 million yen in 1942. DKB, 1942, 63–4. The Nanboku Cotton Manufacturing Company (Nanboku Mengyō) registered an authorized and paid-in capital of 2 million yen in 1942. DKB, 1942, 61.

22. Ch'oe Ch'ang-hak had founded the mining venture in 1914, and made a

fortune in the sale to Mitsui fifteen years later. See Nakanishi Toshiru, *Shin Nihon jinbutsu taikai* [A new directory of prominent Japanese] (Tokyo: Tōhō Keizai Gakusha, 1936), 54; *Chōsen kōrōsha meikan*, 521–2.

Established in 1928, Sansei Mining (Sansei Kōgyō) was listed with an authorized and paid-in capital of five million yen in 1942. DKB, 1942, 23.

23. Nippon Flour Milling Company (Nippon Seifun) held estimated assets on the peninsula in 1945 of 64.5 million yen. JEA 1:156.

24. See Bisson, *Zaibatsu Dissolution*, Appendix. Information on Mitsubishi investments is provided in *Japanese Combines*.

25. DKB, 1942, 45; JEA 1:150.

26. CKN, 1941–2, 122–6. See also Hŏ Su-ryul, "1930 nyŏndae kunyo kongŏphwa chongch'ack," 240–3, 257–9, regarding policy on gold production and development of the Mozan deposits.

27. DKB, 1942, 34; JEA 1:155. The Japanese government itself held over half the shares of the Japan Iron Manufacturing (Nippon Seitetsu). *Japanese Economic Penetration*, 13–14.

28. DKB, 1942, 30; JEA 1:149.

29. Both Mitsubishi and Mitsui were also major shareholders in a state-supported mining venture from 1938. Japan Gold Mining (Nippon Sankin Shinkō) was established in September of 1938 for mining and refining on the peninsula. The company was listed with an authorized capital of fifty million yen in 1941, with thirty million yen paid-in. The Japanese government owned 50% of the shares, and Mitsui, Mitsubishi, and Sumitomo were also major shareholders. CGKKY, 1941, 650–1; Keijō Nippōsha, *Chōsen nenkan, 1942* [Chōsen annual, 1942] (Keijō: Keijō Nippōsha, 1942), 26–7. Kim Yŏn-su joined with Japan Gold Mining and gained state support as well to form Okkye Gold for development of his gold mines in Kangwŏn Province.

30. JEA 1:156. A list of Nichitsu firms and affiliates is provided in DKB, 1942, 254–5. For a more detailed study of Nichitsu investment in Korea, see two essays of Kobayashi Hideo: "1930 nendai Chōsen kōgyōka seisaku no tenkai katei" [Development of a Korean industrialization policy in the 1930s], *Chōsenshi Kenkyūkai Ronbunshū* 3 (1968): 164–70; "1930 nendai Nippon Chisso Hiryō Kabushiki Kaisha no Chōsen e no shishutsu ni tsuite" [The advance of Japan Nitrogenous Fertilizers into Korea in the 1930s], in Yamada Hideo, ed., *Shokuminchi keizaishi no shomondai* [Issues in colonial economic history] (Tokyo: Institute of Developing Economies, 1973), 139–89. The investment portfolio of Noguchi is briefly described in WWJ, 1939, 692–3.

The plant director of the Chōsen Nitrogenous Fertilizers company, Shiraishi Munenari, described the history and present status of the firm in his "Chōsen ni okeru chisso hiryō kōgyō ni tsuite" [The production of nitrogenous fertilizer in Korea], in Chōsen Kōgyō Kyōkai, *Chōsen kōgyō to sono shigen*, pt. 2, 152–68.

31. Chōsen Hydroelectric Power (Chōsen Suiryoku Denki) was listed with an authorized and paid-in capital in 1942 of 150 million yen. DKB, 1942, 20.

32. Investors organized the Chōsen Electricity Transmission Company (Chōsen Sōden) in 1934 with headquarters in Tokyo. The company was listed with an authorized capital of thirty million yen in 1942, and twenty-two million yen paid-in. Chōsen Hydroelectric held 44% of the shares, the ODC 17%, and Nichitsu 8%. DKB, 1942, 20.

33. Government contract published April 30, 1934. Chronology, 51.

34. August 20, 1937. Chronology, 60.

35. *JANIS*, IX40.

36. JEA 1:151. The Chōsen Yalu River Hydro-electric Generation Company (Chōsen Oryokkō Hatsuden) was founded in 1937. The company listed an authorized and paid-in capital of 50 million yen in 1942. DKB, 1942, 21.

37. DKB, 1942, 50.

38. Established in 1935, Chōsen Synthetic Oil (Chōsen Jinzō Sekiyu) listed an authorized and paid-in capital in 1942 of ten million yen. DKB, 1942, 51.

39. The Chōsen Nitrogenous Gunpowder Company (Chōsen Chisso Kayaku) was founded in 1935 with a paid-in capital of 10 million yen and a plant at Hŭngnam. See Hŏ Su-ryul, "1930 nyŏndae kunyo kongŏphwa chongch'aek," 273. The company was listed with estimated total assets in Korea in 1945 of 250 million yen. JEA 1:151; Office of Strategic Services, *Korea. Economic Survey*, 36–7.

40. *JANIS*, ix31.

41. "Chōsen tōka naichi shihon gokorei ni yoru jigyō," 35.

42. Data presented here are based on bank company reports published in CGKKY, 1941.

43. "Chōsen tōka naichi shihon gokorei ni yoru jigyō," 35. Note that the capital investment of Kanegafuchi branch plants, the largest Japanese textile ventures on the peninsula, were not included in this comparison.

44. Foreign Economic Administration, Enemy Branch, Japanese Special Services Staff, *Summary Industrial Survey of Korea*, April 17, 1945, RG 407, National Archives, 114.

45. CGKKY, 1941, 128, 632–3, 635. Kyŏngsŏng raised its paid-in capital to 5 million yen the next year, 7.5 million by 1942, and 10.5 million in 1944. The total estimated assets of Kanegafuchi's textile plants in Seoul and Kwangju in 1945 amounted to 425.5 million yen. The textile plants represented only 37% of the total investment on the peninsula of Kanegafuchi Industries. JEA 1:75, 83, 154.

Tōyō Cotton Spinning (Tōyō Bōseki) was listed with total estimated assets in Korea in 1945 of 262 million yen. JEA 1:159. Dai Nippon Cotton Spinning (Dai Nippon Bōseki) also operated plants on the peninsula, with estimated total assets in 1945 of 360 million yen. JEA 1:152.

46. Sakoma Fusatarō of Sakoma Shōkai in Pusan was a major investor as well. Chūgai Industries (Chūgai Sangyyō) succeeded the Chūgai Investment Company (Chūgai Tōshi) as the major investor in 1941. See pertinent years of CGKKY. Chōsen Spinning was listed with total estimated assets in Korea in 1945 of 285 million yen. JEA 1:150.

47. "Chōsen tōka naichi shihon gokorei ni yoru jigyō," 35.

48. CGKKY, 1941, 654.

49. CGKKY, 1941, 84, 149, 437, 472. Records of business taxes paid in 1942 suggest more parity among the firms than the paid-in capital figures: Mitsukoshi – 16,686 yen; Chōjiya – 14,302 yen; Hwasin – 10,930 yen; and Minakai – 9,551 yen. See Keijo Shōkō Kaigisho, *Keijō shōkō meikan* [A list of prominent commercial ventures] (Keijō: Keijō Shōkō Kaigisho, 1943).

50. See Nakamura Takafusa, *Economic Growth in Prewar Japan*, 203–13. Nakamura highlighted concentration in banking in the interwar years, characterized by mergers and expansion of zaibatsu control.

Chapter 5. Finance

1. See Lew Young-ick, "The Kabo Reform Movement: Korean and Japanese Reform Efforts in Korea, 1894" (Ph.D. diss., Harvard University, 1972), 5–14; Harold F. Cook, *Korea's 1884 Incident* (Seoul: Royal Asiatic Society, 1972), and

Martina Deuchler, *Confucian Gentlemen and Barbarian Envoys* (Seattle: University of Washington, 1977).

2. Recognizing the political and economic power of the Min clan from an area near Ch'ŏngju in North Ch'ungch'ŏng Province, the government-general awarded titles of nobility and financial awards to no less than eight Min families in 1911. A list of the six marquis, three counts, twenty-one viscounts, and forty-five barons appointed by the governor-general is provided in Shakuo Shunjo, *Chōsen heigōshi: ichimei, Chōsen saikinshi,* 607–9.

3. "The banking system was created in advance of the industrial demand for its loans and other financial services, and also in advance of the demand of individual savers for monetary and time deposits. This was achieved by de facto government subsidies combined with the responsiveness of entrepreneurs to the profit opportunities offered by banking." Patrick, "Japan," 277.

4. Pak Hŭng-sŏ reviewed the development of colonial banking, trust, and investment companies in Chapter 2 of his *Hanil Ŭnhaeng sasimnyŏnsa* [A forty-year history of the Hanil Bank] (Seoul: Samsŏng, 1972), 14–77. In Table I–6 (p. 14), the editor provided comparative data on deposits and loans of the "special banks" such as the Bank of Chōsen, the Industrial Bank, and also of the "ordinary" commercial banks. In 1940 the Industrial Bank itself provided better than twice the amount of loans extended by all the ordinary banks combined.

Koh Seung-jae has traced the history of the Bank of Chōsen in his article, "The Role of the Bank of Chōsen (Korea) and the Japanese Expansion in Manchuria and China." A detailed study of Koreans working in the Chōsen Industrial Bank can be found in Karl Moskowitz, "Current Assets." Brief histories and a public record of deposits, loans, dividends, as well as of major administrators and shareholders are available in annual editions of CGKKY.

5. See, for instance, Shin Yong-ha, "Landlordism in the Late Yi Dynasty," *Korea Journal* 18 (June 1978): 25–32, and 18 (July 1978): 22–9.

6. Chōsen Shokusan Ginkō, Chōsabu, "Chōsen ni okeru dochaku shihon no kenkyū [A study of indigenous capital in Korea]," *Shokugin Chosa Geppō* (Apr. 1938): 3.

7. "Chōsen ni okeru dochaku shihon no kenkyū [A study of indigenous capital in Korea], *Shokugin Chosa Geppō,* no. 59 (1943): 3–6.

8. Kim Yŏn-su, "Kim Yŏn-su," in Wŏllo Kiŏbin, eds., *Chaegye hoego* [Memories of the business world] (Seoul: Han'guk Ilbosa, 1981), 1:83–4.

9. Chung Young-iob, "Korean Investment under Japanese Rule," in C. I. Eugene Kim and Doretha E. Mortimore, eds., *Korea's Response to Japan: the Colonial Period, 1910–1945* (Kalamazoo: Western Michigan University, 1977), 33.

10. CGKKY, 1921.

11. More sympathetic than most to Japan's role on the peninsula, Han did not oppose annexation in 1910. See Han Sang-yong, *Kan Soryū Kun o wataru* [Reflections of Han Sang-yong] (Keijō: Kan Saryū Kun Kanreki Kinenkai, 1941), 130. Unlike Kim Yŏn-su or Pak Hŭng-sik, Han Sang-yong accepted appointment as a Councillor on the Central Advisory Council for the government-general (pp. 270–3), and wrote proudly of his connections with prominent Japanese financiers such as Shibusawa Eiichi (pp. 340–4, 362–5). Han's career has been summarized in the following: Abe Kaoru, *Chōsen kōrōsha meikan,* 69; Shimamoto Susumi *Chōsen zaikai no hitobito* [Prominent figures in Korean business circles] (Keijō: Keijō Shishinsha, 1941), 60–1; Cho Ki-jun, *Han'guk kiŏpkasa,* 123–39. See also descriptions of Han Sang-yong in Im Chong-sik, *Ilche ch'imnyak kwa ch'inilp'a* [Pro-Japanese groups and aggression under Japanese imperialism] (Seoul: Ch'ŏngsa, 1982), 112; Kang Tong-jin, *Ilche ŭi Han'guk ch'imnyak chŏngch'aeksa,* 215–16.

12. Hao Yen-P'ing *The Comprador in Nineteenth Century China,* 1; Idem., *The Commercial Revolution in Nineteenth-Century China. The Rise of Sino-Western Mercantile Capitalism* (Berkeley: University of California Press, 1986).

13. See CGKKY, 1921, 1928, 1931. See also Koh Seung-je (Ko Sŭng-je), "The Development of the Modern Banking System in Korea," *Koreana Quarterly* 1, 2(Winter 1959): 82–92.

14. See Suzuki Takeo, "Jihen go Chōsen kinyū [The Manchurian Incident and finance in Chōsen]," lecture no. 10 in his *Chōsen kinyū ron juko* [A discussion of finance in Chōsen: ten lectures] (Keijō: Teikoku Jihō Kōsei Gakkai Chōsen Honbu, 1940); Hatori Junhiro, "Senjika (1937–1945) Chōsen ni okeru tsūka to infureshion" [Inflation in the currency of Chōsen during wartime], in Iinuma Jirō and Kyō Zaigen, eds., *Shokuminchi Chōsen no shakai to teikō* [Society and resistance in colonial Korea] (Tokyo: Miraisha, 1982), 238–81.

15. Park Sung-sang, ed., *The Banking System in Korea* (Seoul: Bank of Korea, 1968), 13.

16. Data on shareholdings can be found in pertinent years of CGKKY and TGKY.

17. A representative list of Min family business activities can be found in Table 1 of this book.

18. The Kyesŏng was listed with a paid-in capital in 1940 of 2 million yen. As the largest shareholder in the Tongil Bank (paid-in capital of 2.75 million yen), the company held some 14,583 shares or 18% of the total shares. Min Kyu-sik and his sons held some 6,300 shares of the Tongil.

19. The Yŏngwha Industrial Company (Yŏnghwa Sanŏp) was founded in February of 1937 for investment in real estate, agricultural land improvement projects, and industry. It was listed in 1941 with an authorized capital of five hundred thousand yen, a paid-in capital of two hundred thousand yen, and with the Yŏngbo (Yŏngbo Hammyŏng Hoesa) and Kyesŏng Companies holding nearly 90% of the total of ten thousand shares. CGKKY, 1941, 35.

20. TGKY (1943), 31:38.

21. Han Sang-yong and others organized the Chosŏn Life Insurance Company (Chosŏn Saengmyŏng Pohŏm) in 1922. The company was registered under President Han Sang-yong in 1940 with an authorized capital of 500 thousand yen and 115 thousand yen paid-in. Pak Hŭng-sik, Hyŏn Chun-ho, and Pang Ui-sŏk were among the directors, with Min Kyu-sik added later as an auditor. Major shareholders included Hyŏn's Hakp'a Agricultural Estate (15%), Han Sang-yong, and others. CGKKY, 1940, 55; TGKY (1943), 31:42.

22. Min Kyu-sik also served as representative director of two breweries. Investors organized the smaller Chosŏn Brewery Company (Chosŏn Yangjo) in 1926, and registered the venture with a paid-in capital of 65 thousand yen in 1940. TGKY (1940), 28:55. The larger Central Brewery (Chung'ang Chujo) was established a decade later, with a paid-in capital in 1940 of 470 thousand yen. Kim Sa-yŏn led the company as president, with Min Kyu-sik and Ha Chun-sŏk serving as directors. CGKKY, 1941, 248.

Ha Chun-sŏk served as president of Chosŏn Engineering (Chosŏn Kongjak) and as a director at Han Kyu-bok's Chosŏn Industry and Management (Chosŏn Kongyŏng). Kim Sa-yŏn was president of Chōsen Yeast (Chōsen Kikuji) with investors Yasuda Kyōjun and other Japanese as the principal shareholders. DKB, 1942, 66. The company was listed with assets in 1945 of 8.5 million yen. JEA 1:152. Kim held directorships on the boards of the Tongil Bank and the South Manchurian Spinning Company, and was appointed to the Central Advisory Council of the government-general from April of 1934. TGKY (1940), 28:184, Executive Section; Nakanishi Toshiru, *Shin Nihon jinbutsu taikai,* 100.

23. The Tōhō Development Company (Tōhō Takushoku) was listed with an authorized capital of 500 thousand yen, and 185 thousand paid-in. CGKKY, 1941, 309; Yamakawa Chikashi, *Jigyō oyobi jinbutsu*, 278–9.

24. CGKKY, 1941, 309.

25. Min Kyu-sik appeared as the sole Korean representative on the board of the Chōsen Trade Promotion Company (Chōsen Bōeki Shinkō). Established in February of 1941 for foreign trade, the Japanese company was listed with an authorized capital of 2 million yen, 1.5 million paid-in. DKB, 1941, 94; TGKY (1943), 31:48. The total assets of the company in 1945 were estimated at 15 million yen. JEA 1:76, 152.

26. The Chōsen Trust Company (Chōsen Shintaku), founded in December of 1932 in Seoul, was listed in 1941 with an authorized capital of 10 million yen, and 2.5 million yen paid-in. CGKKY, 1941, 17–18.

27. Min also served on the board of Ōhashi's Chōsen Beer. A subsidiary of Dainippon Beer (Dainippon Biiru), the Chōsen Beer Company (Chōsen Biiru) was founded in Seoul in August of 1933, and listed by 1942 with an authorized capital of six million yen and three million yen paid-in. DKB, 1942, 65; Yamakawa Chikashi, *Jigyō oyobi jinbutsu*, 247. The company held estimated assets in Korea in 1945 of 50.6 million yen. JEA 1:149.

28. CGKKY, 1931, 370.

29. Regarding Shibusawa's interest in railroad construction in Korea, see Janet Hunter, "Japanese Government Policy, Business Opinion, and the Seoul–Pusan Railway, 1894–1906, *Modern Asian Studies* 11 (1977): 573–9. I have examined Shibusawa's attitudes in the context of Korean nationalist movements at the turn of the century in my dissertation, "Imperial Expansion and Nationalist Resistance," 97–117.

30. WWJ, 1939, 720.

31. CGKKY, 1931, 397–8; Yamakawa Chikashi, *Jigyō oyobi jinbutsu*, 235–6; DKB, 1942, 19.

32. JEA 1:77, 154.

33. Three brief histories of the Hanil Bank are available: a retrospective in the *Donga Ilbo* of March 26, 1933, "Tongil Unhaeng samsimnyŏnsa" [A thirty-year history of the Tongil Bank]; a summary in Ch'oe Yŏng-mo's *Chohŭng Unhaeng 90 nyŏnsa* [A ninety-year history of the Choheung Bank] (Seoul: Choheung Bank, 1987), 87–93; and a review in Koh Seung-jae, *Han'guk kŭmyungsa yŏn'gu*, 34–47.

34. The boldness of the changes was noted in an article of the *Maeil Sinpo* of August 12, 1920. The decision to concentrate family energies on the Hanil sparked long and heated discussions at the Min family home. See Min Pyŏng-do, "Min Pyŏng-do," in Wŏllo Kiŏbin, eds., *Chaegye hoego*, 10:201.

35. Min Tae-sik lead the bank through a relatively stable decade of moderate growth. The bank recorded an annual return of between 7% and 9% from 1918 through 1926, falling to 6% from 1928. See Ch'oe Yŏng-mo, *Chohŭng Ŭnhaeng 90 nyŏnsa*, 92. Branches were opened in Yaesan, South Ch'ungch'ŏng Province, at Wŏnsan and Hamhŭng in South Hamgyŏng Province to the northeast, and at Kimhwa in Kyŏnggi Province.

36. Banking Ordinance of November 24, 1928. See Koh, *Han'guk kumyungsa yŏn'gu*, 44.

37. The addition of Hosŏ capital brought the total paid-in capital to 2.775 million yen, with a number of Hosŏ shareholders now holding large blocks of stock in the Tongil. Out of a total of 80,000 shares, Kim Chin-byŏn, former Hosŏ Bank president, retained 1,935 shares until 1939; Ch'oe Kyu-sŏk, a former Hosŏ director, 1,418 shares until 1942; and Sŏng Hak-hŏn, 1,304 shares until 1939. See CGKKY, pertinent years. Although the executive director of the Hosŏ, Sŏng Ak-hŏn, was appointed

to the same position in the newly named Tongil Bank, no other Hosŏ officers were added. One other change evident from 1931 was the absence of Tae-sik's brother from the administration, after serving as a director of the Hanil from 1920.

38. Continuing problems led to Min Tae-sik's resignation a year later due to "difficulties dating from the takeover of the Hosŏ Bank." Board members interviewed emphasized, however, that every effort would be made to maintain Tae-sik's interest in the bank, and to bring another member of the family into the bank. *Donga Ilbo*, July 22, 1934. The board apparently convinced Tae-sik to stay on as president, and some days later a shareholders group proposed changes in the bank's articles of incorporation to give Min more power over former Hosŏ Bank shareholders. *Donga Ilbo*, July 26, 1934.

39. *Donga Ilbo*, March 26, 1933.

40. Petitions by the shareholders and the intervention of the government-general are described in the *Donga Ilbo* of July 30, 1936; see also Ch'oe Yŏng-mo, *Chohŭng Ŭnhaeng 90 nyŏnsa*, 102–3. The bank reported annual returns on capital of only 3% from 1933 through 1938, rising gradually to 7% by the second half of 1942. The Hansŏng Bank in Seoul also reported a low annual return of only 3% during 1933–1937, but Hyŏn Chun-ho's Honam Bank (paid-in capital, 1.375 million yen) in Kwangju posted annual returns of 7% between 1933 and 1938. *Chohŭrg Ŭnhaeng 90 nyŏnsa*, 75, 99.

Min Kyu-sik found time for quite a diversity of business activities. He served as managing director of the Hanil from 1920 until November of 1930. He founded a family-owned agricultural venture, the Yŏngbo Company, in 1933 and served as representative director. He was also president of the Tōhō Development Company, the Chungyŏng Brewery, the Tongil and then Choheung Banks, and of the Chosŏn Silk Weaving Company (Chosŏn Kyŏnjik), and was a member of the board of directors for the Tonggwang Raw Silk Company, the South Manchurian Spinning Company, the Hwasin Company, and other concerns. He was appointed to the Council of Kyŏnggi Province in 1942, and to the Central Advisory Council in 1945. A resume is available in the archives of the Choheung Bank as well as in documents at the U.S. National Archives: Occupied Areas Files – Korea, "Names and Biographies of Members of Central Advisory Council of Koreans, Target No. 61."

41. Ch'oe Yŏng-mo, *Chohŭng Ŭnhaengsa 90 nyŏnsa*, 103. The Honam Bank held some 1,870 shares in the Tongil from 1934 through 1941. In 1942, Hyŏn Chun-ho's agricultural concern, the Hakp's Company, was listed with 970 shares. See pertinent years of CGKKY. Hyŏn Chun-ho wrote of strong pressure from the colonial administration to change the Honam's persistent nationalist practices of doing business only with Koreans and other policies excluding Japanese nationals. The administration at last ordered the Honam shareholders to choose between the Tongil and the Chōsen Commercial Bank. See Son Chŏng-yŏn, *Musong Hyŏn Chun-ho* [Musong Hyŏn Chun-ho] (Kwangju: Chŏnnam Maeil Sinmunsa, 1977), 267–9.

42. Min Kyu-sik served as president of the newly named Choheung Bank until November, 1945, with a paid-in capital of 5.98 million yen and sixty-five branches.

43. Weekly reports of loans of each branch include information on net assets of the applicant, purpose of the loan, and details about how the money will be used. I was able to gain access to reports for the latter half of 1934 and 1936. See Tongil Bank, Board of Directors, *Ch'wich'eyŏkhoe kyŏllok* [Record of resolutions from meetings of the board of directors], Choheung Bank Archives.

44. CGKKY, 1921–30.

45. I was able to ask Min Tae-sik's son, Min Pyŏng-do, directly about this issue in an interview of September 1987. He emphasized the role of capital control by the Bank of Chōsen, especially after 1936.

46. Shimamoto Susumi, *Chōsen zaikai no hitobito*, 58–9. Another observer noted that Kawaguchi actually ran the bank in the absence of the discouraged president, Min Kyu-sik. See Ch'oe Yŏng-mo, *Chohŭng Ŭnhaeng 90 nyŏnsa*, 102–3. Kawaguchi rather than Min Kyu-sik was listed as representative of the bank in the administration's list of critical industries in 1937. *Keizai Geppō* (July 1937): 809.

47. The Chōsen Trust Company, owned mainly by the Bank of Chōsen and the Industrial Bank, held 1,350 shares in 1941 and 2,106 in 1942. But no other Japanese individual or firm is listed among Tongil major shareholders. See CGKKY. The weak performance of the bank in the 1930s and the uncertain situation of Korean finance from 1939 may well have discouraged Japanese investment. But even without ownership, management control was enough to adjust the dedicated Korean focus of the bank. A comparison of bank records of 1934 and 1936 suggests a significant increase in the number of Japanese nationals receiving loan support from 1936.

48. For details of Japanese control of the bank after 1936, see "Min Pyŏng-do," in *Chaegye hoego* 10:210–12.

49. See Koh Seung-jae, "Hansŏng Ŭnhaeng" [The Hansŏng Bank], *Han'guk kŭmyungsa yŏn'gu*, 14–33.

50. "Min Pyŏng-do," 10:210–12.

51. Maurice Zeitlin, "Corporate Ownership and Control."

52. *Donga Ilbo*, June 18, 1921, p. 2.

Chapter 6. Pak and commerce

1. Japanese merchants often bypassed the traditional Korean "commission merchants" (*kaekchu*) and "brokers" (*yŏgak*). See Cho Ki-jun, "The Impact of the Opening of Korea on its Commerce and Industry," *Korea Journal* 16 (Feb. 1976): 27–44; Pak Wŏn-sŏn, *Kaekchu* [Commission merchants] (Seoul: Yonsei University Press, 1968), 177–80. See also Miyajima Hiroshi, "Chōsen kango kaikaku igo no shōgyōteki nōgyō" [Commercial agriculture after the Kabo reforms in Korea], *Shirin* 57, 6(Nov. 1974): 38–77; Sawamura Tōhei, "Richō makki menseihin yunyū bōeki no hatten" [Developments in the cotton import trade at the close of the Yi dynasty], *Shakai Keizaishi Gaku* 19, 2–3(1953): 57–80. Apart from considerations of both status and productive investment of capital, an uneven competition with Japanese merchants enjoying favorable access to the finance and transportation networks necessary for international trade would have slowed Korean entry into large-scale commerce throughout the colonial period in any case.

2. Kim Chin-ha, ed., *Han'guk muyŏksa* [A history of Korean trade] (Seoul: Han'guk Muyŏk Hyŏphoe, 1972), 192, Table 36.

3. See "Chōsen ni okeru hantōjin shihaika no kaisha jōsei" [The condition of companies under native management in Korea], *Shokugin Chōsa Geppō* 20 (Jan. 1940): 26–9.

4. The stores are described in *Fifty Years*, 126, a company history published in Korean as *Hwasin osimnyŏn*. A chronology of significant events in the company's history can be found in the annual editions of CGKKY, and later in Yŏm Han-Yŏng, *Hoesa yŏn'gam 1955* [Company annual 1955] (Seoul: Taehan Kyŏngje Yŏn'gamsa, 1955). A summary of the company's growth is provided in Yamakawa Chikashi, *Jigyō oyobi jinbutsu*, 434–5. See also "Pak Hŭng-sik," 187, 210.

5. Although the original building on Chongno was destroyed in a fire of 1935, Pak opened a new six-story Hwasin Department Store building in November of 1937. His pride in this accomplishment is apparent in his account of the visit of the Korean prince Yi Wang-ŭn to Hwasin on April 18, 1938. See "Pak Hûng-sik," 211.

6. Chōsen Shōkō Kaigisho, *Zensen shōkō kaigisho hattenshi*, 28.

7. A list of investments is provided in Table 2 of this book.

8. CGKKY, 1927, 326; 1931, 312; 1933, 287; 1941, 414; TGKY (1940), 28: 38, *Fifty Years*, 90–106.

9. The Chejudo Industrial Company (Chejudo Hŭngŏp) was founded in June of 1937 for agricultural development, real estate investment, and finance, with an authorized and paid-in capital in 1941 of five hundred thousand yen. Ha Chun-sŏk served as president, with Pak and Cho Chun-ho as directors. CGKKY, 1941, 315. According to Pak Hŭng-sik, the venture began as a joint investment among the three, but Pak bought out his partners in February of 1941 to become sole owner. The company had purchased three thousand acres at the foot of Mount Halla on Cheju Island for the purpose of cattle raising. *Fifty Years*, 176–8.

10. TGKY (1940), 28:43, (1943), 31:71; CGKKY, 1941, 310; DKB, 1942, 91.

11. Abe Kaoru, *Chōsen kōrōsha meikan*, 100.

12. TGKY (1940), 28:93, (1943), 31:71; DKB, 1942, 87.

13. The Chosŏn Industry and Management Company (Chosŏn Kongyŏng) dated from September 1939. Registered with an authorized capital of 1 million yen and 500 thousand yen paid-in, the company was a joint enterprise managed by Koreans, but with strong Japanese investment by Iwama Makoto (25% of the shares) and others. Pak Hŭng-sik was among the largest indigenous investors, with 5% of the shares. CGKKY, 1941, 606. The board included Pak, Ha Chun-sŏk, Han Sang-yong, Pang Ŭi-sŏk, and Min Kyu-sik.

14. CGKKY, 1941, 182; DKB, 1942, 46; TGKY (1943), 31:39.

15. Among smaller ventures, Pak was also a director of the Chōsen Heian Railway Company (Chōsen Heian Tetsudo), with estimated assets in 1945 of 52 million yen. DKB, 1942, 11; JEA 1:150.

16. CGKKY, 1941, 612.

17. JEA 1:74, 154.

18. CKN, 1941–2, 39.

19. Chōsen Orimono Kyōkai, *Chōsen seni nenkan 1943* [Korean textile annual, 1943] (Keijō: Chikazawa, 1943), 116–17; TGKY (1943), 31:44.

20. JEA 1:76, 152.

21. CKN, 1941–2, Chronology, 30, 39, 48, 65.

22. Shimamoto Susumu, *Chōsen zaikai no hitobito*, 178–9; regarding the Genyōsha, see E. Herbert Norman, "The Genyōsha: A Study in the Origins of Japanese Imperialism," in *Pacific Affairs* 17, 3(Sept. 1944): 261–84, and John Wayne Sabey, "The Gen'yōsha, the Kokuryūkai, and Japanese Expansionism" (Ph.D diss., University of Michigan), 1972.

23. DKB, 1942, 93.

24. TGKY (1941), 29:532.

25. DKB, 1942, 230.

26. DKB, 1942, 75.

27. The Chōsen Aircraft Manufacturing Company (Chōsen Hikoki Kōgyō) was organized by president Pak Hŭng-sik in October of 1944 with an authorized capital of 50 million yen, and estimated assets in 1945 of 49.5 million yen. A plant was built at Anyang outside of Seoul, and a workforce of twenty-eight hundred employees assembled to begin production of aircraft. Representatives from the government-general, the Japanese air force, the Industrial Bank, and the Oriental Development Company served on the board. Pang Ŭi-sŏk and Kim Yŏn-su also served as directors, as did Yi Ki-yŏn of Sŏnil, and Min Kyu-sik was listed as an auditor. See *Fifty Years*, 208–15, *JANIS*, 38; JEA 1:149.

28. JEA 1:49, 81, 153.

29. "Whatever Ōji Paper's feeling against Pak might have been, it was a private one and a question of interests in the trade, and Ōji Paper was obliged to follow the recommendation of Governor-General Ugaki for reasons of policy and Ugaki's prestige." *Fifty Years*, 102. Sŏnil had earlier gained a foothold in Korean newsprint markets at the expense of Ōji Paper.

30. CGKKY, 1941, 148–9.

31. WWJ, 1939, 195.

32. The Chōsen Petroleum Company, Ltd. (Chōsen Sekiyū) was founded in June of 1935 in accord with the Petroleum Business Law of June 30, 1934, to promote Korean fuel sources. Based in Seoul on Ulchi Avenue, the company operated plants in South Hamgyŏng Province. Jigyō to Keizaisha, *Senman sangyō taikan, 1940* [Review of commerce in Chōsen and Manchukuo] (Tokyo: Jigyō to Keizaisha, 1940), 48; Yamakawa, *Jigyō oyobi jinbutsu*, 246–7; DKB, 1942, 58; TGKY (1943), 31:43–4.

33. The company reported an 18% annual dividend in 1938. Yamakawa, *Jigyō oyobi jinbutsu*, 246–7.

34. JEA 1:151.

35. CGKKY, 330; 1940 ed., 437. See also *Senman sangyō taikan*, 94. Hwasin continued the jewelry store business of Sin T'ae-wha on Chongno Avenue that Pak had purchased for 360,000 yen in 1931. *Fifty Years*, 109.

36. Chronology, 45; *Fifty Years*, 113.

37. The Donga Department Store of Ch'oe Nam was located in a building owned by Min Kyu-sik across from the Hwasin on Chongno Avenue. For a brief review of the history of the store, see Cho Ki-jun, *Han'guk kiŏpkasa*, 218–24.

38. TGKY (1943), 31:71.

39. TGKY (1940), 29:41.

40. Allen, "Structure of Interorganizational Elite Cooptation," 393–4. Allen defined the "interlocking directorate" as "any situation in which two or more corporations share one or more directors in common."

41. TGKY (1943), 31:71. The same president and three executive directors appeared in the listing for Hwasin itself in 1943, with Min Kyu-sik and Pang Ŭi-sŏk joining two Japanese on the board.

42. WWJ, 1939, 913.

43. Chōsen Orimono Kyōkai, *Chōsen seni yoran* [Korean textile annual] (Tokyo: Chōsen Orimono Kyōkai, 1943), 122.

44. WWJ, 1943, 71–2. Pak's friendship with Tsuda is described in *Fifty Years*, 131–2.

45. A record of adjustments among business circles on the peninsula can be found in the publications of the Keijō Chamber of Commerce and Industry. See my article, "The Keishō and the Korean Business Elite."

46. *Fifty Years*, 94, 173, 127. Besides loans from these larger banks owned and managed by Japanese, Pak also had to rely on financial relations with Korean banks. For instance, he received a loan of 28 thousand yen from the Tongil Bank in early September of 1934, for the purchase of paper goods. He listed his net worth at 250 thousand yen, with collateral of land worth 40 thousand yen in his hometown area of Yongganggun. See Tongil Bank, *Records*, August 31, 1934, 4. The Sŏnil also received a line of credit in October of that year for 50 thousand yen, on the collateral of 100 thousand yen worth of real estate. *Records*, October 26, 1934, 26.

47. *Fifty Years*, 127–9. There were other examples of administration favor. Governor-General Ugaki intervened on his behalf in 1935 to permit use of the former Chongno Police Station by the Hwasin Store after a disastrous fire destroyed its original site.

48. Born in Japan in 1894, Yoneda was a graduate of Meiji University in Tokyo. He served as manager of the business department and also of the paper department at Sŏnil Paper, and later as a director of Hwasin Commercial and manager of the Trade Section. See Takamiya Taihei, ed., *Chōsenjin meiroku* [A directory of prominent figures in Korea] (Keijō: Keijō Shibosha, 1942), 163; *Fifty Years*, 106.

49. Ko Wŏn-sŏp, *Panminja choesonggi*, 21.

50. Fujiyama was prominent in sugar production and marketing in Taiwan and Manchuria, and very active in business circles in Tokyo. He served on the board of Mitsukoshi Department Store, the Tokyo Stock Exchange, and the Nippon Kyodo Securities Company. He was elected vice-president, and from 1941 president of the Tokyo Chamber of Commerce and Industry. WWJ, 1943, 16.

51. WWJ, 1943, 81.

52. Pak himself described his friendly relations with executives of Kanegafuchi Textile (Kanegafuchi Bōseki), Japan Sugar Manufacture (Dai Nihon Seitō), Meiji Confectionery (Meiji Seika), and Japan Flour (Nisshin Seifun) in *Fifty Years*, 191. The Sŏnil Paper Company established a branch in Pusan in April of 1936 to facilitate commerce with Japan. Ibid., 103.

53. Juhn, Daniel Sungil, "The Development of Korean Entrepreneurship," in Andrew C. Nahm, ed., *Korea under Japanese Colonial Rule* (Kalamazoo: Center for Korean Studies, Western Michigan University, 1973), 122.

54. There was continuity after liberation as well. Pak reorganized his inner circle of investments into Hwasin Industries and Hwasin Trade after liberation. The trade venture was set up in 1946 under Pak's nephew, Pak Pyŏng-gyo, and by 1949 was among the larger trading firms on the peninsula. Kang Se-gyun, *Chŏn'guk sanggong taegam* [A review of the nation's commerce and industry] (Seoul: Chunwoe Sanggong Ch'ŏngbosa, 1949), 7. The Industrial Company later absorbed the trading unit, and in 1955 was registered among major Korean enterprises with an authorized capital of three million hwan, under president Pak Hŭng-sik and vice-president Yi Kyu-jae. Yŏm Han-Yŏng, *Hoesa yŏn'gam 1955*, 424.

55. Imotani Zenichi, *Chōsen keizaishi*, 165–73.

56. *Chosŏn Ilbo*, June 15, 1934; Pak Hung-sik, "Pak Hŭng-sik," 186–7.

57. Ko Wŏn-sŏp, *Panminja choesanggi*, 19.

Chapter 7. Kim and industry

1. Cho Ki-jun, *Han'guk chabonjuŭi sŏngnipsa ron*, 486–501.

2. Duesenberry originally suggested a "demonstration effect" affecting consumer behavior. "People believe that the consumption of high quality goods for any purpose is desirable and important. If they habitually use one set of goods, they can be made dissatisfied with them by a demonstration of the superiority of others. But mere knowledge of the existence of superior goods is not a very effective habit breaker. Frequent contact with them may be. In this field it is not only true that 'what you know won't hurt you,' but that what you do know does hurt you." *Income, Saving and the Theory of Consumer Behavior* (New York: Oxford University Press, 1967), 27. Applied cross-nationally, the thesis would suggest exposure to higher standards of living and the improved products of industrialized nations would stimulate consumption and demand for improved local goods.

3. Chosŏn Ŭnhaeng Chosabu, *Chosŏn kyŏngje yŏnbo 1948* [Annual of the Korean economy, 1948] (Seoul: Chosŏn Ŭnhaeng, 1948), 99; Kim Tu-yong, *Chōsen kindai shakaishi wa*, 234.

4. Chōsen Shokusan Ginkō Chōsabu, "Chōsen ni okeru hantōjin shihaika no kaisha jōsei, 26–7.

5. See Kim Yŏn-su, "Kim Yŏn-su," in *Chaegye hoego*; *Sudang*; also WWJ, 1939, 428, and 1943, 64.

6. See Kim Yong-sŏp, "Hanmal Ilcheha ŭi chijuje. Saryesa: Kobu Kimssiga ŭi chiju kyŏngyŏng kwa chabon chŏnhwan" [System of landownership from the end of the Yi Dynasty through the colonial period. The fourth case: land administration and capital movement in the Kim family of Kobu], *Han'guksa Yŏn'gu* (Feb. 1978), 65–135; *Kyŏngbang*, 48.

7. A list of Kim's investments can be found in Table 3 of this book.

8. *Kyŏngbang*, 50.

9. *Kyŏngbang*, 117, 122–4; CGKKY, 1941, 123–4; TGKY (1943), 31:33. The company was listed by the end of the colonial period with the Samyang Company, Kyŏngsŏng Spinning, and family members as the major shareholders. *Kyŏngbang*, 117.

10. CGKKY, 1935, 239; 1940, 307; *Sudang*, 135–6; TGKY (1940), 28:29; *Samyang*, 88. The family also owned and controlled Samch'ŏk Enterprise (Samch'ŏk Kiŏp), an agricultural venture with headquarters in Manchuria, and an authorized capital of 1 million yen with 250 thousand yen paid-in in 1941. DKB, 1941, 198; *Sudang*, 176–80.

11. *Samyang*, 17–19, 96.

12. The company estimated total holdings prior to 1945 as property with an annual harvest of 150,000 sŏk, or 750,000 sixty-six pound bushels of rice. *Samyang*, 200. Assuming a harvest of about 21 sŏk per chŏngbo (i.e., 2.45 acres) of land, the holdings represented close to 7,000 chŏngbo, or 17,000 acres. The company reported holdings of 2,500 chŏngbo in the Chŏlla area in 1940. The estimated value of these holdings alone would have been about 6.675 million yen. Average prices for land can be found in Chōsen Shokusan Ginkō Kanteifu, *Zensen tenden baibai kakaku oyobi shūekicho* [A study of prices and profits in the purchase and sale of land in Korea] (Keijō: Chōsen Shokusan Ginkō Kanteiful, 1943), 8.

13. Kim Pyŏng-je, ed., *Inmul ŭnhaengsa* [A history of major figures in banking] (Seoul: Ŭnhaenggyesa, 1978), 117–18; *Sudang*, 145–7.

14. The Tonggwang Raw Silk Company (Tonggwang Sengsa) was organized in August of 1935 by Ko Wŏn-dong, a former Posŏng School principal, and Managing Director Kamizawa. Kamizawa had been an executive of a Kobe Raw Silk (Kobe Seisa) affiliate, Taegu Silk Manufacture (Taiku Seishi), with a paid-in capital of one hundred thousand yen. CGKKY, 1941, 142.

The Tonggwang was reorganized in 1941 as Tonggwang Silk Manufacture (Tonggwang Chesa) with a paid-in capital of one million yen. Concentrated investment by the Kyŏngsŏng raised the capital in 1944 to two million yen. CGKKY, 1940, 151; Chōsen Orimono Kyōkai, *Chōsen seni yōran*, 1943, 83; *Kyŏngbang*, 117; Yamakaw, *Jigyō oyobi jinbutsu*, 62.

15. *Samyang*, 84.

16. CGKKY, 1941, 386; DKB, 1942, 26; CKN, 1941–2; Chronology, 15.

17. Founded only in September of 1938, Japan Mining (Nippon Kinsan Shinkō) was registered with an authorized capital of fifty million yen in 1941, and a paid-in capital of thirty million yen. CGKKY, 1941, 650–1. With headquarters in Tokyo and a branch in Seoul, half of Japan Mining's shares were owned by the Japanese government, and the rest by Mitsui, Mitsubishi, and Japan Mining.

18. WWJ, 1943, 6.

19. JEA 1:150.

20. Kim served on the boards of the Chōsen Savings Bank (Chōsen Chochiku

Ginkō) and the Hansŏng Banks, and of three railroads and one utility company. The railroads included the West Chōsen Central Railway, the Chōsen Keitō Railway, and the Keishun Railway companies. Kim was listed among the principal shareholders in the latter two companies, with 2% of both the Keitō and Keishun shares.

The Samyang Company was the second largest shareholder with 9% of the equity in Saitō Kyūtarō's Chōsen Heian Railway (Chōsen Heian Tetsudo). DKB, 1942, 11. The railway's assets in 1945 were estimated at fifty-two million yen. JEA 1:150. Tagawa Tsunejirō of the Ryūzan Construction Company was president of the railway, and the construction company held nearly 9% of the shares as well. Tagawa had succeeded Kada Naoharu as president of the Keijō Chamber of Commerce and Industry. Others on the board of the railway company included Pak Hŭng-sik. DKB, 1942, 10, 21.

21. JEA 1:152.

22. Ibid., 151. Chōsen Refining held stock in other Japanese investments on the peninsula, such as Nippon Magnesite Chemical Industry (Nippon Magunesito Kagaku Kōgyō) with a paid-in capital of 5 million yen in 1942, and Chōsen Gold Industries (Chōsen Sankin Shinkō) with a paid-in capital of 10 million yen in 1941. Total assets of the former in 1945 were estimated at 31.5 million yen, and the latter at 79.5 million yen. JEA 1:156, 150.

23. In sixteen years as president of the Chōsen Industrial Bank (1921–37), Ariga Mitsutoyo played a major role in funding industry and agriculture on the peninsula. He then turned his energies to enterprises on the peninsula closely tied to government support, heading such companies as Chōsen Refining, the Japan High Frequency Heavy Industry Company (Nippon Kōshūsha Jugyō), and the Kankō Hydroelectric Company (Kankō Suiryoku Denki). Yamakawa, *Jigyō oyobi jinbutsu*, 314; Abe, *Chōsen kōrōsha meikan*, 50.

24. *Jigyō to jinbutsu*, 314; WWJ, 1939, 213. Hayashi succeeded Ushijima Seizō as president of the Keishun Railway Company, in which both the Industrial Bank and Ariga were major investors. CGKKY, 1941, 48–9; DKB, 1942, 10; *Chōsen kōrōsha meikan*, 69–70.

25. Kim was a director and major investor in another railway venture with a somewhat longer history but less capital. Investors organized the Chōsen Keitō Railway Company (Chōsen Keitō Tetsudo) in 1928 with headquarters in Suwŏn, and with an authorized capital in 1942 of 5 million yen, 3.45 million yen paid-in. Kim held 2% of the total shares available. CGKKY, 1941, 46–7; DKB, 1942, 10–11.

26. JEA 1:154.

27. DKB, 1942, 10; *Jigyō oyobi jinbutsu*, 429.

28. *Chōsen kōrōsha meikan*, 69.

29. DKB, 1942, 11; *Jigyō oyobi jinbutsu*, 329; WWJ, 1939, 125.

30. JEA 1:157.

31. *Kyŏngbang*, 58; see also *Inch'on*, 156–68; *Sudang*, 150–80. The history was summarized in annual editions of CGKKY. Sudang's father, Chisan Kim Kyŏng-jun, and Sŏng-su's father, Wŏnp'a Kim Ki-jung, were among the largest investors.

32. *Han'guk inmyŏng taesajŏn*, 286; *Chōsen kōrōsha meikan*, 46–7; Chōsen Shokusan Ginkō, *Chōsen Shokusan Ginkō nijūnen shi*, 264, 266; *Kyŏngbang*, 30.

33. See his obituary of September 20, 1939, in Chronology, 26.

34. *Kyŏngbang*, 542–3.

35. Ibid., 71, 542–3.

36. Ibid., 33.

37. Ibid., 141; TGKY, 1940, Executive Section, 235; Keijō Nippōsha, *Chōsen nenkan 1944*, 380.

38. TGKY (1940), 28:9, (1943), 31:21. Ch'oe also served as a director of another

family affiliate, Samsŏng Cotton (Samsŏng Myŏnŏp), with a paid-in capital of 195 thousand yen.

39. See pertinent years of CGKKY; *Kyŏngbang*, 122–3, 516–19.

40. DKB, 1942, 61. The company registered a paid-in capital of 2.8 million yen in 1940, with total assets estimated at 11.5 million yen. CGKKY, 1940, 128. By 1942 the company's paid-in capital had risen to 5 million yen with the addition of assets from South Manchurian Spinning. See DKB, 1942, 61; *Chōsen seni yōran*, 88–9.

41. TGKY, (1943) 31:13–14; *Kyŏngbang*, 517, 519. Kim Yŏn-su's Samyang Company and Yangyŏnghoe, together with Sin Ki-ch'ang, Kim Pong-yŏng, and Ko Kwang-p'yo were listed as major shareholders in 1943.

42. Nakanishi Toshiiru, *Shin Nihonbutsu taikai*, 530.

43. Ibid., 100.

44. TGKY (1940), 28:28, Manchuria Section, (1943), 31:32; DKB, 1942, 159; *Sudang*, 169–76; *Kyŏngbang*, 106–7.

45. U.S. observers made the following report after an on-site inspection of the company's plant in Suchiatun, Liaoning Province, Manchuria, on June 13, 1946. "The plant with 35,000 spindles and about 1,050 looms was built in 1942 and equipped with new machinery from Japan. It was managed and operated by Koreans and had about 3,000 employees. According to the Korean guard, reports were current that the plant was built with Korean rather than with Japanese or Manchurian capital. This could not be checked."

The report continued: "It is clear that the report of the Chinese to the effect that Soviets removed 100% of the equipment from this plant is incorrect, but losses due to the activities of the Soviets may be large. It is also believed that the value of $45,000,000 U.S. (i.e., 675 million yen) on materials removed is exaggerated." Edwin Wendell Pauley, *Report on Japanese Assets in Manchuria to the President of the United States*, Appendix 12, Plant Inspection Report 1-K-8 (Washington, DC: Government Printing Office, July 1946).

46. JEA 2:67.

47. *Kyŏngbang*, 516, 518, 523, 525.

48. See *Kyŏngbang*, 127.

49. A statistical comparison of the two companies, with attention to nationality of stockholders, can be found in Chōsen Shokusan Ginkō, Chōsabu, *Chōsen ni okeru kōgyō kaisha no shihon kōsei chōsa* [A study of capital formation in Korean industrial companies] (Keijō: Chōsen Shokusan Ginkō, 1935), 9–10, Table 2.

50. CGKKY, 1941, 132; TGKY (1943), 31:38.

51. *Kyŏngbang*, 62.

52. Ibid., 523. The Japanese term for subsidy was *hojokin*.

53. *Samyang*, 122, 128–9. The subsidies covered 30% or less of the total investment in each of these projects.

54. *Sudang*, 81. For biographical sketches of Pak, see *Chōsen kōrōsha meikan*, 59; *Han'guk inmyŏng taesajŏn*, 286.

55. I emphasize only industry because there is little material available regarding Kim's agricultural enterprise abroad. The Samyang Company established the Ch'ŏnil Agricultural Estate near Mukden in September of 1937, and the Pansŏk Estate to the north in Kirin Province in the same year. The company later developed the Kyoha, Maeha, Kudae, Taebong, and Kuchi estates as well, with total holdings of over 7,200 acres (3,000 chŏngbo). Kim purchased the Samch'ŏk Company in 1939, a land development company with holdings in Manchuria. *Samyang*, 137–9, 177–80. Though I have as yet located no record of reclamation efforts, these companies may well have received government aid in their development efforts.

56. The Critical Industries Ordinance (Jūyō Sangyō Tōseiho) of March 2, 1937, encouraged and provided support for industrial investment in Manchuria and, on the other hand, restricted support for plant development on the peninsula. Kim turned his attention abroad with a plan to build a Kyŏngsŏng plant in Manchuria, but wrote of being frustrated by the unstable military situation and lack of cooperation from the Japanese military command. Earlier negotiations proved futile with Kyŏngsŏng's machinery supplier, Toyota Weaving of Nagoya (Toyota Shokki) for a joint enterprise. *Kyŏngbang*, 104–7; *Sudang*, 150–9.

57. *Kyŏngbang*, 62.

58. Hyŏn Chun-ho of the Honam Bank also served on the board of the Donga Ilbo Company as auditor from September of 1921 until October of 1923, and later as a director from May of 1937 until publication was suspended in August of 1940. Kim Sang-man, ed., *Donga Ilbosa sa*, 421.

59. One further prominent Korean investor served on the boards of the Kyŏngsŏng and Haedong Heungop companies in the early 1940s: Ch'oe Ch'ang-hak. Among the wealthiest of the indigenous capitalists through 1945, Ch'oe had become famous as the "gold mining king" through development of Samsŏng Mining, sold to Mitsui Mining in 1929. Athough Ch'oe developed his own Taech'ang Industries, he was better known for extensive investments in Japanese enterprises on the peninsula, and his participation on the board of the unofficial government daily, the *Maeil Sinpo*.

Born in 1891, Ch'oe was active in commerce before investing in a successful mining venture, the Samsŏng Company. He also served as a director of Posŏng School, of Kyŏngsŏng, and of the Kim family's Haedong Heungop. He was a major shareholder in the Keijin Enterprise Company, in Tashidō Railway (1.6% of the shares), and in Chōsen Trust (1.7%). CGKKY, 1941, 148–9, 359; DKB, 1942, 10; TGKY (1940), 28:235, Executive Section; Nakanishi, *Shin Nihonbutsu taikai*, 54; *Chōsen kōrōsha meikan*, 521–2. Ch'oe held 1% of the total shares in the North Korean Paper and Chemical Manufacturing Company, a venture with estimated assets of 162 million yen in 1945. JEA 1:153. Active also in finance, Ch'oe was a major shareholder in Chōsen Trust (Chōsen Shintaku). TGKY (1943), 42.

Ch'oe organized Taech'ang Industries (Taech'ang Sanŏp) in 1934 for mining, trade, and finance. The company registered an authorized capital of 2 million yen in 1941, 1.5 million yen paid-in, with Ch'oe himself holding 88% of the shares available. Kim Yŏn-su served as a director of the company. CGKKY, 1941, 359.

60. Takamiya, *Chōsenjin meiroku*, 103.

61. Chōsen Shōkō Kaigisho, *Zensen shōkō kaigisho hattenshi*, Appendix, 54–55; *Chōsen kōrōsha meikan*, 55; *Jigyō oyobi jinbutsu*, 444; Koh Seung-jae, *Han'guk kŭmyungsa yŏn'gu*, 153, 221–2.

62. *Keizai Geppō* (July 1937): 94.

63. *Chōsen kōrōsha meikan*, 827.

64. I present a similar conclusion in "Entrepreneurship in Colonial Korea: Kim Youn-su," *Modern Asian Studies* 22, 1(1988): 165–77.

Chapter 8. *Legacies*

1. For a comparison of Japanese and Korean family systems and their effect on family management and ownership of the chaebŏl, see Hattori Tamio, "The Relationship between Zaibatsu and Family Structure: the Korean Case," in Akio Okochi and Shigeaki Yasuoka, eds., *Family Business in the Era of Industrial Growth* (Tokyo: University of Tokyo Press, 1983), 121–45.

2. Calvin Hoover, "Capitalism," in David L. Sills, ed., *International Encyclo-*

pedia of the Social Sciences, vol. 2 (New York: Macmillan and Free Press, 1968), 294–5.

3. See Ramon H. Myers and Mark R. Peattie, eds., *The Japanese Colonial Empire, 1895–1945* (Princeton: Princeton University Press, 1984); Hyman Kublin, "The Evolution of Japanese Colonialism," 67–84; Bruce Cumings, "The Origins and Development of the Northeast Asian Political Economy: Industrial Sectors, Product Cycles, and Political Consequences," in Frederic C. Deyo, ed., *The Political Economy of the New Asian Industrialism* (Ithaca: Cornell University Press, 1987), 44–83.

4. Bruce Cumings, "The Legacy of Japanese Colonialism in Korea," 489.

5. Allen, "The Structure of Interorganizational Elite Cooperation," 395.

6. Kajimura Hideki, "Minjok chabon kwa yesok chabon," 523. Kang Tong- jin has argued that administration policies after 1919 to split native landowners from tenants and corporate owners from labor were largely successful. *Ilche ŭi Han'guk ch'imnyak chŏngch'aeksa*, 202–16.

7. René Maunier, *The Sociology of Colonies. An Introduction to the Study of Race Contact* (London: Routledge and Kegan Paul, 1949).

8. Hagen Koo, "The Interplay of State, Social Class, and World System," 170. For studies of bureaucratic development in the Republic of Korea, see Lee Hahn-been, *Korea: Time, Change, and Administration* (Honolulu: East–West Center Press, 1968); W.D. Reeve, *The Republic of Korea* (Oxford: Oxford University Press, 1963); and Kim Joungwon, *Divided Korea: Politics of Development, 1945–1972* (Cambridge: Harvard University Press, 1975).

9. Lee Byung-chull of Samsung was the most prominent of the postcolonial business leaders. He was instrumental in the founding of the Federation of Korean Industries in 1961, providing an institutional base for the major business leaders apart from the larger and more diverse Korean Chamber of Commerce and Industry. The list of those prosecuted for "illicit accumulation" in collusion with the Rhee government provides a roster of the successful major business elites in the first fifteen years after liberation, and a glimpse of the new "inner circle." See Ch'oe Yŏng-gyu, *Han'guk hyŏngmyŏng chaep'ansa* [Korean revolution: a history of the litigation], vol. 1 (Seoul: Tonga Publishing, 1962).

10. C. Clyde Mitchell, "Report of the New Korea Company," (Seoul: U.S. Military Government in Korea, National Land Administraton, 1948); Choi Moon Hwan, "A Review of Korea's Land Reform," *Koreana Quarterly* 2, 1(Spring 1960): 55–63; Ban Sung Hwan et al., *Rural Development* (Cambridge: Harvard University Press, 1980).

11. Pak was charged in 1948 with antinationalist activities during the colonial years, but was acquitted the next year. He was convicted in 1961 of "illicit accumulation" of some six hundred million hwan during the intervening decade. Kim Yŏn-su also was tried for antinationalist activities in 1948 and later acquitted. His son, Kim Sang-hŭng of Samyang, was convicted for illicit accumulation in 1961. Ko Wŏn-sŏp, *Panminja choesanggi*.

12. Chosŏn Unhaeng Chosabu, *Chosŏn kyŏngje yŏnbo 1948*, 103–10.

13. U.S. Armed Forces in Korea, 24th Corps, *Intelligence Summary: Korea, Weekly Summary*, July 23, 1948, no. 149, National Archives, p. 992.

14. Morris Wolf, "Memorandum on Restrictions in Korean Constitution upon Private Enterprise," 1954, A.I.D.-Korea, Executive Offices, RG 286, National Archives.

15. Taehan Pangjik Hyŏphoe, ed., *Panghyŏp isimnyŏnsa* [A twenty-year history of the Korean Spinners and Weavers Association] (Seoul: Samsŏng, 1968), 474.

16. C.M. George, "Prerequisites to Economic Viability," July 6, 1955, American

Embassy Seoul, Foreign Service Dispatch 5, RG 59, National Archives, p. 3; Edwin
M. Cronk, "Annual Economic Report 1955, ROK," March 19, 1956, American
Embassy Seoul, Foreign Service Dispatch 294, RG 59, National Archives, pp. 33–4,
47.

17. Taehan Pangjik Hyŏphoe, *Panghyŏp isimnyŏnsa*, 269.

18. Charles R. Frank, Jr., Kwang Suk Kim, and Larry E. Westphal, *Foreign
Trade Regimes and Economic Development: South Korea* (New York: National
Bureau of Economic Research, 1975), 36–9.

19. Former Japanese assets in South Korea were estimated at about 5.2 billion
dollars in 1945. JEA 1:35. However, many of the industrial properties suffered heavy
damage during the Korean War. All but 10% of the original twenty-seven hundred
vested business properties had been sold by July of 1956. Combined Economic
Board, U.N. Command, "Joint ROK/UNC Study of the Economic Reconstruction
Program for Korea," 1957, RG 59, National Archives, p. 19; W.R.F. Steiner, "Study
of Vested Property in Korea," July 8, 1952, A.I.D.-Korea, Executive Office, RG
286, National Archives.

20. The following nine firms each operated at least 30,000 spinning machines:
T'aech'ang, Kŭmsŏng, Chŏnnam, Taehan, Chosŏn, Kyungbang, Tongyang, Samho,
and Taechŏn (29,500 machines). Taehan Pangjik Hyŏphoe, ed., *Sŏmyu yŏnbo 1960*
[Textile annual, 1960] (Seoul: Taehan Pangjik Hyŏphoe, 1960).

21. Han'guk Sanŏp Ŭnhaeng [Korea Reconstruction Bank], "Han'guk myŏn
pangjik kongŏp ŭi chaemu punsŏl" [A financial analysis of the cotton spinning
industry in Korea], *Sanŏp Ŭnhaeng Wŏlbo*, no. 19 (Jan. 1957): 14–15.

22. Han'guk Ŭnhaeng, *Chosa Wŏlbo* [Monthly research review] 14, 11 (Nov.
1960): 40–1.

23. Suh Sang-chul, "Foreign Capital and Development Strategy in Korea,"
Korean Studies 2 (1978): 67–94; Chung Young-iob, "U.S. Economic Aid to South
Korea after World War II," in Andrew C. Nahm, ed., *American–Korean Relations,
1866–1976* (Kalamazoo: Center for Korean Studies, Western Michigan University),
187–217; Anne O. Krueger, *The Developmental Role of the Foreign Aid Sector*
(Cambridge: Harvard University Press, 1979); Kim Yang-hwa, "Miguk ŭi taehan
wŏnjo wa Han'guk ŭi kyŏngje kujo" [U.S. aid to Korea and the structure of the
Korean economy], in Song Kŏn-ho and Pak Hyŏn-ch'ae, eds., *Haebang sasimnyŏn ŭi
chaeinsik, I* [A reexamination of the forty years following liberation] (Seoul:
Tolbegae, 1985), 227–74.

24. Comptroller General of the United States, "U.S. Assistance Program for
Korea, International Cooperation Administration, Department of State, Fiscal Years
1954–1956," 1957, RG 59, National Archives, p. 54.

25. Frank, Kim, and Westphal, *Foreign Trade Regimes and Economic Development*, 35.

26. *Chosa Wŏlbo* 14, 11(Nov. 1960): 210, 212.

27. See my paper, "Concentration in a Weak State: The Early Textile Chaebŏl,"
Journal of Developing Societies, in press.

28. Kang Tong-jin, "Han'guk chaebŏl ŭi hyŏngsŏng kwajŏng kwa kyebo"; Kim
Sŏng-du, "Han'guk tokchŏm chaebŏl hyŏngsŏng ŭi t'ŭgisŏng"; Kim Tae-hwan, "1950
nyŏndae Han'guk kyŏngje ŭi yŏn'gu" [A study of the Korean economy in the 1950s],
in Chin Tŏk-gyu, ed., *1950 nyŏndae insik* [An understanding of the 1950s] (Seoul:
Hangilsa, 1981), 157–256.

29. Kang Se-gyun, *Chŏn'guk sanggong taegam*, 7; *Fifty Years*, 216–19.

30. The holding company including the trading branch was listed in 1955 with the
same paid-in capital, though now listed in the new currency (i.e., hwan) as three
million hwan. See Yŏm Han-yŏng, *Hoesa yŏn'gam 1955*, 435. The unit of currency

in the Republic was changed from wŏn to hwan on February 15, 1953, with an exchange rate of one hundred wŏn for one hwan.

31. Yamada Saburō, *Kankoku kōgyōka no kadai* [The process of industrialization in Korea], Report of the Institute of Asian Economies (Ajia Keizai Kenkyujō), No. 977 (Tokyo: Institute of Asian Economies, 1971), 222–38.

32. "Pak Hŭng-sik," 278. Tungsten served as a leading export for the First Republic, with the government's Korea Tungsten Mining Company responsible for extraction and private traders responsible for exports. See Chang Chi Ryang, "Tungsten Mining in Korea," *Korean Affairs* 2 (May/June 1962): 204–8. Kim Kyong-dong cited a "tungsten dollar incident" of 1952 in which the Rhee government allotted three million dollars of foreign exchange earned from tungsten exports to several entrepreneurs for grain and fertilizer imports. "By taking advantage of the discrepancy in foreign exchange rates and by monopolizing the price, these firms made enormous profits. The government was then offered a large contribution in return for the favor." See his "Political Factors in the Formation of the Entrepreneurial Elite in South Korea," *Asian Survey* 16, 5(May 1976): 468.

33. Ch'oe Hwal, *Sŏmyu yŏnbo 1960* [Textile annual 1960] (Seoul: Taehan Pangjik Hyŏphoe, 1960), 128.

34. Ch'oe Hwal, *Somyu yŏnbo 1959* [Textile annual 1959] (Seoul: Taehan Pangjik Hyŏphoe, 1959), sec. 4, p. 9.

35. *Fifty Years*, 257–9.

36. *Samyang*, 209.

37. Ibid., 213, 220.

38. Ibid., 220.

39. The leading Korean sugar companies in 1956 included the following: Lee Byung-chull's Cheil Sugar, as well as Tongyang, Kanguk, Kŭmsŏng, Haitai, and Taedong. Ibid., 237.

Cheil Sugar dominated the domestic market, producing 48% of the domestically produced sugar sold in the Republic in 1956, 37% in 1957, 54% in 1958, 62% in 1959, and 69% in 1960. Yi Tae-wŏn, *Cheil chedang Samsimnyŏnsa* [A thirty-year history of Cheil Sugar] (Seoul: Cheil Chedang Chusik Hoesa, 1983), 523.

40. Taehan Pangjik Hyŏphoe, *Panghyŏp isimnyŏnsa*, 143. Kyungbang had earlier procured 324 weaving machines in 1954 under a United Nations Korea Reconstruction Agency grant, thereby doubling the total number to 724. Kyungbang accounted for about 13% of the cotton cloth and 7% of the cotton yarn produced on the peninsula that year. See *Sŏmyu yŭnbo 1955*, sec. 1, pp. 6, 11–12.

41. Taehan Sangga Hoeuiso, ed., *Sanŏp Kyŏngje* (Dec. 1958): 75; *Sŏmyu yŏnbo 1959*, sec. 1, p. 3.

42. *Sanŏp Kyŏngje* (Nov. 1959): 75; *Sŏmyu yŏnbo 1960*, sec. 1, p. 5.

43. Cho Ki-jun, "Types of Entrepreneurs in the Modernization Process of the Korean Economy," in Asiatic Research Center, *Report of the International Conference on Problems of Modernization in Asia (June 28–July 7, 1965)* (Seoul: Korea University Asiatic Research Center, 1966), 623.

44. See my paper, "Autonomy and Capacity in Korea's First Republic," presented at the Fifty-ninth Annual Meeting of the Eastern Sociological Association, March 1989.

45. Hirschmeier and Yui, *The Development of Japanese Business*; also Gustav Ranis, "The Community-centered Entrepreneur in Japanese Development," *Explorations in Entrepreneurial History* 8, 2(Dec. 1955): 80–97.

46. See Kang Man-gil, "Reflections on the Centenary of the Opening of Korea," 10–18; Kim Kyong-dong, "Political Factors."

Appendix A

Portfolios

Table 1. *Min family portfolio (1942)*

Directorships	Paid-in capital (yen)[a]
Family-owned companies	
Kyesŏng Company [Kyesŏng]	2 million[b]
Yŏngbo Company [Yŏngbo Hammyŏng Hoesa]	2.5 million[b]
Major joint-stock investments/executive responsibility	
Hanil/Tongil Bank [Tongil Unhaeng]	2.775 million[b]
Chosŏn Silk Weaving [Chosŏn Kyŏnjik]	200 thousand[b]
Joint investments	
Kyŏngsŏng Spinning [Kyŏngsŏng Pangjik]	7.5 million
South Manchurian Spinning [Namman Pangjik]	5 million
Tonggwang Silk [Tonggwang Chesa]	2 million
Chosŏn Trade Promotion [Chosŏn Bōeki Shinkō]	1.5 million
Hwasin [Hwasin]	1 million
Hwasin Trade [Hwasin Muyŏk]	637 thousand
Chosŏn Industry and Management [Chosŏn Kongyŏng]	500 thousand
Chung'ang Brewery [Chung'ang Chujo]	480 thousand
Chosŏn Engineering [Chosŏn Kongjak]:	250,000[b]
Yŏnghwa Industries [Yŏnghwa Sanŏp]:	200,000[b]
Tōhō Development [Tōhō Shokusan]:	185,000[b]
Chosŏn Life Insurance [Chosŏn Saengmyŏng Pohŏm]:	115,000
Chosŏn Brewery [Chosŏn Yangjo]:	65,000
Participation in major Japanese ventures	
Keijō Electric [Keijō Denki]:	12.6 million
Chōsen Beer [Chōsen Biiru]:	3 million
Chōsen Trust [Chōsen Sintaku]:	2.5 million
Chōsen Land Improvement [Chōsen Tochi Kairyō]:	1.125 million

Note: This is a partial list of companies in which Min Tae-sik and Min Kyu-sik were listed as directors in the later colonial years.

[a] Figures indicate the amount of paid-in capital in 1942, or for the latest year available prior to 1942.

[b] The family or a family-owned company appeared among the top few largest stockholders. Unless otherwise indicated, the firms listed are all joint-stock companies.

Source: The table is based on information found in TGKY, CGKKY, and especially in DKB, 1942.

173

Table 2. *Portfolio of Pak Hŭng-sik (1942)*

Directorships	Paid-in capital (yen)[a]
Family-owned companies	
Sŏnil Paper [Sŏnil Chimul]	125 thousand[b]
Hwasin [Hwasin]	1 million[b]
Taedong Industries [Taedong Hŭngŏp]	500 thousand[b]
Major joint-investments/administrative responsibility	
Hwasin Trade [Hwasin Muyŏk]	637 thousand[b]
Joint investments	
Kyŏngsŏng Spinning [Kyŏngsŏng Pangjik]	7.5 million
South Manchurian Spinning [Namman Pangjik]	5 million
Tongil Bank [Tongil Ŭnhaeng]	2.775 million[b]
Honam Bank [Honam Ŭnhaeng]	1.875 million[b]
Chōsen Wholesale Textile [Chōsen Seni Zakka Gensha]	1.5 million
Keijin Enterprise [Keijin Kigyō]	1 million[b]
Daikō Trade [Daikō Bōeki]	500 thousand[b]
Chejudo Industrial [Chejudo Sanŏp]	500 thousand[b]
Chosŏn Industry and Management [Chosŏn Kongyŏng]	500 thousand[b]
Chosŏn Engineering [Chosŏn Kongjak]	250 thousand[b]
Chosŏn Life Insurance [Chosŏn Saengmyŏng Pohŏm]	115 thousand
Participation in major Japanese ventures	
Oriental Development Company [Tōyō Takushoku]	62.5 million
Chōsen Aircraft Industry [Chōsen Hikoki Kōgyō]	50 million
Chōsen Petroleum [Chōsen Sekiyū]	27 million
North Korea Paper and Chemical Manufacture [Hokusen Seishi	10 million
Kagaku Kōgyō]	1.25 million
Chōsen Heian Railway [Chōsen Heian Tetsudo]	

Note: This is a partial list of companies in which Pak Hŭng-sik served on the board of directors in the later colonial years.

[a] Figures indicate the amount of paid-in capital in 1942, or for the latest year available prior to 1942.

[b] The family or a family-owned company appeared among the top few largest stockholders. The firms were all joint-stock companies.

Source: The table is based on information found in TGKY, CGKKY, and especially in DKB, 1942.

Table 3. *Portfolio of Kim Yŏn-su (1942)*

Directorships	Paid-in capital (yen)[a]
Family-owned companies	
Samyangsa [Samyangsa]	3 million[b]
Chung'ang Commerce and Industry [Chung'ang Sanggong]	1 million[b]
Samch'ŏk Enterprises [Samch'ŏk Kiŏp]	250 thousand[b]
Major joint-stock investments/administrative responsibility	
Kyŏngsŏng Spinning [Kyŏngsŏng Pangjik]	7.5 million[b]
Haedong Bank [Haedong Ŭnhaeng]	800 thousand[b]
South Manchurian Spinning [Namman Pangjik]	5 million[b]
Samyang Commercial [Samyang Sangsa]	190 thousand[b]
Joint investments	
Taech'ang Industries [Taech'ang Sanŏp]	1.5 million
Shōwa Kirin Beer [Shōwa Kirin Biiru]	1.2 million
Okkye Gold [Okkye Kinsan]	1 million[b]
Hwasin Trade [Hwasin Muyŏk]	637 thousand[b]
Daikō Trade [Daikō Bōeki]	500 thousand[b]
Chosŏn Engineering [Chosŏn Kongjak]	250 thousand[b]
Chosŏn Life Insurance [Chosŏn Saengmyŏng Pohŏm]	115 thousand[b]
Participation in major Japanese ventures	
Chōsen Aircraft Industry [Chōsen Hikoki Kōgyō]	50 million
Chōsen Petroleum [Chōsen Sekiyū]	27 million
Kankō Hydroelectric [Kankō Suiryoku Denki]	12.5 million[b]
West Chōsen Central Railway [Seisen Chūo Tetsudo]	6 million
Keishun Railway [Keishun Tetsudo]	5 million[b]
Chōsen Refining [Chōsen Seiren]	5 million
Chōsen Keitō Railway [Chōsen Keitō Tetsudo]	3.45 million[b]
Chōsen Tōa Trade [Chōsen Tōa Bōeki]	2.5 million[b]
Chōsen Heian Railway [Chōsen Heian Tetsudo]	1.25 million[b]
Chōsen Books and Printing [Chōsen Shoseki Insatsu]	500 thousand

Note: This is a partial list of companies in which Kim Yŏn-su was listed among the directors in the later colonial years.

[a] Figures indicate the amount of paid-in capital in 1942, or for the latest year available prior to 1942.

[b] The family or a family-owned company appeared among the top few largest stockholders.

Source: The table is based on information found in TGKY, CGKKY, and especially in DKB, 1942.

Appendix B

Brief Biographies

Abe Sen'ichi

Abe joined the government-general in Seoul as secretary just after graduation from Tokyo University in 1919. He was later appointed mayor of P'yŏngyang and then governor of South Kyŏngsang Province. Abe managed the Korean operations of Chōsen Gold Industry, and later organized Okkye Gold with Kim Yŏn-su. Abe served as president of the government's control agency, the Chosen Gold Sales and Purchase Company, during the war years.

Ariga Mitsutoyo

Born in 1873, Ariga joined the Tax Bureau in Japan after graduation from Tokyo Law Academy in 1895. He soon came to Korea as an official in the finance section of the residency-general and the government-general, before appointment as a director and then president of the Industrial Bank at age forty-six in 1919. Successful direction of the bank led to his appointment to the Japanese House of Peers in September of 1934. Retiring from the bank in 1937, Ariga went on to the presidencies of such prominent Japanese firms as Chōsen Refining, the Japan High Frequency Heavy Industry, and Kankō Hydroelectric.

Ch'oe Ch'ang-hak

Born in 1891 in North P'yŏngan Province, Ch'oe gained wealth and presitige as the "gold mining king" through development of Samsŏng Mining, sold to Mitsui Mining in 1929. Although Ch'oe developed his own Taech'ang Industries, he was better known for extensive investments in Japanese enterprises on the peninsula, and his participation on the board of the unofficial government daily, the *Maeil Sinpo*. He was a major shareholder in Keijin Enterprise, Tashidō Railway, Chōsen Trust, and in North Korean Paper and Chemical Manufacturing. Ch'oe also served as a director of Posŏng School, of Kyŏngsŏng, and of the Kim family's Haedong Industries.

Chogō Eiji

Born in 1896, Chogō graduated from the Civil Engineering Department of Tokyo Imperial University in 1919 before joining the Ministry of Interior. He was dispatched to Korea in 1926 to supervise flood control projects and local railroad construction as chief of the Wŏnsan Civil Engineering Station. An advisor for the

Manchuria and Chōsen Trade Association, Chogō later joined the Hwasin chaebŏl as a leading executive. His experience in government and trade fit well with the plans of Pak Hŭng-sik for international trade, first at Sŏnil Paper and later at Hwasin Trade.

Ha Chun-sŏk

Cofounder of Chejudo Industries with Pak Hŭng-sik, Ha served as president of Chosŏn Engineering for manufacture of mining and military equipment. He also appeared as president of Dōka Industries for trade on the Chinese mainland.

Han Sang-yong

Educated in Japan, he returned to Korea at the turn of the century to a career in the Hansŏng Bank. A relative by marriage of Count Yi Wan-yong, Han was welcomed by the aristocratic owners with promotions to managing director (1910–23), and then to a five-year tenure as president. Remaining active in finance, Han later held posts in Korean firms such as Chosŏn Life Insurance, but mainly in prestigious Japanese investments such as Chōsen Trust. He took part as a director and often major investor in a number of other prominent industrial and financial concerns during the colonial years, though seldom as a major stockholder in larger native enterprises.

Hashimoto Keizaburō

Hashimoto graduated from Tokyo Imperial University before entering the ministries of Finance, and later Agriculture and Commerce, rising to the level of vice-minister in both. He went on to the presidencies of Nippon Petroleum and Chōsen Petroleum, directorships at numerous mining and industrial firms, and appointment to the House of Peers.

Hayashi Shigeki

A graduate of Tokyo University in 1912, Hayashi served as director of the Education Bureau of the government-general, and then governor of North Chŏlla Province. Turning later to finance, Hayashi served under Ariga at the Industrial Bank, and as a director from 1933 to 1936. Hayashi gained appointment as executive director of the Keishun Railway, and of Kankō Electric under President Ariga Mitsutoyo.

Hyŏn Chun-ho

Hyŏn (1888–1950), a leading landowner in South Chŏlla Province, owned the Hakp'a Agricultural Estate, and served as president and major owner of the Honam Bank. Hyŏn also served on the board of the *Donga Ilbo* and Posŏng College, and was prominent in various other Korean-owned ventures.

Kada Naoji

Kada worked as a civil engineer in the colony of Taiwan before coming to Korea in 1917 to pursue business interests, originally in lumber. He later served as president of Chōsen Leather, and also of Chōsen Agriculture Promotion. Active also in business policy associations, he served as president of the Keijō Chamber of Commerce and Industry from 1932 to 1939.

Katō Keizaburō

Born in 1874, Katō graduated with a degree in law from Nippon University in 1898. After some years of government service, he won appointment as president of the Hokkaido Industrial Bank in 1924. He went on to a long tenure (1927–37) as president of the Bank of Chōsen, and kept a role in business circles as president of the Chōsen Industrial Association.

Kim Sa-yŏn

Born in Seoul in 1898, Kim graduated from Keio University in Tokyo before becoming active in the Hanil Bank. He later served as president of Chosŏn Yeast, as a director of the Tongil Bank, as a member of the Central Advisory Council from April of 1934, and as auditor of South Manchurian Spinning.

Kim Sŏng-su

The adopted son of Wŏnp'a Kim Ki-jung, Sŏng-su (1891–1955) (pen name Inch'on) graduated from Waseda University in 1912 and returned home as a teacher and administrator at Posŏng Middle School. He founded the famous Kyŏngsŏng Spinning and Weaving Company together with Pak Yŏng-hyo in 1919 and remained at the firm as a director through 1927, and later as an advisor, while maintaining a large block of shares in the company. Sŏng-su founded the prominent vernacular *Donga Ilbo* newspaper in April of 1920, and later helped found Posŏng College. Sŏng-su emerged as a leading political figure in Korea's First Republic and served briefly as vice-president in May of 1951.

Kim Yŏn-su

The son of a prosperous landowner, Kim Yŏn-su (1896–1979) was a native of the Koch'ang area in North Chŏlla Province. He attended middle school in Tokyo and later graduated from the Economics Department of Kyoto Imperial University. Upon his return he took charge of the family's agricultural properties, expanding the family-owned Samyang Company with agricultural estates in Korea and Manchuria, plus holdings in other commercial and industrial ventures. He served as executive director at Kyŏngsŏng Spinning (1922–7) and president (1935–45), and as representative director of the Haedong Bank (1927–38). He devoted his energies in the First Republic to trade and sugar production at the Samyang Company.

Kim Yong-wan

Brother-in-law and business associate of Kim Yŏn-su, Kim originally managed an agricultural estate with the Samyang before joining the management at Kyŏngsŏng Spinning. He assumed the presidency of Kyŏngsŏng soon after liberation, and became a leader in the Korean Chamber of Commerce and Industry, and in the Federation of Korean Industries.

Min Kyu-sik

Born in 1888, the younger brother of Min Tae-sik attended the family's Hwimun School and studied privately before going on for a college degree at Cambridge

University. Returning to Seoul in the spring of 1920, he immediately assumed the post of managing director of the Hanil Bank. Three years later he became president of the family's industrial venture, the Chosŏn Silk Weaving Company. He organized the Yŏngbo agricultural and real estate firm as a holding company for his land-holdings, buildings, and investments in other commercial and industrial ventures. Min Kyu-sik served as president of the Tongil Bank and then the Choheung Bank until 1945, and thereafter as a director. He remained a prominent figure in finance in the First Republic as president of a finance company and later the Korea Commerce and Industry Bank.

Min Pyŏng-do

The eldest son of Min Tae-sik, Pyŏng-do graduated from Keio University in Tokyo. He subsequently assumed executive responsibilities at the family's Kyesŏng firm, and later at the Tongil's main bank in Seoul.

Min Tae-sik

Born the eldest son of Min Yŏng-hwi, Min Tae-sik (1882–1951) was a high-ranking military officer in the administration of Emperor Kojong at the end of the Chosŏn Dynasty, and a government advisor in 1904 just prior to annexation. After travel to the United States, he returned to manage a family mining venture. He organized his agricultural and real estate holdings under the family-owned Kyesŏng Company in 1935, a holding company also for investments in other enterprises. He served as president of the Hanil Bank from 1920, and then of the Tongil (1931–6).

Min Yŏng-hwi

The father of Min Tae-sik and Kyu-sik, Min Yŏng-hwi (1852–1935) (pen name Hajŏng) had enjoyed prominence as an aristocrat and financier at the end of the Chosŏn Dynasty. He was granted a stipend and title of viscount by the government-general in 1910. Investment in the Hanil Bank led to a directorship in August of 1912. Within three years he won executive control, relinquishing the presidency to his son Tae-sik only in 1920.

Nakatomi Keita

Born in 1888, Nakatomi was initially associated with Kobe Commerce (Kobe Shōgyō). An auditor of the Chōsen Industrial Bank, he served on the board of Chōsen Refining and three trading companies: Chōsen Trade Promotion, Chōsen Tōa Trade, and Daikō Trade. Nakatomi appeared as an auditor of both the Kyŏngsŏng and the South Manchurian Spinning ventures.

Noguchi Jun

An engineering graduate of Tokyo University in 1896, Noguchi developed one of the leading prewar zaibatsu through investment in hydroelectric power, chemicals, and refining. He served as founder and president of Japan Nitrogenous Fertilizer and its affiliate, Chōsen Nitrogenous Fertilizer, and was prominent in various hydro-electric ventures on the peninsula as well.

Ōhashi Shintarō

Born in 1863 in Niigata-ken, Ōhashi rose to the presidencies of Keijō Electric, Chōsen Smokeless Coal, Taiwan Electrification, Nippon Glass, and Oyodogawa Hydroelectric Power. He was elected chair of the board of Chōsen Beer, Dai Nippon Brewery, and Electric Chemical Industrial. He appeared as a director of such leading firms as Daiichi Life Insurance, Tokyo Electric Light, Hokkai Hydro-electric Power, Nippon Yūsen, and the Ōji Paper Manufacturing companies among others.

Pak Hŭng-sik

Pak was born in South P'yŏngan Province near Chinnamp'o in northwest Korea in 1903. He parlayed some family landholdings into local printing and cotton investments. He moved to Seoul in 1926 and quickly established Sŏnil Paper Goods. The company's success led to a further investment in his famous and widely successful Hwasin Department Store on Chongno Avenue in Seoul. Pak organized firms for domestic wholesaling and retailing, trading ventures in China and Southeast Asia, and held minority shares in other joint-stock firms. He led the Hwasin chaebŏl through the liberation and the First Republic in the south under Syngman Rhee, specializing in trade and textile production.

Pak Pyŏng-gyo

Nephew of Pak Hŭng-sik, Pak held major blocks of shares and served on the boards of various Hwasin chaebŏl ventures.

Pak Yŏng-ch'ŏl

Pak had graduated from the Officers School of the Japanese Army in 1904 and served with the Japanese military. Returning to Korea in 1912, he served as a county magistrate and later province governor under the colonial administration. Retiring from public office in 1927, he soon became active in finance as president of the Samnam Bank, and auditor of the Oriental Development Company, and president of the Chōsen Commercial Bank (1929–32).

Pak Yŏng-hyo

A cofounder of Kyŏngsŏng Spinning, Pak (1861–1939) had gained prominence as a government official and reformer in the late Chosŏn Dynasty. He received both the title of marquis and an annual stipend from the government-general from 1910. Pak served as a director of the Chōsen Industrial Bank (1918–30), and then as an advisor until 1938. He was appointed to the Central Advisory Council in 1921, and later to the Japanese House of Peers.

Shibuya Reiji

A former Bank of Chōsen Research director with wide knowledge of Manchuria and China, Shibuya served as executive director of both Daikō Trade and Chōsen Dōa Trade. Born in Hokkaido in 1878, Shibuya graduated from Waseda University and served some years with the nationalist Gen'yōsha organization before joining the Bank of Chōsen. He was prominent as well in trade policy associations.

Ugaki Kazushige

A graduate of the Military Academy in 1891, Ugaki (1868–1956) was raised to the rank of general by 1925. He served as Minister of the Army for four separate terms, and later as a Minister of Foreign Affairs. Ugaki served as governor-general in the colony briefly in 1927, and then from 1931 to 1936.

Appendix C

Glossary

Abe Sen'ichi	阿部千一
Akita Hideo	秋田秀穗
Ariga Mitsutoyo	有賀光豐
budan seiji	武斷政治
bunka seiji	文化政治
chaebŏl/zaibatsu	財閥
Changsang T'an'geng	長上炭坑
Cheil Chedang	第一製糖
Chejudo Hŭngŏp	濟州道興業
chido	指導
Cho Chun-ho	趙俊鎬
Cho Kye-hyŏn	曹契鉉
Ch'oe Ch'ang-hak	崔長學
Ch'oe Tū-sŏn	崔斗善
Chogō Eiji	長鄕衛二
Chohŭng Ŭnhaeng	朝興銀行
Chōjiya	丁子屋
Chŏng Chae-hak	鄭在學
chŏnmu/senmu	專務
Chōsen Biiru	朝鮮麥酒
Chōsen Bōeki Shinkō	朝鮮貿易振興
Chōsen Bōshoku	朝鮮紡織
Chōsen Chisso Hiryō	朝鮮窒素肥料
Chōsen Chisso Kayaku	朝鮮窒素火藥
Chōsen Chochiku Ginkō	朝鮮貯蓄銀行
Chōsen Ginkō	朝鮮銀行
Chōsen Heian Tetsudo	朝鮮平安鐵道
Chōsen Hikaku	朝鮮皮革
Chōsen Hikoki Kōgyō	朝鮮飛行工業
Chōsen Jinzō Sekiyu	朝鮮人造石油
Chōsen Jūgyō	朝鮮重業
Chōsen Kanno	朝鮮勸農
Chōsen Keitō Tetsudo	朝鮮京東鐵道

Chōsen Kikuji	朝鮮麴子
Chōsen Kōgyō Kyōkai	朝鮮工業協會
Chōsen Muentan	朝鮮無煙炭
Chōsen Oryokkō Suiryoku Hatsuden	朝鮮鴨綠江水發電
Chōsen Sankin Shinkō	朝鮮產金振興
Chōsen Seiren	朝鮮製煉
Chōsen Sekiyu	朝鮮石油
Chōsen Seni Zakka Gensha	朝鮮纖維貨元卸株
Chōsen Shintaku	朝鮮信託
Chōsen Shokusan Ginkō	朝鮮殖產銀行
Chōsen Shoseki Insatsu	朝鮮書籍印刷
Chōsen Sōden	朝鮮送電
Chōsen Sōtokufu	朝鮮總督府
Chōsen Suiryoku Denki	朝鮮水力電氣
Chōsen Tōa Bōeki	朝鮮東亞貿易
Chōsen Tochi Kairyō	朝鮮土地改良
Chosŏn Ch'ŏngnyŏn Yŏnhaphoe	朝鮮青年聯合會
Chosŏn Kongjak	朝鮮工作
Chosŏn Kongyŏng	朝鮮工營
Chosŏn Kukja	朝鮮麴子
Chosŏn Kyŏnjik	朝鮮絹織
Chosŏn Saengmyŏng	朝鮮生命
Chu Yo-han	朱耀翰
Chūgai Sangyō	中外產業
Chūgai Tōshi	中外投資
Chung'ang Chujo	中央酒製
Chung'ang Sanggong	中央商工
chusik hoesa/kabushiki kaisha	株式會社
Chūsūin	中樞院
ch'wich'eyok/torishimariyaku	取締役
Dai Nippon Bōseki	大日本紡織
Dai Nippon Seitō	大日本製糖
Daikō Bōeki	大興貿易
Donga Ilbo	東亞日報
Fuzan Suisan	釜山水產
Gen'yōsha	玄洋社
Ginkōrei	銀行令
Ha Chun-sŏk	河駿錫
Haedong Hŭngŏp	海東興業
Haedong Ŭnhaeng	海東銀行
Hakp'a Nongjang	鶴玻農場
hammyŏng hoesa/gōmei kaisha	合名會社
Hanil Ŭnhaeng	漢一銀行
Han Kyu-bok	韓圭復
Han Sang-yong (Kan So-ryū)	韓相龍

Hansŏng Ŭnhaeng	韓城銀行
hapcha hoesa/gōshi kaisha	合資會社
Hashimoto Keizaburō	橋元敬三郎
Hayashi Shigeki	林茂樹
Hayashi Shigezō	林繁臧
Hirata Shinpei	平田新平
Hirayama Masao	平山正夫
hoejang/kaichō	會長
Hokusen Seishi Kagaku Kōgyō	北鮮製紙化學工業
Honam Ŭnhaeng	湖南銀行
Hwasin	和信
Hwayohoe	火曜會
Hyŏn Chun-ho	玄俊鎬
Im Hŏn-gyŏng	林憲慶
Ishikawa Shinjirō	市川眞次郎
Iwama Makoto	岩間亮
Kada Naoji	賀田直治
Kaebyŏk	開闢
Kaisharei	會社令
Kamizawa Murasei	神澤紫樓
kamsayŏk/kansayaku	監査役
Kanegafuchi Bōseki	鐘淵紡織
Kankō Suiryoku Denki	漢工水力電氣
Katō Keizaburō	加藤徹三郎
Kawaguchi Makoto	河口亮
Kawamoto Toshimasu	河本駿錫
Keijin Kigyō	京仁企業
Keijō Denki	京城電氣
Keijō Shōkō Kaigijo	京城商工會議所
Keishun Tetsudo	京春鐵道
kengi	建議
Kim Chae-su	金在洙
Kim Hong-jip	金弘集
Kim Ki-jung, Wŏnp'a	金祺中，圓坡
Kim Kyŏng-jung, Chisan	金景中，芝山
Kim Ok-hyŏn	金玉鉉
Kim Sa-yŏn	金思演
Kim Sŏng-su, Inch'on	金性洙，仁村
Kim Yo-hyŏp, Akche	金堯莢，藥濟
Kim Yŏn-su, Sudang	金年洙，秀堂
Kim Yong-wan	金容完
Ko Kwang-p'yo	高光表
Ko Wŏn-dong	高元勳
Kobe Seishi	神戸製絲
Kobe Shōgyō	神戸商業

Kodama Hideo	皇玉秀雄
kŭndae kukka	近代國家
Kyeryong Kŭmsan	鷄龍金山
Kyesŏng	桂成
kyŏllok	結錄
kyŏngjejŏk chŏnbok	經濟的征服
Kyŏngsŏng Chigyu	京成織紐
Kyŏngsŏng Pangjik	京成紡織
maep'an	買辦
Meiji	明治
Meiji Seika	明治製菓
Min Kyu-sik	閔圭植
Min Pyŏng-do	閔丙壽
Min Tae-sik	閔大植
Min Yong-hwi	閔泳微
Minakai	三中井
minjok chabon	民族資本
minjok kaeryang chuŭija	民族改良主義者
minjok kiŏp	民族企業
Mitani Toshiro	三谷俊博
Mitsubishi	三菱
Mitsukoshi	三越
Mitsui	三井
Mitsui Bussan	三井物産
Mozan Tekkō Kaihatsu	茂山鐵礦開發
Mun Sang-u	文尙宇
Naisen ittai	內鮮一體
Nakatomi Keita	中富計太
Namman Pangjik	南滿紡織
Nanboku Mengyō	南北棉業
Nichitsu	日窒
Nippon Chisso Hiryō	日本室素肥料
Nippon Kinsan Shinkō	日本金産振興
Nippon Kōshūsho Jūgyo	日本高周波重業
Nippon Magunesito Kagaku Kōgyō	日本Magunesito化學工業
Nippon Sangyō Keizai Iinkai	日本産業經濟委員會
Nippon Seitetsu	日本製鐵
Nippon Seifun	日本製粉
Noguchi Jun	野口遵
Ōji Seishi	王子製絲
Ōji Shōken	王子證卷
Ōhashi Shintarō	大橋新太郎
Okkye Kinsan	王偊金産
Ōkura Kihachirō	大倉喜八郎
Paek In-gi	白應卽

Pak Hŭng-sik	朴興植
Pak Pyŏng-gyo	朴炳教
Pak Yŏng-ch'ŏl	朴榮哲
Pak Yŏng-hyo	朴泳孝
Pang Ŭi-sŏk	方義錫
Park Chung-hee (Pak Chŏng-hŭi)	朴正熙
Pukp'unghoe	北風會
Rhee Syngman (Yi Sŭng-man)	李丞晚
Ryūsan Kōsaku	龍山工作
sajang/shachō	社長
Sakoma Fusatarō	泊間房太郎
Samch'ŏk Kiŏp	三拓企業
Samyangsa	三養社
sangmu/jōmu	常務
Sansei Kōgyō	三成工業
Shibusawa Eiichi	涉澤榮一
Shibuya Reiji	涉谷禮治
Shiokawa Tōruyoshi	鹽川濟吉
Shiraishi Munenari	白石宗城
Shōwa Kirin Biiru	昭和麒麟麥酒
Sin Ki-ch'ang	申基昌
Sin'ganhoe	新幹會
Sŏnil Chimul	鮮一紙物
Sunch'ang T'angeng	新倉炭坑
Taech'ang Muyŏk	大昌貿易
Taech'ang Sanŏp	大昌產業
Taedong Hŭngŏp	大同興業
taep'yo/daihyo	代表
Tagawa Tsunejirō	田川常治郎
Taguchi Sukeichi	田口弼一
Taiku Seishi	大邱製絲
Taishō	大正
Tanaka Saburō	田中三郎
Tani Takima	谷多喜磨
Teikoku Seima	帝國製麻
t'och'ak chabon	土着資本
Tōhō Shokusan	東邦殖產
Tokyo Kōtō Kōgyō Gakko	東京高等工業學校
Tonggwang Chesa	東光製絲
Tonggwang Sengsa	東光生絲
Tongil Ŭnhaeng	東一銀行
Tōyō Bōseki	東洋紡織
Tōyō Seishi	東洋製絲
Tōyō Takushoku	東洲拓殖
Toyota Bōshoku	豐田紡織

Tsuda Shingo	津田信五
Ushijima Shozō	牛島省三
Watanabe Sadaichirō	渡邊定一郎
Yasuda Kyŏjun	安田慶淳
yesok chabon	隸屬資本
Yi Kang-hyŏn	李康賢
Yi Ki-yŏn	李基衍
Yi Kwang-su	李光洙
Yi Kyu-jae	李圭載
Yi Pyŏng-ch'ŏl (Lee Byung-chull)	李秉哲
Yokose Morio	橫瀨守雄
Yoneda Yasaburo	米田彌三郎
Yŏngbo	永保
Yŏnghwa Sanŏp	永和產業
yūkei kikan	誘掖機關
Yun U-sik	尹宇植
Zenkoku Hyakkaten Kumiai	全國百貨店組合

Bibliography

Asian Languages

Abe Kaoru. *Chōsen kōrōsha meikan* [A list of eminent figures in Korea]. Keijō: Minshū Jironsha, 1935.

Ch'a Ki-byôk, ed. *Ilche ŭi Han'guk sigmin t'ongch'i* [Colonial administration in Korea under Japanese imperial rule]. Seoul: Chŏngŭmsa, 1985.

Cheil Mojik Kongŏp Chusik Hoesa, ed. *Cheil Mojik 20 nyŏn* [Twenty years of Cheil Wool]. Seoul: Cheil Mojik Kongŏp Chusik Hoesa, 1974.

Chin Tŏk-su. "1920 nyŏndae kungnae minjok undong e kwanhan koch'al" [Reflections on domestic national movements in the 1920s]. In Song Kŏng-ho and Kang Man-gil, eds., *Han'guk minjujuŭi ron* [A study of Korean democracy], 140–590. Seoul: Ch'angjak kwa Pip'yŏngsa, 1982.

Cho Ki-jun. *Han'guk kiŏpkasa* [A history of Korean entrepreneurs]. Seoul: Pagyŏngsa, 1973.

Han'guk chabonjuŭi sŏngnipsa ron [A study of the development of capitalism in Korea]. Seoul: Taegwangsa, 1977.

Han'guk kyŏnjesa [An economic history of Korea]. Seoul: Ilsinsa, 1985.

"Han'guk chabonjuŭi hyŏngsŏnggi ŭi kiŏbin yŏn'gu" [Studies of entrepreneurs in the formation of Korean capitalism], *Haksulwŏn nonmunjip* (1987): 8–125.

Ch'oe Hwal. *Sŏmyu yŏnbo 1955* [Textile annual 1955]. Seoul: Taehan Pangjik Hyŏphoe, 1955.

Sŏmyu yŏnbo 1960 [Textile annual 1960]. Seoul: Taehan Pangjik Hyŏphoe, 1960.

Ch'oe Yŏng-gyu. *Han'guk hyŏngmyŏng chaep'ansa* [Korean revolution: a history of the litigation], vol. 1. Seoul: Tonga Publishing, 1962.

Ch'oe Yŏng-mo. *Chohŭng Ŭnhaeng 90 nyŏnsa* [A ninety-year history of the Choheung Bank]. Seoul: Choheung Bank, 1987.

Chōsen Kōgyō Kyōkai. *Chōsen kōjō meiran* [List of factories in Korea]. Keijō: Chōsen Kōgyō Kyōkai, 1932, 1936, 1940.

Chōsen no kōgyō to sono shigen [Industry and industrial resources in Korea], edited by Shibuya Reiji. Keijō: Chōsen Kōgyō Kyōkai, 1937.

Chōsen Orimono Kyōkai. *Chōsen seni yōran* [Korean textile annual], edited by Hashiguchi Hideko. Keijō: Chōsen Orimono Kyōkai, 1943.

Chōsen Shōkō Kaigisho. *Zensen shōkō kaigisho hattenshi* [A history of the development of chambers of commerce and industry in Korea], edited by Kuninaka Reisui. Pusan: Fuzan Nippōsha, 1935.

Chōsen Shokusan Ginkō (Chōsen Industrial Bank). *Chōsen Shokusan Ginkō nijūnen shi* [A twenty-year history of the Chōsen Industrial Bank]. Keijō: Industrial Bank, 1938.

Chōsen Shokusan Ginkō, Chōsabu. *Chōsen ni okeru kōgyō kaisha no shihon kōsei chōsa* [A study of capital formation in Korean industrial companies]. Keijō: Chōsen Shokusan Ginkō, 1935.

"Chōsen ni okeru dochaku shihon no kenkyū" [A study of indigenous capital in Korea]. *Shokugin Chosa Geppō* (Apr. 1938): 1–8.

"Chōsen no kōgyō go kōjō" [Industrial factories in Korea]. *Shokugin Chōsa Geppō*, no. 58 (Dec. 1939): 53–94.

"Chōsen ni okeru hantōjin shihaika no kaisha jōsei" [The condition of companies under native management in Korea]. *Shokugin Chōsa Geppō* (Jan. 1940): 25–64.

"Chōsen tōka naichi shihon go kore ni yoru jigyō" [The enterprises of Japanese capital invested in Korea]. *Shokugin Chōsa Geppō*, no. 65 (June 1940): 12–43.

"Chōsen shikin mondai no shindankai" [A new phase in the problem of capital in Korea], part 2. *Shokugin Chōsa Geppō*, no. 76 (May 1941): 35–44; no. 77 (June 1941): 15–38.

"Chōsen ni okeru dochaku shihon no kenkyū" [A study of indigenous capital in Korea]. *Shokugin Chōsa Geppō* (1943): 1–9.

Chōsen Shokusan Ginkō Kanteifu. *Zensen tanden baibai kakaku oyobi shūekicho* [A study of prices and profits in the purchase and sale of land in Korea]. Keijō: Chōsen Shokusan Ginkō Kanteifu, 1943.

Chōsen Sōtokufu. *Chōsen Sōtokufu Kanbo, 1928.* [Official Gazette of the Government-General, 1928]. Keijō: Chōsen Sōtokufu, 1928.

Hōreishū [Collection of laws]. Keijō: Chōsen Sōtokufu, 1936.

Chōsen hōrei shūran [A collection of legislation in Korea]. Tokyo: Teikoku Chihō Kyōsei Gakkai Chōsen Honbu, 1938.

Shisei sanjūnen shi [A thirty-year history of administration]. Appendix: "Nempyō" [chronology]. Keijō: Chōsen Insatsu Kabushiki Kaisha, 1940. (Cited as Chronology.)

Chōsen Tōkanfu. *Kanbo* [Official Gazette]. Keijō: Residency-General, 1960–9.

Chosŏn Ŭnhaeng Chosabu. *Chosôn kyŏngje yŏnbo 1948* [Annual of the Korean economy, 1948], edited by Chang Ki-yŏng. Seoul: Chosŏn Ŭnhaeng, 1948.

Chu Chong-hwan. *Chaebŏl kyŏngje non: sanŏp chojik nonjŏk chŏpkŭn* [An economic study of the chaebŏl, from the perspective of industrial organization]. Seoul: Chŏngŭm Munhwasa, 1985.

Donga Ilbosa. *Donga Ilbo.* Seoul: Donga Ilbosa.

Donga Ilbo Sasŏl P'yŏnch'an Wiwŏnhoe, ed. *Donga Ilbo sasŏl nonjip* 1 (1920–1940) [Collection of editorials from the *Donga Ilbo*]. Seoul: Donga Ilbosa, 1977. (Cited as DISN.)

Han Pae-ho. "Samil undong chikhu ŭi Chosŏn singminji chŏngch'aek" [Colonial policy in Korea immediately after the March First Movement]. In Ch'a Ki-byŏk, ed., *Ilche ŭi Han'guk singmin t'ongch'i* [Colonial administration in Korea under the Japanese Empire], 78–107. Seoul: Chŏngŭmsa, 1985.

Han Sang-yong. *Kan Soryŭ Kun o wataru* [Reflections of Han Sang-yong]. Keijō: Kan Soryū Kun Kanreki Kinenkai, 1941.

Han'guk Inmyŏng Taesajŏn P'yŏnch'an Wiwŏnhoe, ed. *Han'guk inmyŏng taesajŏn* [A dictionary of eminent Koreans]. Seoul: Singu Munhwasa, 1967.

Han'guk Sanŏp Ŭnhaeng. "Han'guk myŏn pangjik kongŏp ŭi chaemu punsŏl" [A financial analysis of the cotton spinning industry in Korea]. *Sanop Ŭnhaeng Wŏlbo*, no. 19 (Jan. 1957): 14–27.

Han'guk Ŭnhaeng. *Chosa Wŏlbo* [Monthly Research Review] 14, 11(Nov. 1960).

Hanil Ŭnhaeng. *Hanil Unhaeng osipnyŏnsa* [A fifty-year history of the Hanil Bank], edited by Kim Yu-sŏng. Seoul: Samsŏng, 1982.

Hatori Junhiro. "Senjika (1937–1945) Chōsen ni okeru tsūka to infureshion"

[Inflation in the currency of Chōsen during wartime]. In Iinuma Jirō and Kyō Zaigen, eds., *Shokuminchi Chōsen no shakai to teikō* [Society and resistance in colonial Korea], 238–81. Tokyo: Miraisha, 1982.

Hŏ Su-ryul. "1930 nyŏndae kunyo kongŏphwa chŏngch'aek kwa Ilbon chabon ŭi chinch'ul" [The industrialization policy for military needs in the 1930s, and the advance of Japanese monopoly capital]. In Ch'a Ki-byŏk, ed., *Ilche ŭi Han'guk singmin t'ongch'i* [The colonial administration of Korea under Japanese rule], 228–88. Seoul: Chŏngŭmsa, 1985.

Hong Sŏng-yu. *Han'guk kyŏngje ŭi chabon ch'ukchŏk ŭi kwajŏng* [The process of capital accumulation in the Korean economy]. Seoul: Korea University Press, 1965.

Hwang Myŏng-su. *Kiŏpkasa yŏn'gu* [Studies in entrepreneurship]. Seoul: Ch'ŏndae Publishing, 1983.

Ikeshima Hiroyuki. "Nihon ni okeru kigyōhō no keisei to tenkai" [The formation and development of enterprise legislation in Japan]. In Takayanagi Shinichi and Fujita, *Shihonsugihō no keisei to tenkai* [The formation and development of capitalist law], 205–58. Tokyo: University of Tokyo Press, 1973.

Im Chong-sik. *Ilche ch'imnyak ch'inilp'a* [Pro-Japanese groups and aggression under Japanese imperialism]. Seoul: Ch'ŏngsa, 1982.

Imotani Zenichi. *Chōsen keizaishi* [A history of the Korean economy]. Tokyo: Daitōkaku, 1955.

Inch'on Kinyŏmhoe. *Inch'on Kim Sŏng-su chŏn* [A biography of Inch'on Kim Sŏng-su]. Seoul: Inch'on Kinyŏmhoe, 1976. (Cited as *Inch'on.*)

Jigyō to Keizaisha. *Senman sangyō taikan, 1940* [Review of commerce in Chōsen and Manchukuo, 1940), edited by Naitō Hatoya. Tokyo: Jigyō to Keizaishi, 1940.

Jōyaku Kyoku Hōkika. "Nihon tōchi jidai no Chōsen" [Korea under Japanese rule]. *Gaichi Hōseishi* 4 (March 1966): 61–98.

Kaebyŏksa. *Kaebyŏk*. Seoul: Kaebyŏksa, 1920–5.

Kajimura Hideki. *Chōsen ni okeru shibon shugi no keisei to tenkai* [The structure and development of capitalism in Korea]. Tokyo: Ryūkei Shosha, 1977.

"Minjok chabon kwa yesok chabon" [National capital and dependent capital]. In Kajimura Hideki et al., *Han'guk kŭndae kyŏngjesa yŏn'gu* [Studies of modern Korean history], 516–27. Seoul: 1983.

Kang Tong-jin. "Han'guk chaebŏl ŭi hyŏngsŏng kwajŏng kwa kyebo" [Background and development of Korean conglomerates]. *Chŏnggyŏng Yŏn'gu* 2, 11 (Nov. 1966): 121–8.

Ilche ŭi Han'guk ch'imnyak chŏngch'aeksa: 1920 nyŏndae rŭl chungsim ŭro [The political policy of penetration in Korea under Japanese rule: the 1920s]. Seoul: Hangilsa, 1980.

Kang Se-gyun. *Chŏn'guk sanggong taegam* [A review of the nation's commerce and industry]. Seoul: Chunwoe Sanggong Ch'ŏngbosa, 1949.

Kang Tŏk-sang and Kajimura Hideki. "Nitteika Chōsen no hōritsu seido ni tsuite" [The legal system in Korea under the Japanese Empire]. In Fukushima Masao, ed., *Nihonhō to Ajia. Niida Noboru Hakasei Tsuite Ronbunshū* [Japanese law and Asia: essays in memory of Dr. Niida Noboru], no. 3, 319–37. Tokyo: Keiso Shobo, 1974.

Keijō Nippōsha. *Chōsen nenkan, 1944* [Chōsen annual, 1944], edited by Yokomizu Mitsuteru. Also 1942 edition. Keijō: Keijō Nippōsha, 1944.

Keijō Shōkō Kaigisho. *Tōkei nempō 1940* [Statistical annual, 1940]. Keijō: Keijō Shōkō Kaigisho, 1940.

Keijō Shōkō Kaigisho nijūgo nenshi [A twenty-five year history of the Keijō

Chamber of Commerce and Industry], edited by Itō Seiyoshi. Keijō: Keijō Shōkō Kaigisho, 1941.

Keijō shōkō meikan [A list of prominent commercial ventures], edited by Sugiyama Shigeichi. Keijō: Keijō Shōkō Kaigisho, 1943.

Kim Chin-ha, ed. *Han'guk muyŏksa* [A history of Korean trade]. Seoul: Han'guk Muyŏk Hyŏphoe, 1972.

Kim Chun-yŏp and Kim Ch'ang-sun. *Han'guk kongsanjuŭi undongsa* [A history of the Korean Communist Movement], vol. 2. Seoul: Korea University Press, 1969.

Kim Pyŏng-je, ed. *Inmul ŭnhaengsa* [A history of major figures in banking]. Seoul: Ŭnhaenggyesa, 1978.

Kim Sang-hong, ed. *Sudang Kim Yŏn-su* [*Sudang Kim Yŏn-su*]. Seoul: Sudang Kinyŏm Saŏphoe, 1971. (Cited as *Sudang.*)

Samyang yuksimnyŏn, 1924–1984 [Sixty years of the Samyang, 1924–1984]. Seoul: Chusik Hoesa Samyangsa, 1984. (Cited as *Samyang.*)

Kim Sang-man, ed. *Donga Ilbosa sa* [A history of the Donga Ilbo Company]. Seoul: Donga Ilbosa, 1975.

Kim Sŏng-du. "Han'guk tokchŏm chaebŏl hyŏngsŏng ŭi t'ŭgisŏng" [Unique characteristics in the formation of Korean conglomerates: the inefficient and uneconomical nature of Korean conglomerates]. *Sasanggye* (Sept. 1968): 108–22.

Kim Tae-hwan. "1950 nyŏndae Han'guk kyŏngje ŭi yŏn'gu" [A study of the Korean economy in the 1950s]. In Chin Tŏk-gyu, ed., *1950 nyŏndae insik* [An understanding of the 1950s], 157–256. Seoul: Hangilsa, 1981.

Kim Tu-yong. *Chōsen kindai keizaishi wa* [Reflections on the recent history of the economy in Korea]. Tokyo: Kyōdo Shōbo, 1947.

Kim Yang-hwa. "Miguk ŭi taehan wŏnjo wa Han'guk ŭi kyŏngje kujo" [U.S. aid to Korea and the structure of the Korean economy]. In Song Kŏn-ho and Pak Hyŏn-ch'ae, eds., *Haebang sasimnyŏn ŭi chaeinsik, I* [A reexamination of the forty years following liberation], 227–74. Seoul: Tolbegae, 1985.

Kim Yong-sŏp. "Hanmal Ilcheha ŭi chijuje. Saryesa: Kobu Kimssiga ûi chiju kyŏngyŏng kwa chabon chŏnhwan" [System of landownership from the end of the Yi Dynasty through the colonial period. The fourth case: land administration and capital movement in the Kim family of Kobu]. *Han'guksa Yŏn'gu* (Feb. 1978): 65–135.

Kim Yŏn-su. "Kim Yŏn-su." In Wŏllo Kiŏbin, eds., *Chaegye hoego* (Memories of the business world], vol. 1, 19–276. Seoul: Han'guk Ilbosa, 1981.

Ko Wŏn-sŏp. *Panminja choesanggi* [A record of charges against the antinationalists]. Seoul: Paegyŏp Munhwasa, 1949.

Kobayashi Hideo. "1930 nendai Chōsen kōgyōka seisaku no tenkai katei" [Development of a Korean industrialization policy in the 1930s]. *Chōsenshi Kenkyūkai Ronbunshū* 3 (1968): 141–74.

"1930 nendai Nippon Chisso Hiryō Kabushiki Kaisha no Chōsen e no shishutsu ni tsuite" [The advance of Japan Nitrogenous Fertilizers into Korea in the 1930s]. In Yamada Hideo, ed., *Shokuminchi keizaishi no shomondai* [Issues in colonial economic history], 139–89. Tokyo: Institute of Developing Economies, 1973.

Koh Seung-jae (Ko Sŭng-je). *Han'guk kŭmyungsa yŏn'gu* [Studies in the history of Korean finance]. Seoul: Ilchogak, 1970.

Han'guk kyŏngyŏngsa yŏn'gu [Studies in the history of business management in Korea]. Seoul: Samwha, 1975.

Kunsa Hyŏngmyŏng P'yŏnch'an Wiwŏnhoe. *Han'guk kunsa hyŏngmyŏngsa* [History of the military revolution in Korea], vol. 1, pt. 1. Seoul: Kugga Chaegŏn Ch'oego Hoeui, Han'guk Kunsa Hyŏngmyŏngsa P'yŏnch'an Wiwŏnhoe, 1963.

Maeil Sinbosa. *Maeil Sinbo* [Daily News]. Keijo: Maeil Sinbosa.

Min Pyŏng-do. "Min Pyŏng-do" [Min Pyŏng-do]." In Wŏllo Kiŏbin, eds., *Chaegye hoego*, vol. 10, 195–256. Seoul: Han'guk Ilbosa, 1981.

Miyajima Hiroshi. "Chōsen kango kaikaku igo no shōgyōteki nōgyō" [Commercial agriculture after the Kabo reforms in Korea]. *Shirin* 57, 6 (Nov. 1974): 38–77.

"Chosŏn t'oji chosa saŏp yŏn'gu sŏsŏl" [An introduction to studies on the land survey in Korea]. In Kajimura Hideki, ed., *Han'guk kŭndae kyŏngje yŏn'gu* [Studies in the modern economic history of Korea], 299–330. Seoul: Sagyejŏl Printing, 1983.

Nakanishi Toshiru. *Shin Nihon jinbutsu taikai* [A new directory of prominent Japanese]. Tokyo: Tōhō Keizai Gakusha, 1936.

Ohashi Seizaburō et al., eds. *Chōsen sangyō shishin* [A guide to industry in Korea]. Tokyo: Kawabata Kentarō, 1915.

Pak Hŭng-sik. "Pak Hŭng-sik." In Wŏllo Kiŏbin, eds., *Chaegye hoego* [Memories of the business world], 171–257. Seoul: Han'guk Ilbosa, 1981.

Pak Hŭng-sŏ, ed. *Hanil Ŭnhaeng sasimnyŏnsa* [A forty-year history of the Hanil Bank]. Seoul: Samsŏng, 1972.

Pak In-hwan, ed. *Kyŏngbang Yuksimnyŏn* [Sixty years of the Kyŏngsŏng Spinning and Weaving Company]. Seoul: Samhwa Publishing, 1980. (Cited as *Kyŏngbang*.)

Pak Kwŏn-sang, ed. *Donga Ilbo nonsŏl yuksimnyŏn* [Sixty years of editorials in the *Donga Ilbo*]. Seoul: Donga Ilbosa, 1980. (Cited as DINY.)

Pak Wŏn-sŏn. *Kaekchu* [Commission merchants]. Seoul: Yonsei University Press, 1968.

Sawamura Tōhei. "Richō makki menseihin yunyū bōeki no hatten" [Developments in the cotton import trade at the close of the Yi dynasty]. *Shakai Keizaishi Gaku* 19, 2–3 (1953): 57–80.

Shakuo Shunjō. *Chōsen heigōshi: ichimei, Chōsen saikinshi* [Annexation of Korea: the first chapter, Korea's recent history]. Keijō: Chōsen oyobi Manshūsha, 1926.

Shikata Hiroshi. *Chōsen ni okeru kindai shihonshugi no seiritsu katei* [The formation of a modern capitalism in Korea]. In the series, *Chōsen Shakai Keizaishi Kenkyū* [Studies in the social and economic history of Korea]. Keijō: Daigaku Hōbun Gakkai, 1933.

Shimamoto Susumu. *Chōsen zaikai no hitobito* [Prominent figures in Korean business circles]. Keijō: Keijō Shishinsha, 1941.

Shiraishi Munenari. "Chōsen ni okeru chisso hiryō kōgyō ni tsuite" [The production of nitrogenous fertilizer in Korea]. In *Chōsen no kōgyō to sono shigen* [Industry and industrial resources in Korea], pt. 2, 152–68. Keijō: Chōsen Kōgyō Kyōkai, 1937.

Sin Sŏk-ho, ed. "Samil undong ŭi chŏn'gae" [The unfolding of the March First Movement]. In Donga Ilbo, ed., *Samil undong osipchunyŏn kinyŏmjip* [A fifty-year memorial volume of the March First Movement]. Seoul: Donga Ilbosa, 1963.

Son Chōng-yŏn. *Musong Hyŏn Chun-ho* [Musong Hyŏn Chun-ho)]. Kwangju: Chŏnnam Maeil Sinmunsa, 1977.

Song Kŏn-ho. *Han'guk minjujuŭi ŭi t'amgu* [A study of democracy in Korea]. Seoul: Hangilsa, 1978.

Suzuki Takeo. "Jihen go Chōsen kinyū [The Manchurian Incident and finance in Chōsen]," lecture no. 10 of *Chōsen kinyū ron juko* [A discussion of finance in Chōsen: ten lectures]. Keijō: Teikoku Jihō Kōsei Gakkai Chōsen Honbu, 1940.

Chōsen keizai no shin kōsō [New ideas in the Korean economy]. Tokyo: Taikaidō Insatsu Kabushiki Kaisha, 1942.

Taehan Pangjik Hyŏphoe, ed. *Sŏmyu yŏnbo 1960* [Textile annual, 1960]. Seoul: Taehan Pangjik Hyŏphoe, 1960.

Panghyŏp isimnyŏnsa [A twenty-year history of the Korean Spinners and Weavers Association]. Seoul: Samsŏng, 1968.

Taehan Sanggong Hoeuiso, ed. *Sanŏp Kyŏngye* [Industrial economy]. Monthly.

Takamiya Taihei, ed. *Chōsenjin meiroku* [A directory of prominent figures in Korea]. Keijō: Keijō Shibosha, 1942.

Takasugi Tōgō. *Chōsen kinyū kikan hattatsushi* [A history of the development of financial institutions in Korea]. Keijō: Jitsugyō Taimususha, 1940.

Teikoku Kōshinjo. *Teikoku ginkō kaisha yōroku* [A list of banks and corporations in the empire]. Tokyo: Teikoku Kōshinjo, annual. (Cited as TGKY.)

Tōa Keizai Shinpōsha. *Chōsen ginkō kaisha kumiai yōroku* [A list of banks, firms and partnerships in Korea], edited by Nakamura Sukeryō. Keijō: Tōa Keizai Shinpōsha, annual. (Cited as CGKKY.)

Tongil Bank, Board of Directors. *Ch'wich'eyŏkhoe kyŏllok* [Record of resolutions from meetings of the board of directors]. Seoul: Choheung Bank Archives.

Tōyō Keizai Shinpōsha. *Dairiku kaisha benran* [Handbook of companies on the continent], edited by Akihishi Sawano. Tokyo: Tōyō Keizai Shinpōsha, 1942. (Cited as DKB.)

Chōsen nenkan, 1942 [Korean annual, 1942]. Tokyo: Tōa Keizai Shinpōsha, 1942.

Wŏllo Kiŏbin, eds. *Chaegye hoego* [Memories of the business world]. Seoul: Han'guk Ilbosa, 1981.

Yamabe Kentarō. *Nihon tōchika no Chōsen* [Korea under Japanese rule]. Tokyo: Iwanami Shoten, 1971.

Yamada Saburō. *Kankoku kōgyōka no kadai* [The process of industrialization in Korea]. Report of the Institute of Asian Economies (Ajia Keizai Kenkyūjō), no. 977. Tokyo: Institute of Asian Economies, 1971.

Yamakawa Chikashi. *Jigyō oyobi jinbutsu* [Enterprise and entrepreneurs]. Tokyo: Tokyo Dempō Tsūshinsha, 1941.

Yi Tae-wŏn. *Cheil chedang samsimnyŏnsa* [A thirty-year history of Cheil Sugar]. Seoul: Cheil Chedang Chusik Hoesa, 1983.

Yŏm Han-yŏng. *Hoesa yŏn'gam 1955* [Company annual 1955]. Seoul: Taehan Kyŏngje Yŏn'gamsa, 1955.

Zenkoku Keizai Chōsa Kikan Rengōkai, Chōsen Shibu. *Chōsen keizai nempō 1941–1942* [Annual of the Korean economy, 1941–1942]. Tokyo: Kaizōsha, 1943. (Cited as CKN.)

English Language

Allen, Michael Patrick. "The Structure of Interorganizational Elite Cooptation: Interlocking Corporate Directorates." *American Sociological Review* 39 (1974): 393–406.

American Advisory Staff, Department of Justice. "Draft of Study on the Administration of Justice in Korea under the Japanese and in South Korea under the United States Army Military Government in Korea to 15 August 1948." (Seoul: USAMGIK, 1948). RG 407, Box 2067, National Archives.

Baker, Edward J. "The Role of Legal Reforms in the Japanese Annexation and Rule of Korea, 1905–1919." In David McCann et al., eds., *Studies on Korea in Transition*, 17–42. Honolulu: Center for Korean Studies, 1979.

Balandier, G. "The Colonial Situation: A Theoretical Approach." In Immanuel

Wallerstein, ed., *Social Change. The Colonial Situation*, 34–61. New York: John Wiley, 1966.

Baldwin, Frank. "The March First Movement: Korean Challenge and Japanese Response." Ph.D. diss., Columbia University, 1969.

Ban Sung Hwan et al. *Rural Development.* Cambridge: Harvard University Press, 1980.

Bendix, Reinhard. "Industrialization, Ideologies, and Social Structure." *American Sociological Review* 24, 5(Oct. 1959): 613–23.

Bisson, T. A. *Zaibatsu Dissolution in Japan.* Westport, CT: Greenwood Press, 1976.

Brudnoy, David. "Japan's Experiment in Korea." *Monumenta Nipponica* 25, 1–2 (1970): 155–95.

Cardoso, F. H., and E. Faletto. *Dependency and Development in Latin America.* Berkeley: University of California Press, 1979.

Chandler, Alfred D. "The United States: Seedbed of Managerial Capitalism." In Alfred D. Chandler and Herman Deems, eds., *Managerial Hierarchies: Comparative Perspectives on the Rise of the Modern Industrial Empire*, 9–40. Cambridge: Harvard University Press, 1980.

Chang, Chi Ryang. "Tungsten Mining in Korea." *Korean Affairs* 2(May/June 1962): 204–8.

Chang Yunshik. "Colonization as Planned Change: The Korean Case." *Modern Asian Studies* 5, 2(1971):161–86.

Chen, Edward I-te. "The Attempt to Integrate the Empire: Legal Perspectives." In Ramon H. Myers and Mark R. Peattie, eds., *The Japanese Colonial Empire, 1895–1945*, 240–74. Princeton: Princeton University Press, 1984.

Cho Ki-jun. "Types of Entrepreneurs in the Modernization Process of the Korean Economy." In Asiatic Research Center *Report of the International Conference on the Problems of Modernization in Asia, June 28–July 7, 1965*, 616–26. Seoul: Korea University Asiatic Research Center, 1966.

"The Impact of the Opening of Korea on its Commerce and Industry." *Korea Journal* 16(Feb. 1976): 27–44.

Choi Moon Hwan. "A Review of Korea's land Reform." *Koreana Quarterly* 2, 1 (Spring 1960): 55–63.

Chung Young-iob. "Korean Investment under Japanese Rule." In C. I. Eugene Kim and Doretha E. Mortimore, eds., *Korea's Response to Japan: the Colonial Period, 1910–1945*, 15–41. Kalamazoo: Western Michigan University, 1977.

"U.S. Economic Aid to South Korea After World War II." In Andrew C. Nahm, ed., *American–Korean Relations, 1866–1976*, 187–217. Kalamazoo: Center for Korean Studies, Western Michigan University, 1979.

Civil Property Custodian, External Assets Division, General Headquarters, Supreme Commander of Allied Forces in the Pacific. *Japanese External Assets as of August 1945.* September 30, 1948, vol. 1, "Korea" and vol. 2, "Manchuria." RG 59. National Archives. (Cited as JEA.)

Clark, Rodney. *The Japanese Company.* New Haven: Yale University Press, 1979.

Cohen, Jerome. *Japan's Economy in War and Reconstruction.* Minneapolis: University of Minnesota Press, 1949.

Combined Economic Board, U.N. Command. "Joint ROK/UNC Study of the Economic Reconstruction Program for Korea." 1957. RG 59. National Archives.

Comptroller General of the United States. "U.S. Assistance Program for Korea, International Cooperation Administration, Department of State, Fiscal Years 1954–1956." 1957. RG. 59. National Archives.

Cook, Harold F. *Korea's 1884 Incident.* Seoul: Royal Asiatic Society, 1972.

Cronk, Edwin M. "Annual Economic Report 1955, ROK." March 29, 1956. American Embassy Seoul, Foreign Service Dispatch 294, RG 59. National Archives.

Cumings Bruce. "The Legacy of Japanese Colonialism in Korea." In Ramon H. Myers and Mark R. Peattie, eds., *The Japanese Colonial Empire, 1895–1945*, 478–96. Princeton: Princeton University Press, 1984.

"The Origins and Development of the Northeast Asian Political Economy: Industrial Sectors, Product Cycles, and Political Consequences." In Frederic C. Deyo, ed., *The Political Economy of the New Asian Industrialism*, 44–83. Ithaca: Cornell University Press, 1987.

Deuchler, Martina. *Confucian Gentlemen and Barbarian Envoys*. Seattle: University of Washington, 1977.

Deyo, Frederic C. *Dependent Development and Industrial Order: an Asian Case Study*. New York: Praeger, 1981.

ed. *The Political Economy of the New Asian Industrialism*. Ithaca: Cornell University Press, 1987.

Dong Wonmo. "Japanese Colonial Policy and Practice in Korea, 1905–1945: A Study in Assimilation." Ph.D. diss., Georgetown University, 1965.

Dore, Ronald. *British Factory – Japanese Factory*. Berkeley: University of California Press, 1973.

Dos Santos, Theontonio. "The Structure of Dependence." *The American Economic Review* 60, 2(1970).

Duesenberry, James S. *Income, Saving and the Theory of Consumer Behavior*. New York: Oxford University Press, 1967.

Edwards, Corwin D., et al. *Report of Mission on Japanese Combines*. March 1946. General Headquarters, Supreme Commander for the Allied Powers. RG 407. National Archives.

Evans, Peter. *Dependent Development. The Alliance of Multinational, State and Local Capital in Brazil*. Princeton: Princeton University Press, 1979.

Evans, Peter B., and Dietrich Rueschemeyer. "The State and Economic Transformation: Toward an Analysis of the Conditions Underlying Effective Intervention." In Peter B. Evans, Dietrich Rueschemeyer, and Theda Skocpol, eds., *Bringing the State Back In*, 44–77. Cambridge, Eng.: Cambridge University Press, 1985.

Foreign Economic Administration, Enemy Branch, Japanese Special Services Staff. *Summary Industrial Survey of Korea*. April 17, 1945. RG 407. National Archives.

Japanese Economic Penetration into Korea as of 1940 as Shown by an Analysis of Corporations Operating in Korea. October 23, 1945, State Department. RG 407, Box 2052. National Archives.

Frank, Charles R., Jr., Kwang Suk Kim, and Larry E. Westphal. *Foreign Trade Regimes and Economic Development: South Korea*. New York: National Bureau of Economic Research, 1975.

Geertz, Clifford. *The Interpretation of Culture*. New York: Basic, 1973.

George, C. M. "Prerequisites to Economic Viability." July 6, 1955. American Embassy Seoul, Foreign Service Dispatch 5, RG 59. National Archives.

Gerschenkron, Alexander. "Economic Backwardness in Historical Perspective." In Alexander Gerschenkron, *A Book of Essays*, 5–30. Cambridge: Harvard Belknap, 1966.

Gold, Thomas B. *State and Society in the Taiwan Miracle*. New York: Sharpe, 1986.

Government-General of Chōsen. *Annual Report on Reforms and Progress in Chōsen*, 1910–1937. Keijō: Government-General, annual. (Cited as *Annual Report*.)

Chōsen in Pictures. Keijo: Government-General, 1921.

Gragert, Edwin. "Landownership Change in Korea under Japanese Colonial Rule: 1900–1935." Ph.D. diss., Columbia University, 1982.

Haggard, Stephen, and Chung-In Moon. "The South Korean State in the International Economy: Liberal, Dependent, or Mercantile." In John Gerald Ruggie, ed., *The Antinomies of Interdependence: National Welfare and the International Division of Labor*, 131–89. New York: Columbia University, 1983.

Hao Yen-P'ing. *The Comprador in Nineteenth Century China: Bridge between East and West*. Cambridge: Harvard University Press, 1970.

The Commercial Revolution in Nineteenth-Century China. The Rise of Sino-Western Mercantile Capitalism. Berkeley: University of California Press, 1986.

Hattori Tamio. "The Relationship between Zaibatsu and Family Structure: the Korean Case." In Akio Okochi and Shigeaki Yasuoka, eds., *Family Business in the Era of Industrial Growth*, 121–45. Vol. 10 of the International Conference on Business History. Tokyo: University of Tokyo Press, 1983.

Heidenheimer, Arnold J., and Frank C. Langdon. *Business Associations and the Financing of Political Parties. A Comparative Study of the Evolution of Practices in Germany, Norway and Japan*. The Hague: Martinus Nijhoff, 1968.

Hirschman, Albert. *The Strategy of Economic Development*. New Haven: Yale University Press, 1958.

Hirschmeier, Johannes. "Shibusawa Eiichi: Industrial Pioneer." In William W. Lockwood, ed., *The State and Economic Enterprise in Japan*, 209–47. Princeton: Princeton University Press, 1965.

Hirschmeier, Johannes, and Tsunehiko Yui. *The Development of Japanese Business*. Cambridge: Harvard University Press, 1975.

Hoover, Calvin B. "Capitalism." In David L. Sills, ed., *International Encyclopedia of the Social Sciences*, vol. 2, 294–302. New York: Macmillan and Free Press, 1968.

Horie Yazuzō. "Modern Entrepreneurship in Meiji Japan." In William W. Lockwood, ed., *The State and Economic Enterprise in Japan*, 183–208. Princeton: Princeton University Press, 1965.

Hulbert, Homer. "The New Century." *The Korea Review* 1, 1(1901):3–16.

Hunter, Janet. "Japanese Government Policy, Business Opinion, and the Seoul–Pusan Railway, 1894–1906. *Modern Asian Studies* 11(1977): 573–9.

Ishida Takeshi. "The Development of Interest Groups and the Pattern of Political Modernization in Japan." In Robert E. Ward, ed., *Political Development in Modern Japan*, 293–326. Princeton: Princeton University Press, 1968.

Jacobs, Norman. *The Korean Road to Modernization and Development*. Urbana: University of Illinois Press, 1985.

Johnson, Chalmers. "Political Institutions and Economic Performance: The Government–Business Relationship in Japan, South Korea, and Taiwan." In Frederick C. Deyo, ed., *The Political Economy of the New Asian Industrialism*, 136–64. Ithaca: Cornell University Press, 1987.

Joint Army–Navy Intelligence Studies (JANIS) Publishing Board. *Joint Army-Navy Intelligence Study of Korea, including Tsushima and Quelpart*. April 1945. RG 407. Box 2103. National Archives. (Cited as *JANIS*.)

Jones, Leroy P., and Il Sakong. *Government, Business, and Entrepreneurship in Economic Development: The Korean Case*. Cambridge: Harvard University Press, 1980.

Juhn, Daniel Sungil. "Entrepreneurship in an Underdeveloped Economy: the Case of Korea, 1890–1940." D.B.A. diss., George Washington University, 1965.

"The Development of Korean Entrepreneurship." 113–136 in Andrew C. Nahm, ed., *Korea under Japanese Colonial Rule*. Kalamazoo: Center for Korean Studies, Western Michigan University, 1973.

Kamesaka Tsunesaburo, ed. *Who's Who in Japan with Manchoukuo and China,*

1939–1940. Also 1943–1944 vol. Tokyo: Who's Who in Japan Publishing Office, 1939. (Cited as WWJ.)

Kang Man-gil. "The Modernization of Korea from the Historical Point of View." *Asiatic Research Bulletin* 6, 1(March 1963): 1–6.

"Reflections on the Centenary of the Opening of Korea." Korea Journal 16, 2(Feb. 1976): 10–18.

Kim Han-kyo. "The Japanese Colonial Administration in Korea: An Overview." In Andrew C. Nahm, ed., *Korea under Japanese Colonial Rule*, 41–55. Kalamazoo: Center for Korean Studies, Western Michigan University, 1973.

Kim Hyun-kil. "Land Use Policy in Korea with Special Reference to the Oriental Development Company." Ph.D. diss., University of Washington, 1971.

Kim Joungwon. *Divided Korea: Politics of Development, 1945–1972*. Cambridge: Harvard University Press, 1975.

Kim Kwang-tiek. "Industrialization of Korea under Japanese Rule: A Case Study." Ph.D. diss., University of Maryland, 1974.

Kim Kyong-dong. "Political Factors in the Formation of the Entrepreneurial Elite in South Korea." *Asian Survey* 16, 5(May 1976): 465–77.

Kim Wŏn-tae, ed. *Fifty Years of Whashin*. Seoul: Whashin Industrial Company, 1977. (Cited as *Fifty Years*.)

Koh Masuda, ed. *New Japanese–English Dictionary*. Tokyo: Kenkyūsha, 1974.

Koh Seung-jae. "The Development of the Modern Banking System in Korea." *Koreana Quarterly* 1, 2(Winter 1959): 82–92.

"The Role of the Bank of Chōsen (Korea) and the Japanese Expansion in Manchuria and China." *Journal of Social Sciences and Humanities* 32(June 1970): 25–36.

Koo Hagen. "The Interplay of State, Social Class, and World System in East Asian Development: The Cases of South Korea and Taiwan." In Frederic C. Deyo, ed., *The Political Economy of the New Asian Industrialism*, 165–81. Ithaca: Cornell University Press, 1987.

Korea Branch of the Royal Asiatic Society. "Tables of the McCune-Reischauer System for the Romanization of Korean." *Transactions of the Korea Branch of the Royal Asiatic Society* 38(Oct. 1961): 121–8.

Krasner, Stephen. *Defending the National Interest: Raw Materials Investments and U.S. Foreign Policy*. Princeton: Princeton University Press, 1978.

Krueger, Anne O. *The Developmental Role of the Foreign Aid Sector*. Cambridge: Harvard University Press, 1979.

Kublin, Hyman. "The Evolution of Japanese Colonialism." *Comparative Studies in Society and History* 2, 1(Oct. 1959): 67–84.

Lee Chong-sik. *The Patterns of Korean Nationalism*. Berkeley: University of California Press, 1963.

Lee Hahn-been. *Korea: Time, Change, and Administration*. Honolulu: East–West Center Press, 1968.

Lee Hoon K. *Land Utilization and Rural Economy in Korea*. New York: Greenwood, 1969.

Lew Young-ick. "The Kabo Reform Movement: Korean and Japanese Reform Efforts in Korea, 1894." Ph.D. diss., Harvard University, 1972.

Lockwood, William W. "The State and Economic Enterprise in Modern Japan, 1868–1939." In Simon Kuznets, Wilbert E. Moore, and Joseph J. Spengler, eds., *Economic Growth: Brazil, India, Japan*, 537–602. Durham: Duke University Press, 1955.

McNamara, Dennis L. "Imperial Expansion and Nationalist Resistance: Japan in Korea, 1876–1910." Ph.D. diss., Harvard University, 1983.

"A Frontier Ideology: Meiji Japan and the Korean Frontier." *The Journal of International Studies* (Sophia University, Tokyo) 12(Jan. 1984): 43–64.

"Comparative Colonial Response: Korea and Taiwan, 1895–1919." *Korean Studies* 10(1986): 54–68.

"Korea and Brazil at the Turn of the Century: Trade, Elites and Foreign Ties." In Kyong-dong Kim, ed., *Dependency Issues in Korean Development: Comparative Perspectives*, 496–511. Seoul: Seoul National University Press, 1987.

"Entrepreneurship in Colonial Korea: Kim Youn-su." *Modern Asian Studies* 22, 1(1988): 165–77.

"Autonomy and Capacity in Korea's First Republic." Paper presented at the Fifty-ninth Annual Meeting of the Eastern Sociological Association, March 1989.

"The Keishō and the Korean Business Elite." *Journal of Asian Studies* 48, 2(May 1989): 310–23.

"Concentration in a Weak State: The Early Textile Chaebŏl." *Journal of Developing Societies*, in press.

Mann, Michael. "The Autonomous Power of the State: Its Origins, Mechanisms and Results." *Archives Européennes de Sociologie* 25(1984): 185–213.

Marshall, Byron. *Capitalism and Nationalism in Prewar Japan. The Ideology of the Business Elite, 1868–1941*. Stanford: Stanford University Press, 1967.

Mason, Edward, et al., eds. *The Economic and Social Modernization of the Republic of Korea*. Cambridge: Harvard University Press, 1980.

Maunier, René. *The Sociology of Colonies. An Introduction to the Study of Race Contact*. Edited and translated by E. O. Lorimer. 2 vols. London: Routledge and Kegan Paul, 1949.

Military Intelligence Service, War Department General Staff. "Historical Sketch of Japanese Administration in Korea since 1910." In *Survey of Korea*, Appendix 8. Washington, DC: War Department, June 15, 1943.

Mills, C. Wright. *The Power Elite*. New York: Oxford University Press, 1956.

  The Sociological Imagination. New York: Oxford University Press, 1959.

Mitchell, C. Clyde. "Report of the New Korea Company." Seoul: U.S. Military Government in Korea, National Land Administration, 1948.

Miyamoto Matao. "The Position and Role of Family Business in the Development of the Japanese Company System." In Akio Okochi and Shigeaki Yasuoka, eds., *Family Business in the Era of Industrial Growth: Its Ownership and Management*, 39–91. Proceedings of the Fuji Conferece, an International Conference on Business History, vol. 10. Tokyo: Tokyo University Press, 1983.

Molony, Barbara. "Japan's Strategic Investment in High Technology in Korea, 1925–1945." Paper presented at the Association for Asian Studies, March 1984.

Moskowitz, Karl. "The Creation of the Oriental Development Company: Japanese Illusion Meets Korean Reality." In James B. Palais, ed., *Occasional Papers on Korea*, no. 1, 73–109. Seattle: Joint Committee on Korean Studies of the American Council of Learned Societies and the Social Science Research Council, 1974.

"Current Assets: The Employees of Japanese Banks in Colonial Korea." Ph.D. diss., Harvard University, 1979.

Moulton, Harold G. *Japan. An Economic and Financial Appraisal*. Washington DC: Brookings, 1931.

Myrdal, Gunnar. *Asian Drama*. London: Penguin, 1968.

Myers, Ramon H., and Mark. R. Peattie, eds. *The Japanese Colonial Empire, 1895–1945*. Princeton, Princeton University Press, 1984.

Nahm, Andrew C., ed. *Korea Under Japanese Colonial Rule*. Kalamazoo. Center for

Korean Studies, Western Michigan University, 1973.

Nakagawa Keiichiro. "Business Strategy and Industrial Structure in Pre–World-War-II Japan." In Nakagawa Keiichiro, ed., *Strategy and Structure of Big Business*, 3–38. Proceedings of the first Fuji Conference on Business History. Tokyo: Tokyo University Press, 1976.

Nakamura Takafusa. *Economic Growth in Prewar Japan*. New Haven: Yale University Press, 1983.

Nakamura, James I. "Incentives, Productivity Gaps, and Agricultural Growth Rates in Prewar Japan, Taiwan, and Korea." In Bernard S. Silberman and H. D. Harootunian, eds., *Japan in Crisis, Essays in Taishō Democracy*, 329–73. Princeton: Princeton University Press, 1974.

Norman, E. Herbert. "The Genyōsha: A Study in the Origins of Japanese Imperialism." *Pacific Affairs* 17, 3(Sept. 1944): 261–84.

Office of Strategic Services, Research and Analysis Branch, Department of State (Far Eastern Section). *Korea. Economic Survey*. August 5, 1942. Research and Analysis (R & A) 744. RG 59. National Archives.

O'Neill, P. G. *Japanese Names*. A Comprehensive Index by Characters and Readings. New York: Weatherhill, 1972.

Pak Ki-hyuk et al. *A Study of Land Tenure System in Korea*. Seoul: Korea Land Economics Research Center, 1966.

Park Soon Won. "The Emergence of a Factory Labor Force in Colonial Korea: A Case Study of the Onoda Cement Factory." Ph.D. diss., Harvard University, 1985.

Park Sung-sang, ed. *The Banking System in Korea*. Seoul: Bank of Korea, 1968.

Patrick, Hugh. "Japan, 1868–1914." In Rondo Cameron et al., eds., *Banking in the Early Stages of Modernization*, 239–89. London: Oxford, 1967.

Pauley, Edwin Wendell. *Report on Japanese Assets in Manchuria to the President of the United States*. Washington DC: Government Printing Office, July 1946.

Ranis, Gustav. "The Community-centered Entrepreneur in Japanese Development." *Explorations in Entrepreneurial History* 8, 2(Dec. 1955): 80–97.

Reeve, W. D. *The Republic of Korea*. Oxford: Oxford University Press, 1963.

Residency-General of Korea. *Annual Report for 1907 on Reforms and Progress in Korea*. Keijō: Residency-General, 1908.

Robinson, Michael. "Colonial Publication Policy and the Korean Nationalist Movement." In Ramon Meyers and Mark Peattie, eds., *The Japanese Colonial Empire*, 312–46. Princeton: Princeton University Press, 1983.

Cultural Nationalism in Colonial Korea, 1920–1925. Seattle: University of Washington Press, 1988.

Rosovsky, Henry. *Capital Formation in Japan, 1868–1940*. New York: Free Press, 1961.

Sabey, John Wayne. "The Gen'yōsha, the Kokuryūkai, and Japanese Expansionism." Ph.D. diss., University of Michigan, 1972.

Scalapino, Robert A. *Democracy and the Party Movement in Prewar Japan. The Failure of the First Attempt*. Berkeley: University of California Press, 1953.

Schumpeter, Joseph. *The Theory of Economic Development*. New Brunswick, NJ: Transaction, 1983.

The Strategy of Economic Development. New Haven: Yale University Press, 1958.

Seki, Keizo. *The Cotton Industry of Japan*. Tokyo: Maruzen, 1956.

Shin Yong-ha. "Landlordism in the Late Yi Dynasty." *Korea Journal* 18(June 1978): 25–32, and 18(July 1978): 22–9.

Skocpol, Theda. *States and Social Revolutions: A Comparative Analysis of France,*

Russia and China. Cambridge, Eng.: Cambridge University Press, 1979.

Statistical Research Division of the Office of Administration. *Summation of U.S. Army Military Government Activities in Korea,* vol. 2, June 1946. Report to the Military Governor of U.S. Army Military Government in Korea. RG 407. Box 2105. National Archives.

Steiner, W. R. F. "Study of Vested Property in Korea." July 8, 1952. A.I.D-Korea, Executive Office. RG 286. National Archives.

Stepan, Alfred. *The State and Society: Peru in Comparative Perspective.* Princeton: Princeton University Press, 1978.

Suh Dae-sook. *The Korean Communist Movement, 1918–1948.* Princeton: Princeton University Press, 1967.

Suh Sang-chul. *Growth and Structural Change in the Korean Economy, 1910–1940.* Cambridge: Harvard University Press, 1978.

    "Foreign Capital and Development Strategy in Korea." *Korean Studies* 2(1978): 67–94.

Tiedemann, Arthur E. "Big Business and Politics in Prewar Japan." In James William Morley, ed., *Dilemmas of Growth in Prewar Japan,* 267–316. Princeton: Princeton University Press, 1971.

U.S. Adjutant General's Office. "Names and Biographies of Members of Central Advisory Council of Koreans." 1945. Adjutant General's Office. RG 407. National Archives.

U.S. Armed Forces in Korea, 24th Corps. *Intelligence Summary: Korea, Weekly Summary,* July 23, 1948. No. 149. National Archives.

U.S. Department of State, Office of Advisor to the Commanding General, U.S. Forces Korea. *A Review of Fiscal Operations of the U.S. Military Government in Korea.* December 1, 1946. RG 407. Box 2058. National Archives.

Useem, Michael. "The Social Organization of the American Business Elite and Participation of Corporation Directors in the Governance of American Institutions." *American Sociological Review* 44(Aug. 1979): 553–72.

    The Inner Circle. Large Corporations and the Rise of Business Political Activity in the U.S. and the U.K. New York: Oxford, 1984.

Wells, K. M. "The Rationale of Korean Economic Nationalism under Japanese Colonial Rule, 1922–1932: the Case of Cho Man-sik's Products Promotion Society." *Modern Asian Studies* 19, 4(1985): 823–59.

Wilken, Paul. *Entrepreneurship. A Comparative and Historical Study.* Norwood, NJ: Ablex, 1979.

Wolf, Morris. "Memorandum on Restrictions in Korean Constitution upon Private Enterprise." 1954. A.I.D.-Korea. Executive Offices. RG 286. National Archives.

Yanaga Chitoshi. *Big Business in Japanese Politics.* New Haven: Yale University Press, 1968.

Yanihara Tadao. "The Problems of Japanese Administration in Korea." *Pacific Affairs* 11, 2(June 1938): 198–207.

Yasuoka Shigeaki. "The Tradition of Family Business in the Strategic Decision Process and Management Structure of Zaibatsu Business: Mitsui, Sumitomo, and Mitsubishi." In Nakagawa Keiichiro, ed., *Strategy and Structure of Big Business,* 81–101. Tokyo: Tokyo University Press, 1976.

    "Capital Ownership in Family Companies: Japanese Firms Compared with Those in Other Countries." In Akio Okochi and Yasuoka Shigeaki, eds., *Family Business in the Era of Industrial Growth: Its Ownership and Management,* 1–32. Vol. 10 of Proceedings of the Fuji Conference and International Conference on Business History. Tokyo: University of Tokyo Press, 1983.

Yi Kyu-tae. *The Modern Transformation of Korea*. Seoul: Sejong Publishers, 1970.

Zeitlin, Maurice. "Corporate Ownership and Control: the Large Corporation and the Capitalist Class." *American Journal of Sociology* 79, 5(1974): 1073–119.

Index